Advance Praise for

In the Interest of Justice

"As a mental health advocate and host of *State of Mind,* I often talk about the importance of staying mentally strong. But sometimes life tests that strength in unimaginable ways. This book is a testament to resilience—written during an incredibly painful time by dear friends who have endured more than anyone ever should. Yet, through their suffering, they've shown an unwavering strength, fueled by the love of family and friends. It's a reminder that even in our darkest moments, love carries us forward. Their story is heartbreaking, but it is also powerful, raw, and deeply inspiring. I am honored to share it with you."

—**Maurice Benard**, The *New York Times* Bestselling author, three-time Emmy winner, and host of *State of Mind* podcast

"Throughout my years of knowing Martha Byrne and her legal struggle to shed light on the corruption within the US Department of Justice and the FBI, it has become clear through her in-depth research and analysis into the misguided FBI investigation of her husband and the Bureau's collusion with China's CCP that anyone reading this book would be forced to question the integrity of justice within these two agencies. Outstanding work, Martha."

—**Timothy P. Gill Sr.**, Former Senior US Government Intelligence Officer (FBI)

"The tumultuous journey of Michael and Martha McMahon is a window into a corrupt Federal Government operating in apparent collusion with Chinese Communist Intelligence. Michael is a highly decorated veteran NYPD detective who retired after he was injured in the line of duty and worked as a private investigator. He took on a typical client, a character unbeknownst to Michael, that turned out to have incestuous ties to China. Years later, in an egregious case of overreach, the Federal Bureau of Investigation decides to charge Michael under the Foreign Agent Registration Act, while the corrupt DOJ and FBI chose to work with and protect the Chinese Foreign Intelligence operative for years. This story reflects the firsthand account of the bizarre, upside down worldview of a political globalist agenda. A must read to understand the treachery of the Deep State against the American Citizen."

—**Colonel John Mills** (Ret.) and Former Director, Cybersecurity Policy, Strategy, and International Affairs, Office of the Secretary of Defense

"Martha gives the reader a firsthand account of how a justice system which was supposed to seek the truth, chose instead to bring a case against an innocent American hero, her husband Michael. With Martha's faith and trust in God's plan, she went to the front lines against the DOJ to defend her husband, exposing the dark forces in the government who tried to destroy her family."

—**Ed Martin**, US Attorney for the District of Columbia

IN THE INTEREST OF JUSTICE

One Woman's Fight Against a Weaponized Justice Department to Save Her Husband

MARTHA BYRNE

A POST HILL PRESS BOOK
ISBN: 979-8-89565-144-5
ISBN (eBook): 979-8-89565-145-2

In the Interest of Justice:
One Woman's Fight Against a Weaponized Justice Department to Save Her Husband

Cover design by Jim Villaflores
Cover photo by Barry Morgenstein
Cover hair and make-up by Maureen Walsh

This book, as well as any other Post Hill Press publications, may be purchased in bulk quantities at a special discounted rate. Contact orders@posthillpress.com for more information.

This is a work of nonfiction. All people, locations, events, and situations are portrayed to the best of the author's memory.

Post Hill Press
New York • Nashville
posthillpress.com

Published in the United States of America
1 2 3 4 5 6 7 8 9 10

This book is dedicated to my three incredible children, Michael, Max, and Ann Marie. Your love and support have carried your father and me through our greatest challenge as a family. As your parents, we hope we have been an example to show you to never give up no matter what life throws in your path. We pray you will always fight for the greater good because of what you have witnessed. I promise you will never regret doing the right thing. My three beautiful souls, it won't always be easy, but your positive actions will be felt and then repeated in others. Thank you for every hug and encouraging word. We love you to the moon and back.

My mother Mary Adele,

Since I was a child you encouraged me to be fearless. One of the things you taught me, is that life is all about education. Every experience is a lesson and many can be costly. During this horrific assault on your family, you put your own pain aside to nurture and unselfishly help us. Whether it was dissecting the case over a cup of coffee or your daily insights to strengthen my resolve, I could not have survived this horrific attack without you. Love you "meems."

For the VINMAN. Thanks for making Mike go out for "one more" on February 6th 1993. If he didn't listen to his big brother, there would be no Mike & Martha, Mikey, Max and Ann Marie. I owe you everything KID! Xoxo

Mike,

Thank you for trusting me to fight for your life. I would do it a thousand times over without a blink of an eye. The foundation we have built together can never be broken. I love you.

Thanks be to God,

I am your forever faithful servant. Thank you for showing me countless times you entrusted me with this insurmountable task. Please continue to watch over our beautiful family. Amen.

CONTENTS

FOREWORD

What you're about to read is a story of resilience, of courage, and of a man and a family who refused to be beaten by what looked like unbeatable odds. Mike McMahon is an American hero who dedicated his life and career to the rule of law.

And then the very government entrusted with that rule of law turned on him.

He started his career by answering the call to public service. He worked as a police sergeant in the war zone of the crime-ravaged '90s in New York City. He racked up literally scores of awards—making his living in places where most normal people would be terrified to walk out of their doors in the morning.

When a car accident cut his career short, Mike did what many cops do when they pull the pin and retire—he went into private investigation. He was doing a job he knew and that he was good at. He did right by his clients and he paid his bills. It's the American dream in a nutshell.

Then one day, through no fault of his own he was blindsided. His home was raided by the FBI. He found himself caught in a political dragnet. Suddenly his world was turned upside down. His accounts were frozen and he was stuck with a sky-high bail that was higher than that of the foreign agents and one that a guy with a family of five couldn't ever realistically imagine covering.

So now he didn't just have to think about how his family was going to keep a roof over their heads; he now had the prospect of being a retired cop going through the duration of a federal criminal trial while in prison. I don't have to tell you what those odds are.

What the folks at the FBI didn't count on was Mike's wife: Martha Byrne.

Martha is the kind of spouse that makes it possible for guys like Mike to do the job. She's dedicated, loving, and absolutely tireless. She's how we came to know about Mike's situation in the first place.

When Mike started going through this meat grinder, Martha jumped into action. A force of nature in her own right, she's an Emmy winner who gained national fame as an actress—and she put every single bit of personal and professional capital she had into restoring her husband's freedom and his good name.

It was in the course of her advocacy that she called in the Pipe Hitter Foundation, something we started after Eddie got out of the navy.

We know a thing or two about going through the wringer on an unjust and politically driven case like this. Just like with Mike, the system that Eddie had given his whole professional life to turned on him and our family in a heartbeat. That's why we started PHF and it's why we didn't hesitate to jump in and get involved. But this story isn't about me or our organization. We at the foundation are just honored to play the small part that we could in Mike's story.

People like Mike dedicate and risk their lives protecting our families and communities while maintaining that thin line that separates chaos and order.

And then suddenly, Mike was on the wrong side of it. Treated no better than the violent and vicious criminals he used to put away.

That's when Andrea and I got to know him and when the PHF got involved. This is precisely the kind of case we take up at the Pipe Hitter Foundation.

I hope that, by the time you finish this book, you're just as inspired by Mike and Martha as we have been these last few years.

—Eddie and Andrea Gallagher

INTRODUCTION

My name is Martha Byrne. Many know me as the Emmy Award–winning actress who played Lily Walsh and twin sister Jersey showgirl Rose D'Angelo on *As the World Turns*. In my four-decade career in the entertainment business I have played many roles. My most important and cherished role happened behind the camera. In 1993 I met a real-life hero in NYPD Detective Michael McMahon, who chose me to be his wife. After meeting Michael, work took second position to being a wife and a mother to Michael, Max, Ann Marie, and a dog named Rudy. I have been truly blessed throughout my life.

In October of 2020 our lives changed forever with a predawn knock on our front door. It was the FBI there to arrest my husband. Michael McMahon has never broken the law in his life, he enforces the law. He is a highly decorated hero who went above and beyond the call of duty to serve and protect. One of the good guys and the standard every cop and human being should strive to be.

How could the FBI and the Department of Justice get it so wrong? The journey our family has taken to find the answers is on the pages you are about to embark upon. We learned that even if you live your life with honor and integrity it will mean nothing if the FBI puts a target on your back. If our greatest national security threat China and the Chinese Communist Party are involved, the rule of law becomes subjective and the innocent are sacrificed. Destroying our family was an acceptable government plan to achieve their perceived goal for the greater good of the country. That was their biggest mistake. The lioness will protect her cubs to the detriment of her own well-being. It is instinctual to stand at the front lines against anyone who tries to harm her family. This primal instinct has driven me since the day the FBI violated the sanctity of my family.

This is our story.

CHAPTER ONE

OCTOBER 28, 2020, 5:45AM

OUR FIFTY-FIVE-POUND LABRADOR mix started to bark in the middle of the night, as he often does. We had realized years ago that Rudy would bark at night simply because he was afraid of the dark. Since then, his nocturnal woofs have barely registered with me. On this night I was comfy in bed under a mountain of covers, soothed by the white noise coming from the air purifier. No way was I getting up for Rudy. I cracked an eyelid and saw Mike was asleep next to me.

Then I faintly heard "DING DONG" under Rudy's barking. After a pause I heard "DING DONG DING DONG DING DONG," accompanied by feverish BANGING on the front door. I realized someone really was at the door. BANG BANG BANG!! DING DONG DING DONG!! I heard Mike roll out of bed in the dark and walk toward our bedroom door. Rudy's barking intensified as Mike stepped out. I had to go with him and see who it was. I had gotten hot during the night and had on only a shirt and underwear. I frantically looked for my pajama bottoms on the floor but couldn't find them in the dark. I found my robe but couldn't find the belt. I was anxious to get to the door, so I quickly put the robe on and held it closed.

As I rounded the corner of our hallway, I saw Mike, wearing only a T-shirt and underwear, standing in our foyer looking out the beveled-glass side panel of the front door. The top panel of the center door also had beveled glass. We could only make out dark images and what appeared to be flashlights shining through. With his background in law enforcement Mike was reluctant to open the door. The banging continued and I started to panic. I could feel my face start to go numb, thinking this is our worst nightmare coming true: One of our children was dead.

Everything went into slow motion. I struggled to focus. The voice in my head started to prepare me for the news I was convinced was coming. Which child was dead? Maybe it was my oldest, Mikey, maybe it was Max. When was the last time I saw them? I tried to remember but couldn't. The people on our front steps continued to bang the door harder, demanding Mike open it. I heard someone say, "Michael McMahon!" I started to panic further. Our twenty-two-year-old son has the same name, we call him "Mikey." I tried to remember when we went to bed the night before and if he had come home or not. I couldn't. Did he go out after Mike and I went to bed? Did someone pick him up? Was he in a car accident? Was he downstairs and were they there to arrest him? I was paralyzed with fear.

When my husband heard his name, he reluctantly opened the door. Several men in FBI tactical gear pushed their way into the foyer, which became very tight. Mike asked if they were there for our son and they said, no, they were there for him. Mike let the rest of the FBI agents into the foyer just as our son emerged from the basement. Mikey was wearing only pajama bottoms and seemed dazed, maybe in shock. One of the FBI agents instructed both my son and me to go to the living room just a few feet away. Our home is a split-level and the living room has a clear view of the foyer. Mikey sat on the couch and stared at his father, standing in his underwear, surrounded by FBI agents. Mike asked the lead agent if they were there about Paul Bergrin. The agent said, "No, but I know you from that case. It wasn't the first time you were on my board."

I heard this exchange, as did Mikey. Mikey looked at me and said, "Did you hear what he just said, that it wasn't the first time dad was on his board?" I was standing in the living room with my robe open and a bit disoriented, but I found that remark concerning. They asked Mike if he had any guns in the house. He told them his guns were in the safe downstairs in his office. No one asked where the office was located or if one of us could take them there. They never went downstairs. Mike was led down the hallway to our bedroom to allow him to go to the bathroom and put on clothes. I followed close behind as my daughter Ann Marie, who was fourteen at the time, emerged from her bedroom. She asked what was going on, with a look of fear and confusion. I told her to go back to her room, that everything was fine. She did so and closed her bedroom door.

As I tried to follow Mike into our bedroom, an agent blocked my path and told me to go back to the living room. Our son Max, who was eighteen, never came out of his bedroom down the hall from Ann Marie's. Back in the living room in my robe, I tried to make small talk with a female FBI agent. I asked what this was about. She didn't answer. I made a joke about our dog being the only criminal in the house and all the agents chuckled. Rudy made friends with all the agents, wagging his tail and demanding pets. His presence helped keep the mood civil. Mikey and I sat on separate couches trying to process what was happening. The female agent softened a bit and told me the charge had something to do with China. I laughed at the prospect of Mike having any connection to China.

The female agent stopped talking as Mike came down the hallway now fully dressed, escorted by the arresting officer. I asked the agent if I could hug him goodbye and the agent said yes. Mike handed me his phone and said, "Call Brian." Mike asked the agent if he wanted to go to his office downstairs where he kept his guns, computers, cameras, and records. The agent declined. Mike walked casually out the front door and was never handcuffed in our home. The last person to exit was the female agent who handed me the arrest warrant. The entire experience was respectful and calm. It felt like it was all a dream.

They didn't tell me where they were taking Mike, but the female agent assured me he would be home by that afternoon.

Once they had left, I told Mikey to remain calm, that I would figure this out, and not to worry. Ann Marie and Max came out of their rooms. I told Ann Marie the same—everything will be fine. Her dad didn't do anything wrong, it was clearly a mistake, I would handle it, go to school. I had no idea what I was talking about but all three of my children looked to me for answers. My instinct was to proceed as normal, that this mistake would be rectified by the end of the school day, nothing to worry about.

After Ann Marie got on the bus to school, I got to work. Mikey was in the basement, Max in his room. I called my mother, who lives in an apartment on our property, to tell her what happened. She had a million questions and I had no answers. I knew the next call had to be to my longtime friend Lisa Brown. Lisa had played my TV mother on *As the World Turns* starting in 1985 and we had remained friends ever since. I spoke to Lisa every day. She was married to a very successful defense attorney, Brian Neary. Mike had worked for Brian as a PI for years. I considered Lisa and Brian family. I called her about an hour after the FBI had left the house. She told me I should have called her earlier. I said I didn't want to wake her. She hung up and told Brian what happened as he was walking out the door to go to his office. When Lisa called back a few minutes later she said Brian had "steam coming out of his ears."

Brian loved Mike. Lisa told me not to worry, he was on it. Brian called me from his car and asked if I knew where Mike had been taken. "No." I read what was on the arrest warrant and both of us were baffled by the charges—failure to register as a foreign agent and interstate stalking. Brian said he needed to make some calls and would get back to me. When he called back, he had some disturbing news. Mike was not the only person arrested that morning. The DOJ was going to have a press conference in DC about the case. Mike's name will be mentioned. I started to feel sick to my stomach. A press conference?! From

DC?! With the head of the FBI?! My head began to freeze up and my heart started racing. I felt like I was going to pass out.

Brian asked me if Mike had ever worked on Chinese cases. I said yes but was not sure of the details. He asked if Mike ever put a note on a door of a Chinese client or subject that I could recall. I remembered Mike had worked on a case that took him to an office in lower Manhattan. The subjects of surveillance were Chinese, working in a law office. Mike said the occupants yelled at him for taking pictures through the window of the office door after the occupants refused to open it. Mike left his business card in the door. Brian asked, "Mike doesn't speak Chinese, right?" He knew the answer. "No." Brian informed me the press conference was going to be on C-SPAN and to expect the press to come to the house.

I was still in my robe with no pants. I needed to get off the phone and get dressed. There was no time to collapse in fear; I had to go into high gear to protect my family. I recalled a friend of mine whose husband was arrested and his case had made the national news. She packed a bag for her three kids and sent them to their grandmother's house before the press arrived at her home. That wasn't an option; my children's only grandmother was in her apartment on our property. Where do I send the kids? I didn't have much time to think before the press conference started on C-SPAN. I would watch with the hope this was all a mistake and that they would take this opportunity to say as much. Maybe Mike had cleared everything up wherever he was and now it would be over.

The press conference began with John Demers, US assistant attorney general for the National Security Division, walking to the microphone. He looked to be in his fifties, wearing a suit and tie.

Here are portions of the transcript from the press conference:

> *John Demers:* Good morning. Today, I'm joined by FBI Director, Chris Wray, and remotely by the acting US attorney for the Eastern District of New York, Seth DuCharme, to announce charges against eight

individuals for acting as agents of the People's Republic of China while taking part in an illegal Chinese law enforcement operation known as Fox Hunt. Five of these individuals were arrested across the country this morning. The rest we believe are in China. Since 2014, at the direction of Chinese General Secretary Xi Jinping, China has been engaged in a global operation known as Fox Hunt. China describes Fox Hunt as an international anti-corruption campaign in which it seeks to locate legitimate fugitives around the world to bring them back for trial in China.

There are many established ways that rule-of-law-abiding nations conduct international law enforcement activity. This simply isn't one of them. Operation Fox Hunt is just one of many ways in which China disregards the rule of law. With today's charges, we have turned the PRC's [People's Republic of China] Operation Fox Hunt on its head. The hunters became the hunted, the pursuers the pursued. The five defendants the FBI arrested this morning on these charges of illegally doing the bidding of the Chinese government now face the prospect of prison.

The conduct giving rise to this case investigated by the FBI and prosecuted by the National Security Division and EDNY [United States District Court for the Eastern District of New York] was shocking, but standard operating procedure for Operation Fox Hunt. US Attorney DuCharme will provide more details of the alleged crimes, but at its core, this was a large scale and wide-ranging conspiracy in which several representatives from the Chinese government traveled with the elderly father of the New Jersey–based victim in an effort to threaten him to return to China. The same scheme also included leaving menacing notes on the victim's door, imprisoning the victim's sister in China and harassing the victim's daughter online. The case is charged in part as a conspiracy to act in the United States as illegal agents of a foreign government. The department is committed to the aggressive use of this statute, an important tool in our fight against the illegal foreign activity here, as well as other national security and criminal tools to combat China's Operation Fox Hunt and any other unauthorized illegal activity within the United States.

Christopher Wray: Good morning. Today's charges reflect yet another example of China's ongoing and widespread lawless behavior and our refusal to tolerate it. Simply put, it's outrageous that China thinks it can come to our shores, conduct illegal operations, and bend people here in the United States to their will. In this case, once victims reported China's harassment to the FBI, we began a multi-year investigation in order to bring the perpetrators to justice and vindicate the rule of law, and the FBI is proud to have this investigation culminate in criminal charges, the first of their kind, charges that will help China understand that surveilling, stalking, harassing, and blackmailing our citizens and lawful permanent residents carry serious risks.

As Assistant Attorney General Demers described, Fox Hunt is a sweeping bid by General Secretary Xi and the Chinese Communist Party to target Chinese nationals here in the United States and across the world who are viewed as threats to the regime. These are not the actions we would expect from a responsible nation state. Instead they are more what we would expect from organized criminal syndicate.

Seth DuCharme: Thanks very much, Director Wray. It's my pleasure to be able to participate in today's announcement with you and AAG Demers. To my knowledge, this is the first case of its kind and I think it is significant for a number of reasons. What makes the case really stand out is that it directly involves the efforts of a foreign power to conduct unilateral activity here on US soil in violation of our laws. More specifically, the charges announced today include conspiring to violate 18 USC 851, which relates to the illegal activity by foreign agents operating in the US without notice or permission to the attorney general and conspiring to violate Title 18 United States Code Section 2261, which relates to interstate stalking. Today's arrest of five defendants here in the United States arose from a long-term investigation that we've worked collectively with the FBI, our partners in NSD [Department of Justice's National Security Division] and a number of other agencies, and we've worked with offices across the country because unfortunately, the conduct spans multiple states.

The criminal conduct...involves people in the United States and people overseas, who were working at the behest of government officials in the People's Republic of China, and they were engaged in an international and interstate campaign to threaten, harass and surveil our victim, who we've referred to as John Doe-1, and we're going to try to do our best to protect the anonymity of that victim. John Doe-1 is a US resident.

Complaint on file is over forty pages and rich with facts, but essentially what it says is that over a three-year period, members of the PRC government directed several individuals to engage in unsanctioned and illegal conduct in the United States on behalf of the People's Republic of China for the purpose of coercing a person, John Doe-1, to return to the People's Republic of China, and we believe they did so because John Doe-1 and another victim, his spouse, are alleged by the Chinese government to have committed some violations of Chinese law.

But rather than go through the appropriate channels with the US government to pursue those charges, PRC officials and these defendants in this case engaged in extrajudicial conduct that really violates not only US law, but the types of norms and principles of comity that we would expect from a foreign government. The charged conspiracy involved efforts to pressure John Doe-1 directly, and also by taking actions that affected his family members, including his wife, his adult daughter, and other family members who resided in the United States and some who resided overseas in China. The effort was sustained, relentless over years. It involved some discreet acts to frighten, intimidate, and coerce John Doe, and it involves some shockingly overt attitude.

It involves surveillance, including we believe with use of night vision goggles, involved leaving threatening notes on the victims' doors, and I think perhaps most distressingly, targeting the victim's daughter. The efforts also involved seeking the assistance of a US-based private investigator to bend him to the will of this unlawful mission. To get into just a few of the specifics, one of the notes read, for example, "If you are willing to go back to the mainland and spend 10 years in prison, your wife and children will be safe and all right. That's the end of the matter." This is conduct we would not tolerate from our own citizens, certainly not from our own officials. It constitutes stalking and it is certainly not conduct that we will tolerate when conducted unilaterally by a foreign government with no notice and without the permission of the United States government.

Speaker 2: We will now begin the question-and-answer session. The first question comes from Aruna Viswanatha, please go ahead, from *The Wall Street Journal.*

Aruna Viswanatha: Hi, thanks for doing this. So, as you mentioned, I think John Demers mentioned, this has been going on since 2014, and this is the first time you have brought some cases here. Have you seen an escalation in this trend of harassment efforts over the past year or two? Or what kind of change have you seen? Are they being more aggressive about targeting these people? Our understanding is there are at least two dozen sort of publicly identified targets in the US.

Christopher Wray: So I don't know that I could give you a quantitative assessment of the trend, but I think it's fair to say that this is, as I said in my opening remarks, far from an isolated incident, that it's become all too common, not just here in the United States, but in a number of other countries around the world who also respect the rule of law, and some of the conduct that we've seen here is really beyond the pale and needs to be stopped in the most firm manner possible. Thank you. Thank you.

Speaker 2: The next question comes from Nick Schifrin from PBS. Please go ahead.

Nick Schifrin: Thanks for doing this. Can you discuss who the five who you've arrested are, who you believe they were working for, and how they entered the United States, whether they lied on visa applications? You've mentioned Xi Jinping multiple times. I can imagine that you have connections to these people to PRC officials, but do you have personal evidence or evidence that Xi Jinping personally was involved with this? Thanks.

> *Seth DuCharme:* So this is Seth. I'm not sure who the question was directed to, but I can talk about the defendants a little bit. So, with respect to the five defendants who were arrested today, just briefly, Hongru Jin was a thirty-year-old naturalized US citizen. He resided in Queens, New York. Jin participated in the scheme to stalk our victim, John Doe-1, in or about April of 2017 by assisting with the travel and logistics planning for Zhu Feng and some PRC officials, as well as assisting with the surveillance on John Doe-1 and his father. With respect to Zhu Yong, I can tell you that Yong, who's also known as Jason, he's a sixty-four-year-old PRC citizen and a legal permanent resident of the United States. He resides in Flushing, New York. He was involved in hiring the private investigator, Michael McMahon, to help investigate and surveil and ultimately stalk John Doe-1 on behalf of the PRC government.
>
> Michael McMahon is a fifty-three-year-old US citizen. He's a licensed private detective in New Jersey, and he was essentially recruited and hired to assist with surveillance and conducting other aspects of the operation. Rong Jing is a thirty-eight-year-old US legal permanent resident and PRC citizen. He resides in California. His role essentially was seeking location information for people in the United States on behalf of the PRC government. Then with respect to the fifth defendant who is arrested today, Zheng Congying, he's a twenty-four-year-old PRC citizen and a legal permanent resident. Zheng resided in Brooklyn during the relevant time period, at least, and now he resides out in California where he was arrested earlier this morning. So hopefully that's some helpful background on the defendants and responsive to your question. Thank you.

All I remember hearing was "Michael McMahon," "stalking," and "organized criminal syndicate." It was surreal to say the least but there was no time to analyze it. I went to Mikey's room with a suitcase and told him the press would be coming soon. He would have to go somewhere with his brother and sister for a few days. They could go to one of my sisters' homes nearby if necessary. Mikey started to pack and waited for instructions. I was trying to maintain my composure. I was working remotely at the time and due to participate in a Zoom call with twelve people at 9:00 AM I called a coworker I trusted to let him know what happened but told him I would still make the call. I asked him not to tell our boss. He agreed. I was on that Zoom at 9:00 AM and held it together like it was a normal day.

By the time the Zoom meeting was over, the press began to arrive outside. There wasn't time for Mikey to leave and Ann Marie was in school. I felt trapped. I couldn't go pick her up at school now that the press was there. I only had a few hours before she was due home to figure out how to handle her return. I thought it was better for her to be at school for the time being. The person who usually helped me make these decisions was taken away by the FBI. I was on my own. More cars started showing up. I called my mother, updated her on what was going on, and told her not to speak to the press. She offered to walk to the mailbox to assess the situation. At eighty-four she looked frail but there is no one tougher. I knew she could handle it, so I said OK.

Once the press saw her walk down the driveway multiple reporters came out of their cars and photographed her. They did not ask her any questions and she returned to her apartment. The test run showed they weren't going to come on our property or ring the doorbell. They would have done that already. I realized why. They were waiting for their target, Mike. I wanted to go up to their cars and give them a piece of my mind. I have children! Mike will not speak to you! I stopped myself. I decided to write a note and put it on our front door in case they got impatient. The note said, "No comment." Our attorney warned me no one should speak to the press. No comments were to be made by anyone but our lawyer if the press became aggressive. It was very cold, so they stayed in their cars most of the time. I pulled all the shades and told Mikey no one was going anywhere. If they approached my mother, they would certainly approach my kids. Hopefully they would go away once they realized Mike wasn't home and no one would talk to them.

They didn't. I asked my coworker to cover for me in the afternoon while I awaited instructions from our attorney. I checked outside every few minutes and noticed reporters starting to knock on our neighbors' doors! We didn't socialize often with our neighbors, but they are nice people. I felt terrible. Our quiet neighborhood was infiltrated by the press and I'm sure our neighbors knew how to use Google.

When Brian finally called back, he outlined the charges to me. Mike was charged with failing to register as a foreign agent of China and interstate stalking. There was NO WAY Mike would work for China or stalk anyone. Not possible. Absurd. Insane. They must have him confused with someone else. Who else was charged? Who are these people? My brain became overwhelmed with questions but there wasn't any time to even consider the answers. The press was here watching our every move and my boys were looking for me to fix it. Max had to go to work, so I told him not to engage with the media. As he left I saw the press exit their cars and start to take his picture. I was furious but I couldn't go out and confront them. Not yet. I knew nothing other than what I heard at the press conference and read on the search warrant.

My phone rang from an unrecognizable number. It was Mike. He was very calm and didn't tell me much. He was using the phone of one of the FBI agents. He informed me he was on his way to Brooklyn to be processed and told me to let his older brother Vinny know. Got it! Brian called and instructed me to be at his office in Hackensack for a conference to set bail for Mike. They were asking for $500,000 cash bail. I needed to find the deed to our home and bring it with me. I was to bring copies of our retirement savings and other important documents. Mike had everything organized in a file and all were easy to find. Vinny would also have to cosign the document for bail and put his own assets up for Mike's release. I hung up the phone, gathered all the documents in a folder and waited to be picked up.

Brian Neary's office is a testimony to his long and successful career as a defense attorney. Every inch of the walls is covered with pieces of nostalgia from his alma mater, Notre Dame, or photos of Brian with the who's who of New Jersey politics. He received his law degree from NYU but his Fighting Irish pride was ever present. Brian is well respected in the Garden State and a staple in New Jersey defense litigation. His office overlooks the golden dome of the Bergen County Courthouse building in Hackensack. Vinny and I sat in silence on his leather couch as Brian walked in holding the criminal complaint against Mike. Brian stopped in front of his mahogany desk, not looking up from the document. "This case won't be heard until 2022." My mouth dropped. What was he talking about, 2022?! That was two years from now! It's not possible this will not be over in a matter of a few weeks once everything is cleared up! I mentally dismissed that statement as Brian just preparing me for the worst-case possibility. I had no understanding of the federal court system or any court system for that matter. Brian was our ray of hope to help navigate this and I trusted him with our lives.

The bail hearing with the judge was an audio conference call. With COVID-19 in full force everything was being done remotely. Vinny and I let the judge know we were putting up our homes for bail. Mike would be free to go once the paperwork came through. The hearing only took a few minutes; I heard Mike's voice briefly and it was over. Where was he? I was anxious to get home to our kids. Vinny dropped me off, I gave him Mike's phone, and he headed to Brooklyn to pick up Mike. The press was still outside my house and photographed me as I exited Vinny's car. I knew once Mike came home the press situation would get ugly for all of us. I walked in and let the kids know Brian was working everything out. The perplexed expressions on the children's faces were extremely hard for me to take as their mother. Mikey being the oldest, I needed him to stay strong for the younger two. It would all be handled by Brian, not to worry. I don't know if the children believed me, but my only job was to calm their fear. Their father would be home soon and I knew that would help.

The sun started to set and the temperature plummeted. I looked out and noticed ice forming on the car windows of the media and it brought me a small bit of satisfaction. Maybe the weather would deter them and they would leave before Mike came home.

I got a call from Vinny's phone. It was Mike and he was a few minutes from home. I told him the press was still out front and to find a different way into the house. The back perimeter of our property has a chain link fence and our neighborhood is extremely dark at night. Vinny parked on the street behind our house. Mike snuck through our neighbor's yard, climbed over the fence in the dark and was not seen by anyone. We waited anxiously downstairs as Mike appeared at the sliding doors to the backyard. We all hugged him as he nervously said, "I can't believe it." His demeanor was calm, which immediately helped the kids relax. He said the *New York Post* already had a story online with multiple pictures of Mike and me, including one taken at Gracie Mansion from an Emmy Award party given by the Mayor of New York. I couldn't believe the headline "EX-NYPD IS CHINA MUSCLE" (*New York Post* story).

The article was a horror show. It was a cut-and-paste from the criminal complaint and only focused on Mike being ex-NYPD. They brazenly used the NYPD as clickbait yet did not mention anything about Mike's prolific career as a detective and then a sergeant in the Bronx. He had over one thousand arrests and seventy-eight medals, including the department's second-highest honor, the Combat Cross, for a gang-involved shooting in the Bronx. He became a school safety sergeant in charge of forty public and private schools in the Bronx. At the start of his career, he was a member of the elite Street Crime Unit of New York City, made up of two hundred handpicked officers who cleaned up the entire city. Instead, they spun the story to paint Mike as a thug and heavy for the CCP (Chinese Communist Party) who harassed and stalked a Chinese man and his family in New Jersey. The article attributed the acts of others to Mike and painted a very dirty picture. How could the media get it so wrong? How did they get this online before Mike even got home from processing? It was awful. Is this really happening? Sadly, it was just the beginning.

Mike wanted to review our Ring camera footage from the arrest that morning. He strongly believed this nightmare was due to another case he worked on for the government, the Paul Bergrin case he mentioned in the foyer. The footage would have captured the FBI agent's admission that he knew Mike from that case and it wasn't the first time he was "on his board." When we went to review the footage on the Ring app, it was gone. Where did it go? We had overnight clips from before and since the arrest but the window of the time the FBI was at the house was gone. That had never happened before. Did the FBI erase it remotely? How did it just disappear? Mike and I started to understand this was a well-coordinated attack on our family.

The next day the story was in the print edition of the *New York Post* with a full-page picture of Mike with former NYPD Commissioner Ray Kelly. We had met Ray Kelly a year prior at a Christmas Midnight Mass at St. Patrick's Cathedral in midtown. We were guests of Cardinal Dolan through a mutual friend. I took a picture of Mike and Ray Kelly and Mike used it on his LinkedIn page. In the background of the picture hung a gigantic painting of Pope John Paul II, looking over the two men. It was a great night we would never forget. Now that photo had become a nightmare, attaching Commissioner Kelly for no reason. My hatred for the media—after what had been a lifelong symbiotic relationship—was now at fever pitch. The *New York Post* is the ninth-most-read paper in the country. My children, our friends, and family would now have to see this. It was all lies, and I was furious. Our lawyer said to stay quiet. Let it pass. Don't post anything online. We obeyed.

It immediately got worse. The story went to the wire and every major news outlet picked it up, including local, national, and international news. The world thought my husband was a traitor working for our greatest enemy, China. I knew this story wasn't going away anytime soon. My entire family was in danger.

CHAPTER TWO

THE KIDS RETREATED TO THEIR ROOMS for the night after we assured them that we had everything under control. The press went home after failing to capture a photo of Mike. They even went so far as to shine a bright light into our living room, hoping someone would peek out. We purposely stayed away from the internet, knowing that whatever we might read would only upset both of us. There was no time for that.

With the kids out of earshot, Mike filled me in on what happened after he stepped out of our house that morning. Agent McCarthy handcuffed him on our walkway right outside our front door. McCarthy almost seemed apologetic that he had to do it. Mike was placed in the back seat of an unmarked vehicle being driven by the female agent who was in our house. McCarthy was seated next to Mike. After a few minutes McCarthy asked if our son Mikey, "the one on the couch," was the baby featured on the TV show, *A Baby Story*. That was a popular show on The Learning Channel where each episode featured the birth of a child. (Our baby story was actually about Max, not Mikey.) How bizarre, I thought, for McCarthy to ask Mike if the child who just witnessed his father being arrested in his underwear is the same child featured on a TV show.

From the moment McCarthy entered our home that morning he was amped up like the *Wolf of Wall Street*. He was excessively chatty, his movements were erratic, and his tactics were sloppy. Had he ever executed an arrest warrant before? I would bet not. I couldn't believe this guy took the time to go to YouTube and watch our thirty-minute episode of *A Baby Story*—and he still arrested Mike. The episode featured details of Mike's long and honorable tenure on the NYPD and his career-ending car accident while on a high-speed chase in the Bronx. McCarthy knew Mike was a hero. He knew I was an Emmy-winning actress. He was giddy pinching a guy like Mike.

When McCarthy asked Mike about *A Baby Story*, Mike bristled but didn't answer. He remained silent for a bit then pushed McCarthy about the Bergrin case. Mike asked McCarthy how he "knew" him from that case. McCarthy said that his office mate was the case agent on the Bergrin case. Mike said, "Shawn Brokos?" Hearing that question the female driver adjusted herself and shot McCarthy a look in the rearview mirror to signal him to "shut up." Knowing he had said too much, McCarthy told Mike there would be no more talking until they got to the office. At that point Mike was convinced he had been targeted because of the Paul Bergrin case.

They brought Mike to a warehouse-style building in Woodland Park, New Jersey. There was no signage on the building and there were two side-door loading docks. Mike had made over a thousand arrests while on the NYPD and knew this was not a typical processing center. He was taken to a small room to be interrogated. While Mike naively saw all law enforcement as brothers, he knew the FBI and the NYPD had a sordid history. When the FBI was exposed for not sharing intelligence with the NYPD about 9/11, it created a permanent distrust of the bureau. At the same time, Mike had never had an issue working with federal agents. He had heard stories about this strained partnership, but he could never imagine anyone in law enforcement setting up a colleague. To do so would violate the oath. Any officer who acted in this manner would be considered a traitor who should be stripped of the badge. This was the overwhelming sentiment among Mike and his colleagues. On the morning of October 28, 2020, Mike had no idea he was walking into the lion's den.

Lawyers tell anyone who is arrested not to talk to the cops. Mike would be the first person to advise someone the same. Yet in this moment Mike chose to speak, and it would work in his favor. Mike hadn't planned on doing so, but his overwhelming instinct to help kicked in. One of the men present was EDNY Investigator John Ross who was former NYPD. This made Mike feel like he had someone in the room he could trust; an NYPD brother wouldn't screw him over. Once Mike signed off that he would speak without a lawyer, it threw McCarthy into a tailspin. McCarthy began fumbling through papers and texting frantically, claiming it was with his daughter. I believe with certainly he was texting FBI Case Agent Christopher Bruno to alert him that Mike was actually talking, (Bruno was in Connecticut arresting Jason Zhu). McCarthy had no clue what he was doing and knew little about the case, which worked to Mike's advantage. Ross said little as he was not part of the four-year investigation.

Over the ninety minutes Mike was interrogated, he was shown a series of text messages. One read, "I think if we harass Xu park outside his house and let him know we're out there, I did that on another case." (NOT SHOWN TO MIKE WAS JOHNNY'S REPLY "We can't harass Xu like that lol.") It had been more than four years since Mike had worked on this case, so he was trying to understand the context. He took a few moments before suggesting that maybe it was a typo. He had no idea why he would type something like that. He then realized what "I did that on another case" referred to and explained to McCarthy in detail that he had worked on a case in Little Ferry, New Jersey, where a man was accused of stealing money from a construction company. Mike was hired with another PI to document the day in the life of the accused subject. Mike parked in front of the man's house and photographed the construction work he was doing and the shiny new car in the driveway.

McCarthy quickly got off the subject once he learned the subject of surveillance in the Little Ferry case was not Chinese. He then asked about Mike's friend, Greg Finning. This made Mike extremely uncomfortable. Greg worked with Mike on the NYPD in the 1990s and then left to become an agent in the New York Drug Enforcement Agency office. He was highly regarded by his peers for his work on international money laundering and drug trafficking cases. He eventually retired from the DEA to join a prestigious investigative firm in New York City.

McCarthy made a comment about Finning doing favors for Mike. Mike's mind began to race. He had no idea what McCarthy was referring to and he did not respond. Not getting any movement on Finning, McCarthy showed Mike more texts, which started to spark his memory. One text between Mike and Greg mentioned a man named Brian O'Rourke. Mike told McCarthy he had met an active FBI agent (O'Rourke) at the gym in 2017. The two had mutual friends and shared a few law enforcement war stories.

At this gym encounter, Mike told Agent O'Rourke about the case, describing how he followed a Chinese man in New Jersey who had stolen money from a construction company in China. Mike recalled O'Rourke asking if the man he was following had a "red line" on him. During the interrogation Mike remembered the word "red" but not the actual term "Red Notice." A Red Notice is an international alert for a wanted person. If the US doesn't have an extradition agreement with the issuing country, in this case China, it is unenforceable. O'Rourke assured Mike it sounded like a civil matter and did not instruct him to take any further action. Again, McCarthy moved on and didn't ask more about FBI Agent O'Rourke.

Mike was then shown pictures of two of his former NYPD coworkers Eric Gallowitz and Mike Kelly who also had gone on to become private investigators. Both men had worked with Mike every day on the previous case involving the Chinese man. Mike's chest tightened and he became emotional. Much to Mike's relief, McCarthy told Mike the two had not been arrested. Mike was shown more text messages, but with so much time having passed, it was all a bit confusing. Mike kept asking if he had been used by his Chinese client. A smug McCarthy said, "They weren't part of a construction company, I can tell you that."

Surprisingly, Mike recalled quite a bit about the subject he was tasked to follow. He had worked one day of surveillance in October 2016, and four days of surveillance in April of 2017. He spent the first hour of his interrogation explaining how he had been told the Chinese man had stolen money from a family construction business. The client was trying to see if he was living large on the ill-gotten gains. This is common in cases where money is alleged to have been stolen from a business. The investigative procedure is to do asset searches, follow the subject to account for residences, cars, and so forth. If the victim of the alleged theft wishes to sue the person in civil court the victim must provide evidence. Mike mentioned the words "civil matter" approximately fifteen times in the first hour of his interrogation.

Then McCarthy asked about the subject's father coming from China in April of 2017 to see his son. Mike believed the father came here to convince the son to return the stolen money. Neither Mike nor the other two PIs saw any red flags regarding that visit. Near the end of the interview and after Mike learned he had obviously been used, John Ross asked Mike why he thought they wanted the subject to return to China. Mike said, "I guess to prosecute him."

After a pause, Mike asked, "Was I duped?" At that point, the agents presented Mike with information confirming that he had been used by Chinese agents. Mike was devastated. In all his years he had never had any issue with any client. He prided himself on his work and due diligence.

The agents wrapped up the interview and left Mike alone in the room. The interview was civil and friendly. There were no hot lights or high-pressure tactics. Mike felt it had gone well, even though he was gut-punched knowing he had been used for some purpose yet to be identified. Mike never committed any crime and hoped his willingness to talk would help resolve the matter.

Outside the interrogation room, Mike was relaxed. He chatted with four FBI agents, at one point asking them if they knew a man named Terry McGee. Mike had worked with Terry during his Street Crime years on the NYPD in the early '90s. They all knew Terry. Terry was a beloved member of the NYPD who was paralyzed after an accident while on an overseas assignment. Terry continued to work and became an ambassador for the department.

Mike started telling some crazy stories from his days working with Terry. As the conversation went on, Mike learned that Terry had worked with McCarthy and Case Agent Christopher Bruno in the same FBI field office in Red Bank, New Jersey. Small world. Just then McCarthy walked past the group and was mildly curious about what they were discussing.

Before leaving to be processed in Brooklyn, Mike was free to go to the bathroom on his own. Upon his return, he was finally handed the criminal complaint against him. For the first time Mike saw the charges: violating the Foreign Agents Registration Act (FARA) and interstate stalking surrounding Operation Fox Hunt. Now furious, Mike told Agent McCarthy to tell his supervisor he had "no fucking idea what Fox Hunt or FARA was!!" The complaint was dense with allegations of stalking and harassment. It included an alleged stalking of the subject's daughter living in California by a rogue private investigator who was a paid confidential informant for the FBI. An incident at the New Jersey home of the alleged victim that occurred almost two years after Mike had completed his work on this case was included. The complaint said Mike witnessed a public meeting between the alleged victim and his father, who was forced here from China in April of 2017. There were countless accusations that had absolutely nothing to do with Mike and he was incensed! Stalking?! How could he be charged with actions done by individuals he never met? What the hell was happening?! McCarthy became uncomfortable, and offered to let Mike use his personal phone to call me. The next time I heard Mike's voice was when he appeared in front of the judge for the bail hearing.

At home that night, it was getting late but our adrenaline was running high and we got to work. Mike told me that after reading the complaint he had asked John Ross, "Is my life over?" Ross answered,

"Just do your proffer and you'll be fine." (A proffer is a presentation to the government with evidence of your innocence.) That gave Mike some comfort coming from a former NYPD member. I felt the same relief that someone involved seemed to see the same glaring problems with this arrest. Mike had texted Mike Kelly and Eric Gallowitz after his brother Vinny gave him back his phone. He texted them saying he would need them as witnesses. They never responded. Had they seen the news? Had the FBI lied to them about Mike? Mike was reeling. He looked through his phone to see if he still had all the texts he was shown at his interrogation. He did, and we pulled every file that may be related to the case.

Mike had purchased a new phone in 2018 and transferred everything to it from his old phone. This simple act gave us a footprint of Mike's timeline on the case. He had saved every text message, invoice, contract, background search, and more. He got frustrated because he was sure he must have had handwritten notes and recordings of any meetings somewhere. Since the arrest was four years after the time in question, some items may have been shredded. The fact that he had bought a new phone in 2018 and transferred all the information was a miracle. We printed up every email and text message and started to piece together Mike's role in this. Our dining room became our situation room with hundreds of pages of files pulled to review.

We figured there must be a clue in these files as to what exactly happened. The FBI doesn't just raid your house without cause. So far, we hadn't seen anything in the complaint or at the interrogation that showed a crime. We started building a timeline and we found the person who first contacted Mike, "Emily Hsu." "Emily" was a translator in Queens who initially contacted Mike in the fall of 2016. She wasn't on the list of people arrested that day, but we weren't sure if she was Coconspirator #1 or #2 identified in the complaint or an anonymous confidential informant. For a minute we thought about calling her but decided against it, not knowing what role she played.

We started with what we knew. Emily was the owner of a translation company in Queens called Transperfect Language Services.

Mike had a $5,000 retainer bank check with her company name and a signed contract from her client in need of Mike's services. We collected copies of all her emails and put them in chronological order. We also pulled all the emails, text messages, invoices, and surveillance reports involving "Johnny," "Jason," "Eric Yan," Eric Gallowitz, Greg Finning, and Mike Kelly. We mapped it out quickly and found there wasn't much to review. Unsurprisingly, our facts showed a run-of-the-mill case for any private investigator.

Early the next morning we heard a knock at our door, before the press had returned to the street. It was Greg Finning, armed with bagels and coffee. He seemed genuinely concerned for Mike. Mike was visibly anxious because he had to tell Greg his name came up in the interrogation. Mike took a deep breath and told Greg the FBI had brought up their text messages to each other. Since Mike had only a minimal understanding of the case, he had little more to share.

When Greg heard this news, he seemed to panic and pace back and forth in our living room. His concern about his friend seemed to disappear. After leaving the DEA, Greg had subcontracted Mike several times as a freelance PI on cases for the investigation company he worked for. Instead of sitting down and taking some time to dive into Mike's case, Greg shut down and quickly left. Mike was sick. He had been falsely arrested and called a traitor, and now one of his best friends had emotionally abandoned him.

There was no time to wallow in that hurt, as we had work to do. We went to Brian Neary's office and filed into his conference room. Brian employed several attorneys at his firm, many of whom had worked with Mike over the years. Everyone was shocked and disgusted that Mike had been arrested. Not one person believed anything that was in the media.

Brian had asked and associate who was a former US attorney to join this case. Hearing her take on the case gave Mike and me some hope. There was no crime, yet the DOJ somehow cut and pasted a conspiracy out of thin air. How could they arrest Mike for doing his job?

Brian felt this case needed some additional support on the legal team. His firm didn't often handle national security cases. When Mike was a private investigator, he had worked for an attorney named Larry Lustberg, who was a highly respected defense attorney and well-versed in federal law, having tried many cases with the DOJ. Larry had forty years of experience under his belt and was a director at Gibbons Law Firm. He was lead defense counsel on several high-profile cases throughout his illustrious career. Mike was Larry's go-to private investigator when he needed someone to get the job done. He also loved Mike personally and agreed to join our team. We knew we could not afford any of this, but we did what we could to retain Larry and Brian to get the ball rolling. Larry added Attorney Genna Conti to our defense team. Genna was handpicked by Larry for the coveted position to be mentored and work by his side. Mike had worked with Genna as a private investigator on several cases and was incredibly impressed with her as an attorney. This case was personal to every lawyer who was going to touch it because of how they felt about Mike. Every single one of them was outraged and 100 percent behind us. Our team was strong and would surely be successful getting this thrown out. We left Brian's office cautiously optimistic but still in shock.

I tried to keep things as normal as possible with my kids. I couldn't let myself break down; it wasn't an option. I was working full time and navigating this nightmare. I managed to hold it together in Mike's presence. It wasn't easy. I knew if he saw me cry, he would be overwhelmed by misplaced guilt. I prayed a lot. I spoke to Lisa Brown and my mother every day, as they were my trusted outlets to vent to and think out loud with. I took a lot of calls in my bathroom out of earshot of the kids and Mike.

The next trip to Neary's office threw this case in the first of many unexpected directions. In our research into the subject of Mike's surveillance, Jin Xu, we discovered an article from *The Wall Street Journal* regarding the CCP using lawfare to intimidate dissidents in the US by suing them in civil court. The article was published on July 29, 2020. The article featured photos of Jin Xu and his wife, Fang Liu, who were on China's Most Wanted list and accused of bribes and corruption. According to the article, they were painted as victims of the CCP and being dragged through our American court system to pressure them to return to China. There was no mention in that article about the couple being followed by private investigators or being visited multiple times by Chinese agents since 2016. There were no details of the crimes they committed listed in the civil lawsuit against the couple, other than accusations of stealing money from a Chinese business. The article mentioned that Jin Xu had a government position when he lived in China, while Fang Liu worked for an insurance company in China. It was a fairly innocuous article but now we had to dig in to see if it played any role in our case.

At Neary's office we called up PACER, a landing site for court documents. We printed anything we could find from that civil lawsuit against Jin Xu and Fang Liu. One other party listed as a defendant was Yan Liu (Fang Liu's sister), and someone named Xu Bai was mentioned but not as a defendant. Along with the parties named there were multiple LLCs listed, including JLifetime LLC. We made copies of hundreds of pages and took them home to read. I didn't even know what I was looking for in those documents so I would highlight what I thought might be somehow relevant. The documents were overwhelming and my head was spinning so I put the case aside and would return to it if I found a connection with Mike's case.

We started to get a better picture of who Mike was following back in 2016. These people are being sued for approximately $30 million in the United States and are wanted in China. The civil lawsuit against them has hundreds of pages of evidence against them. Is the lawsuit legit or, as the *WSJ* claimed, just a way for the Chinese Communist Party to harass a dissident who defied it. The allegations of fraud seem to fit what Mike was told back in 2016. Mike's client wanted him to find assets. How many homes does the subject own? Cars? Does the subject work anywhere? Go to a fancy gym or apartment? Do relatives own properties or have other large expenses of record? Private investigators call cases like this, documenting, "a day in the life."

In the case of Jin Xu, Mike felt his client had been victimized and was trying to help locate his stolen money. PIs only have access to public records and there are plenty of open-source records for review. PIs in New Jersey have to be approved by the DMV to search license plates and disclose the use of the information. In this case Mike ran one plate to confirm info provided to him by his client. That plate came back to a Mercedes Benz owned and registered to someone named Xu Bai at an address provided to Mike by his client. This confirmed the subject of Mike's surveillance had something to do with the registered owner. It also showed the vehicle was an asset valued at approximately eighty thousand dollars.

In Mike's email exchanges with his client, he informed him the address provided was owned by an LLC, not a person. This is not common in residential properties unless it's a rental property. This particular property was not a rental. The owner of the home was JLifetime LLC. In April of 2017 Mike found a second home that he believed might be owned by the subject. A simple search showed the second home was also owned by JLifetime LLC. Mike sent an email and what's called a TLO report to his client showing both homes were owned by the same entity and he told him, "Your (stolen) money is in JLifetime." I remembered the civil lawsuit. One of the LLCs listed as being sued was JLifetime. JLifetime is owned by Yan Liu.

The story seemed to be coming together and going in our favor. The civil lawsuit was a compelling piece of evidence to prove there was a civil lane to this case for which Mike was hired. He was never asked to do anything illegal, because of course he wouldn't, but the facts seemed to be going in Mike's direction. Did the government know about this civil case? What was revealed in the civil case and the timeline of events surrounding it would become a vital part of the puzzle.

In the beginning, Larry was intrigued about the civil lawsuit. It proved Mike had a connection to it, but we had no idea if it would clear him. Larry was thrilled that Mike had saved everything related to this case and started planning a proffer for the government. While it was abundantly clear Mike was innocent, Larry warned us what we were up against. The odds are stacked on the side of the government. They successfully indict 99 percent of people and win 99 percent of cases brought to trial. Those are some tough odds to fight. Still, there was no way we weren't fighting this and Larry agreed. Having been a defense attorney for decades, this was one case he knew we should fight.

Larry and Genna put together a proffer for the government showing Mike's defense. It's always a risky move giving the government a map of where we were going with the case. We hoped once they realized Mike had saved all his evidence and kept impeccable records they would back off. Our proffer was a forty-page PowerPoint presentation with texts, emails, photos, reports, bank records, and a timeline. Mike and I both worked tirelessly to provide everything we could find to present to the government.

After the proffer was presented to the government they emailed some questions. Mike was happy to provide the answers and was cooperative. Then the government scheduled a reverse proffer. This would be the government's response to the evidence we presented. Would they offer Mike a plea deal? There was no way he would take a deal but it's quite common to offer one. We made our first trip to EDNY courthouse in Brooklyn with Larry, Genna, and Brian. Mike would finally get to see the players who did this to him all in one room. I was not permitted to go inside due to COVID restrictions, so I got coffee and sat on a bench. The streets were eerily quiet since COVID had shut down the world. It wasn't the city I was used to. I was extremely anxious so I started to walk up and down the street. Within a half hour I saw two men walking towards me. One was over six foot tall with wavy brown hair, the other significantly shorter. I knew instinctively it was EDNY Chief Craig Heeren, the lead prosecutor on Mike's case. I had never seen him before but I knew it was him. As the two men walked passed me, I followed a short distance behind them and tried to listen to what they were saying. He didn't even look at me as he passed, oblivious I was the woman behind the man he was prosecuting. They were both smiling and laughing, clearly on their way to lunch. Clearly the seriousness of this situation was not weighing on Heeren as it was on Mike. Heeren carried himself as if he didn't have a care in the world. Whatever happened in that meeting, it was irrelevant based on his nose planted in the air strolling through the quiet Brooklyn streets. I looked back at the courthouse and saw a grayish-haired man open a side door to accept his food delivery. If my instinct was right, it was US Attorney Matthew Haggans, also part of the prosecution team grabbing his food with a smile. Just another day at the office for these guys, destroying my husband's life.

When Mike exited he told me the meeting was pointless. The FBI Newark case agent Christopher Bruno was in attendance and said nothing. Heeren laid out how much time Mike would serve if found guilty. The entire meeting lasted fifteen minutes. Absolutely nothing was accomplished by dragging everyone in over the Brooklyn Bridge except more billable hours for our lawyers. I asked Mike what Heeren and Haggans looked like and sure enough I was right about both men.

As we were waiting for the news about the presentation, we heard that an article about Fox Hunt was coming out in ProPublica, written by Sebastian Rotella. I was in a panic not knowing how he would portray Mike in the story. Larry had done a brief interview with Sebastian and gave him a quote, but my view of the media was tarnished after the awful coverage of Mike's arrest. The EDNY also knew this article was coming and I was sure they were not happy.

The night before the ProPublica article came out, I was a wreck. I wanted to read it before Mike saw it to prepare him for what may or may not be in it. At this point the public perception was that my husband was a Chinese asset. This article could be devastating in our quest to get the truth out there. I was very naive in those early days, believing that the press would do their job.

I immediately opened my phone before the sun came up and read the article. It was extremely long and filled with fascinating information. The story of Mike's case from this investigative journalist was earth-shattering. We learned more from that article than anything the government had shared so far. It provided details about the man behind this operation, HuJi, who was a police officer in China and the head of repatriating Chinese citizens from other countries. He was a world traveler and highly touted in China for his successful missions to get people back to the mainland to face punishment. The Chinese agent's attempts to repatriate the subject of Mike's surveillance were done in secret. Mike was purposely kept in the dark. As former law enforcement, the Chinese agents would never share their plan with Mike.

The article was fair to Mike and included a supportive quote from Larry that this was a routine PI case for any investigator. I think anyone who read the article could get a broad understanding of these Fox Hunt operations. Of course, this article was not good for the government. It exposed their lack of skill in investigating these Chinese agents while on our soil. They let Chinese bad actors use our country like a revolving door. Our country not only trained Chinese cops with our own law enforcement officials, but allowed them to tour our colleges and take courses. It was embarrassing to say the least. I'm sure this article did not sit well with the government.

Soon after the article came out we got a call indicating that the DOJ would be putting out a superseding indictment against Mike, adding charges of conspiracy. I believe this move was to distract from the article. There was nothing in the superseding indictment that hadn't been told before, with the exception of naming two formerly unnamed "coconspirators." In this indictment the named two coconspirators were at large in China. It was a distraction planted to override the ProPublica article. The article helped us in more ways than the government was even aware. It appeared details about the activities of the Chinese agents had been obtained from a source inside the government.

At the same time, the superseding indictment got the government more press, including in our local media. The articles, which included Mike's picture, featured him as a Chinese asset. I reached out to one of the writers via Facebook and let him know how upset I was. I never heard back.

The frustrating part of the ProPublica article was that the government seemed to know everything about the Chinese agents, yet they went after Mike. Why? I made a list of the people mentioned in the article to align them with Mike's emails and texts. Things started to come together. The men Mike communicated with used their real names with the exception of HuJi. HuJi used the alias "Eric Yan" with Mike. "Johnny" and "Jason" were his middlemen. We learned from the article that HuJi had toured residential areas in New Jersey with "Johnny" during the summer of 2016. The article did not specify any addresses but we could deduce that Mike had been to the same areas when he was hired in the fall of 2016. The story seemed straightforward. In reading it, I still couldn't figure out what crime the government believed Mike had committed. We were still mostly in the dark as we waited for the government to drop the first batch of discovery for us to read.

My brain started to work overtime and I couldn't think about anything else. Mike wasn't doing well and I had no idea how to fix it. I would make him walk with me every morning. Sometimes we wouldn't talk, we would just walk. Mike does not have a temper, but I could feel his anger boiling right under the surface. I wasn't walking on eggshells, but I had to read his temperature every day and proceed as such. In my mind there was no way we wouldn't fight this. I knew if Mike gave in to the pressure of the government, I would lose him forever. The idea of a plea deal was nonnegotiable. He did nothing wrong. Justice would most certainly prevail. We just had to fight.

The first batch of discovery delivered to Neary's office was multiple binders filled with information about the case. I was permitted to look at the sensitive material, but I was under a protective order so I could not discuss what I saw with anyone or take materials home. I could take notes, but the notes had to stay at the office. This case had been deemed a national security case, which put us at a grave disadvantage. That was the point. By handcuffing us to our lawyer's office we were on the meter for every minute we spent there. The first batch was all paperwork, nothing digital. It would take me approximately one or two hours to read through each binder.

From day one I realized the total amount of discovery was overwhelming, 99 percent of which had nothing to do with Mike. We were looking for any connection to the Chinese government where they included Mike and there wasn't a single one. We knew from Mike's materials he had nothing in his possession that connected him, but we had no idea if the Chinese agents had some chatter about him, which may have been the reason the government went after Mike. There was nothing. Trying to prove the negative in a case like this is more challenging than a case where there is overwhelming evidence. Defense attorneys usually use their skills to minimize the amount of damage intended to punish their client. In our case, we were trying to find the connection the government saw but could not. The paper trail evidence was minimal.

Back to our timeline:

"Emily Hsu" from Transperfect Language Services hired Mike in September of 2016. He received a TD Bank retainer check for $5,000 and a signed retainer agreement from Jason Zhu stating he would be responsible for any legal fees of McMahon Investigative Group if Mike was accused of liability in this case.

A wire transfer of $6,000 from the Bank of China in Chinese was received with the words, "ERIC'S TRAVEL" written in English in the memo. Our banking info on the document was in English, the rest was in Chinese.

A few wire transfers of small amounts of money were sent to personal and business accounts.

Every surveillance report and invoice with details of the work done was provided.

Invoices from private investigators Mike Kelly and Eric Gallowitz for their work were included. Checks from McMahon Investigative Group to the two PIs were documented.

One mystery that kept me up at night was the fact that "Emily Hsu," the translator, had not been arrested. All roads led back to her as point zero to this case, yet we heard nothing about her. So, I started digging. There is no such person as "Emily Hsu." Her real name is Lina Xu. From her first contact with Mike she used an alias. Lina Xu was a Chinese translator and her company name was Transperfect Language Services. When we Googled Transperfect Language Services it landed on a very impressive website. Transperfect Language Services listed client were a who's who of large corporations and federal agencies, including the FBI. That was interesting. Was she an FBI asset using the translation company as her cover or was it just a strange coincidence?

I looked further at the emails "Emily" exchanged with Mike. I noticed she had used another name for her business. Even though the business name on the check used to pay Mike was Transperfect Language Services, she used the name Transaccurate Language Services in her emails. The bottom line was she lied to Mike from day one by using an alias. I asked myself "Who is this woman and how did she find Mike to work on this case?" She claimed to be just the liaison for her client, Jason Zhu, who only spoke Chinese. She was merely a conduit to pass on the information to Mike provided to her by Zhu. The information included names, date of birth, Social Security numbers, Chinese passport numbers, photographs of the subjects and family members, a photo of a New Jersey license plate on a Mercedes Benz. It was obvious someone else had already looked into these people prior to Mike being hired. But who? Another PI? Chinese agents? Someone had seen that Mercedes in the US at some point and took that picture. Little did I know how important that photograph would become.

When Mike was contacted by "Emily" in 2016 and given Jin Xu's name, he immediately looked him up. He found a photo of Jin Xu on a wanted list from *China Daily*, CCP's daily newspaper, along with ninety-nine others who were wanted for financial crimes. Mike texts Emily inquiring about this. "I just did some checks on him. Looks like he's wanted in China for corruption". Emily responds, " OK, would you think it will be ok to share this information with Mr. Zhu? OR should I not pass this inf(ormation) to him."

Mike—"I'm sure he knows this but he didn't tell us." "I think he should have." "He's wanted for corruption, embezzlement and taking bribes. If you google his name you will see the photo you sent me."

Emily—"I see, I think now I know what's going on with Jin Xu's case." Emily never follows up on this statement to Mike. Remember, Mike was hired to find assets of this man who allegedly stole money from a family construction business. The accusations against Jin Xu in China lined up with the allegation that he was a thief.

Having retired from the NYPD in 2003, Mike was no longer a member of law enforcement; he was a civilian and a PI. He shared the info about Jin Xu being a wanted man with the two other PIs who worked with him on this case. Mike was working on a civil matter for a client and that was it. The government's take was Mike must have known, or should have known, that he was being hired by the Chinese government because the men he met with at a Panera Bread and Brian Neary's law office in 2016 were Chinese. The fact was Jin Xu could be wanted for criminal acts in China and could also be investigated for civil matters in the US.

There was never any indication his client wanted Mike to approach Jin Xu to pressure him to return the money. Quite the opposite. Mike had no discussion about what HuJi ("Eric Yan") planned to do with the information Mike provided. Private investigators do not have access to federal documents such as tax returns, visa applications, or credit card statements. Bank records can be obtained but are often not able to be corroborated and aren't guaranteed facts. During Mike's interrogation Agent McCarthy seemed shocked Mike could get bank records, saying the FBI would need a warrant. Not true for PIs. There are many companies that do it and it's not illegal. Here you have an FBI agent who is shocked PIs can run bank records. Did he not know that? McCarthy seemed completely uninformed across the board.

Looking back, I was haunted by McCarthy's words in our foyer when Mike asked, "Are you here about the Paul Bergrin case?" and he said, "No, but I know you from that case. It's not the first time you were on my board." I knew we were dealing with personal bias against Mike. If Mike had been targeted because of his work on the Bergrin case, it was time to explore why.

CHAPTER THREE

On February 13, 2001, Mike was involved in a high-speed car chase through the Bronx while in active pursuit of a perpetrator who had violently assaulted his girlfriend and threatened a cop. The lead car in the chase, occupied by the perp, purposely steered his car directly into the front passenger side of the patrol car where Mike was seated. This action caused the patrol car to smash into a telephone pole at fifty miles an hour, allowing the perp to continue to evade the cops. Mike's car looked like an accordion. He was extracted from the wreck and transported to Jacobi Medical Center with a broken hip and fractured neck vertebrae. A live feed from an ABC News chopper documented every brazen move the perpetrator made during the chase, which ultimately ended in his capture.

As I watched news footage of the incident from the *As the World Turns* makeup room in Brooklyn, I had no idea that Mike was in that car. Within an hour I got a call telling me Mike had been severely injured and someone from the NYPD would come pick me up. It is never a good sign for a spouse to receive an escort. Mayor Rudy Guiliani and Police Commissioner Bernard Kerik had done a press conference in front of the hospital after visiting Mike in the emergency room.

When I arrived at the hospital, the halls were lined with fellow officers there to support Mike and our family. Mike was highly medicated and in bad shape when I first saw him in the ER cubicle. It was the first time since we met that the reality of his work hit me. Mike always assured me that his job was not a daily struggle to stay alive. Now I saw the truth with my own eyes and the possibility of losing him at the job he loved overwhelmed me.

After six long months of rehabilitation, the medical assessment held that Mike could return to his NYPD job but be relegated to restricted duty only. His first day back to the Forty-Third Precinct was September 9, 2001. Two days later, September 11, 2001, our country suffered the worst terrorist attack ever on US soil. Mike was forbidden to respond to Ground Zero. He was assigned to whatever his supervisors needed, mostly transporting police personnel to Ground Zero or One Police Plaza. Despite his requests to help, his restricted duty status would not allow that authorization. Mike watched coworkers pile into vans headed to Manhattan. Some never came back. He worked the phones, trying to answer panicked family members making desperate attempts to find their loved ones.

At the end of their shifts, the men and women of the NYPD would return to the precinct covered with dirt after working the Pile. Mike witnessed one patrol car after another returning covered in thick dust and ash. One day a van returned from the Pile and Mike turned on the interior ventilation fan. The dust that came out of the vents overtook him and he began to cough uncontrollably. Every day those men and women were exposed to that toxic dust. Not one of those heroes would have stopped doing their jobs. Unfortunately, illnesses continued to be diagnosed and funerals were held for those that had succumbed to the silent terrorist attack on their bodies.

After months of restricted duty, in mid-2002, it was time for Mike to be reevaluated by the NYPD medical board to determine if he could return to unrestricted duty. Stripped down to his underwear, he was directed to perform specific physical challenges. After a full evaluation, the board decided Mike's disability could cause potential liability to a coworker. He was ordered to retire.

Mike's forced retirement devastated him. It was a huge adjustment to lose his identity as a police officer. Mike had taken the NYPD test at age sixteen with his older brothers. Even though he was too young to join the force he scored in the low nineties. He was called to join the department at eighteen. Knowing he would be turned down because of his age, he decided not to go down to One Police Plaza. His father insisted he go so the NYPD brass wouldn't think he had blown off the department. His dad was convinced they would remove him from the list if he didn't show up.

Mike was right. The lieutenant who checked in the potential recruits saw Mike's age and told him to go home. His name remained on the list and Mike went on with his life not knowing if he would hear from them again. He graduated from Clarkstown North High School in New City, New York, and earned his associate degree in criminal justice from Rockland Community College. While preparing to transfer to Iona College to complete his bachelor's degree, Mike got the call to join the NYPD. He went on to distinguish himself as a decorated NYPD officer with fourteen years of service to the community he was proud to protect. Due to a career-ending injury it had come to an abrupt end. In March of 2003, Sergeant and former Detective Michael McMahon walked out of the Forty-Third Precinct in the Bronx and never returned. I've seen him cry only a few times in our thirty years together and the day he got the call ordering him to retire was one of those times. He would forever miss his job.

There were some difficult life adjustments to be made. We already had one son, Mikey, and our second son, Max, had arrived in September of 2002. We were no longer mandated to live in New York state and together made the decision to move to New Jersey closer to my family. Once in our new home, the boys had their dad 24/7. I saw it was a gift to the children and Mike loved being with them. However, I could see there was something missing for Mike. I tried to keep his spirits up, but I could tell he was struggling. I was working crazy hours at *As the World Turns*, the boys were growing, and schedules were constantly changing. Since I was often at the Brooklyn studio five days a week, Mike kept busy with their school activities and coaching all their youth sports teams.

Even with his plate full, Mike decided to take on the massive challenge of building us a new home. I knew something was still missing, but I was at a loss as to what to do. I decided to ask Lisa Brown if her husband Brian could use Mike as an investigator for his law firm. Brian said he would be more than happy to have Mike on his team. This was a positive development, but Mike was less than enthusiastic. He saw it as a favor, which didn't sit well with him. I knew I had to push him to do it. Despite all he was doing in our lives, I was concerned about him. As his wife and the mother of his children, I had to intervene.

Mike began to work for Brian in 2005. Initially, he would drive Brian so he could conduct business calls to discuss cases with his clients. There were also many trips to jails to meet clients. Their car rides became both interesting and entertaining for Mike. Lisa and I used to joke our husbands were "off on another caper." They shared a love of Notre Dame's football team, and their "soap diva" wives. Mike would come home with a smile and I started to feel like he was on the right track. Brian started assigning Mike a few cases to do interviews and gather information. This reengaged Mike's incredible instincts honed during his time as an NYPD detective.

The "mental muscle" to solve a crime had returned. Seeing Mike's potential, Brian assigned him bigger cases and began to refer him to his colleagues. Due to his vast field experience as a cop, defense attorneys loved his take on cases. When his client list began to grow, Mike decided it was time to open his own PI business, McMahon Investigative Group. The business took off. He investigated cases for billionaires, politicians, and celebrities. His client list included the Vatican and even a presidential candidate. His success rate was excellent and it didn't take long for the word to spread.

In 2010, Mike began to work for defense attorney Larry Lustberg, who became our lead defense attorney in this case. It was quite a feather in Mike's cap to be hired by a renowned global firm employing over two hundred staff attorneys. Larry was a highly sought-after lawyer who handled the most interesting cases and clients. Mike worked on several cases with Larry and he became a valued asset to the firm.

Larry's Gibbons law firm had a long-standing client in Paul Bergrin, a former New Jersey US Attorney. Bergrin had been tried and convicted of racketeering, sex trafficking, money laundering, and murder in a Newark federal court. He was given six life sentences and in 2012 was temporarily serving out his time in a maximum-security prison in Brooklyn, New York. Upon his conviction in 2013, Bergrin refused to accept that he would spend the rest of his life in prison. As a seasoned attorney he knew his legal rights and every loophole he could explore to appeal his case, the cost of which would be paid by US taxpayers. Bergrin had no available funds left for his defense, so Larry Lustberg at Gibbons was assigned to represent him through the Criminal Justice Act. The CJA allows every American a right to an attorney if the person charged "cannot afford one." The government had assessed that Bergrin had such a right. Larry brought in Mike as a CJA investigator whose cost would be reimbursed by his client, the government.

Mike was enthusiastic about joining Larry's team on this case in 2013. The Bergrin story was front-page news for months and Mike had been closely following it. Mike recalls a warning from Larry if he worked on this case, something was going to happen to him. Mike laughed it off, asking, "Like what?" Mike had dismissed it at the time. He had dealt with some vile criminals before, why would this guy be any different?

When Mike joined the team it was on Paul's fourth appeal. He was the last in a long list of prior investigators who had worked on this case. In reviewing the background material, Mike came across details never covered in the media. He was blown away by the information he read. This case was unlike any he had ever worked on in his career. For clarity, *New Yorker* magazine named Paul Bergrin the "baddest attorney in U.S. history." They weren't kidding. Bergrin testified as a character witness for two former US attorney colleagues charged with corruption. This was a big "no-no" that brought embarrassment to the Newark office. After that he became persona non grata to his coworkers in the Newark US Attorney's office after. Colleagues systematically began to punish Bergrin. They stopped assigning him cases, which infuriated him. He couldn't take it anymore and, as was the intent of the US Attorney's office, he quit.

Their victory was short lived. Bergrin opened his own law firm right in Newark and defended some of the most dangerous criminals in the world. He was now on the outside, tormenting the US attorneys who were once his colleagues. He became highly successful at winning homicide cases. The word quickly spread in Newark that he was the man if you needed a ruthless defense attorney. His ego exploded and his greed knew no limit. If a client was locked up for running a prostitution ring, Bergrin would take over the client's prostitute business during the client's incarceration and pocket the cash that came with it. If a client was a sentenced drug dealer, Bergrin followed the same pattern and became richer for it.

Bergrin was living the true gangster life. He would pull up on street corners in his $200,000 Bentley, looking for clients. Criminals respected him and his street persona meshed with their street life. Defense attorneys were either grateful or jealous of not being the ones chosen to defend these mobsters anymore. Bergrin's clients were murderers, cartel members, pimps, drug dealers, and sex traffickers. There was never a shortage of bad guys and his business thrived. A federal investigation was probably opened against Bergrin before the ink was dry on his new business cards.

In court, Bergrin would taunt the prosecutors and too often come out on the winning side. This was unheard of in federal court. Bergrin was up to no good and prosecutors knew it. Their goal was to take him down. The Newark FBI worked hand in hand with the DEA and the Newark US Attorney's office on the case against Bergrin, who had become public enemy number one in Newark. It was all-hands-on-deck to arrest and prosecute him and put him in prison. The FBI used confidential informants (CIs) to gather intelligence on Bergrin. These informants became a direct line to the target. The federal government has a responsibility to protect those CIs, who are paid thousands in cash to further the bureau's case.

The Bergrin case was dangerous. There was a "life and death" element to the investigation. The tasks to gather incriminating evidence became more dangerous. The informants would do anything to avoid going to prison. The New Jersey Attorney's office suspected that Bergrin had arranged for the elimination of witnesses set to testify against his clients. The disappearance of witnesses would explain all the "winning" cases he handled in Newark. No witnesses, no case.

The death of Kemo McCray, a confidential informant, was a horrific stain on the FBI. McCray should have been afforded full protection. This worst-case scenario happened when female FBI case agent, Shawn Brokos, was in charge of the case. The government alleged that Bergrin had been provided information that McCray was an informant and told the "Crew" during a meeting, to win this case against him, Kemo must go. The Bergrin case coined the phrases "No Kemo, No Case," "No Witness, No Case."

Some informants provide more valuable information than others. Some can't handle the pressure but do it to stay out of jail for their own misdeeds. For any CI in a Bergrin case, every day could be their last as people kept showing up dead at a disturbing rate.

When Bergrin was finally arrested, he chose to represent himself, a risky move and not advisable. The government assigned a standby counsel just in case. At trial, during cross-examination of prosecution witness FBI Agent Shawn Brokos, he shamed her for failing to protect the murdered confidential informant Kemo McCray. Brokos seethed but had no recourse. All eyes were on Brokos, who admitted on the stand she had failed to protect a confidential informant who had requested witness protection just weeks prior to his murder. It was an embarrassment for both Brokos and the entire DOJ to have a notorious criminal and primary subject of their investigation cross-examine an FBI case agent. It was a never-ending nightmare for the

FBI. This case involved multiple federal agencies and was constantly covered by the media.

The trial lasted for three long and exhausting weeks. Despite his dramatic display in Newark Federal Court, Paul Bergrin was found guilty of all twenty-three charges. He was given six life sentences. Since this was a federal case there was no chance of parole. The guilty verdict only fueled him to add gas to his appeal process. This was a legal game for him and he thrived on it. He used his legal skills to work his way through the system.

Larry Lustberg hired Mike to work on Bergrin's fourth post-trial appeal motion. He was handed multiple binders filled with thousands of pages of previous court documents to review. When I didn't hear from Mike for a few hours, I would find him in his office engrossed in the mountains of discovery evidence. Even for a seasoned detective like Mike, this case was both fascinating and challenging. Out of the gate, Mike was assigned to do dozens of witness interviews and submit written reports. Many of those witnesses, Mike would later learn, were in the Witness Protection Program or had left the program. Mike was ready to dive in but first he wanted to meet Bergrin face to face.

Investigators don't get many, if any, cases like this. Mike was astounded by the magnitude of Bergrin's alleged criminal activities. The opportunity to personally sit opposite this convicted felon, relegated to solitary confinement, was what true investigators live for. Bergrin had been convicted to six life sentences and the reality of freedom was not on the table. Bergrin had the legal right to execute an appeal as all defendants do. Mike felt his role as the investigator would assist Larry and wanted to contribute in any way he could.

When you visit a federal prison, you have to fill out paperwork with basic information such as name, address, phone number, date of birth, and even your Social Security number, and get preapproved for a one-on-one, face-to-face visit. Those identifying details are kept in a federal database. That process put Mike on the radar of the federal government every time he visited a federal facility. Remember, Mike was a paid CJA investigator for the Bergrin defense, the cost being reimbursed by the government. Mike's meeting with Bergrin was brief but he was left with a distinct impression of the man. After Mike introduced himself, Bergrin immediately began giving Mike orders. Mike had only two hours on his initial visit and Bergrin didn't waste any time. He tasked Mike with finding certain witnesses and provided some addresses. Mike reminded him that he was new to the case and cautioned Bergrin that his knowledge of his case was limited.

Anything Bergrin said was confidential but Mike knew he was dealing with a very dangerous person. He looked Mike dead in the eyes while speaking without blinking. His charming pretense might well disarm a lesser investigator. Mike took his notes and walked out of Brooklyn Federal Prison, never to return to visit Paul Bergrin again. Paul was soon transferred to Terre Haute, Indiana then later to ADX Florence, in Colorado, to be in solitary confinement twenty-three hours a day. All communications after that were limited through the prison email system, CorrLinks, which Mike distrusted and believed was being monitored. Group phone calls were conducted through Larry at his law office.

Mike began drawing up a list of approximately seventy-five interviewees. Many of the witnesses refused to be interviewed, others had simply disappeared. Mike always left his business card with those he interviewed. Sometimes the subject would advise Mike they would be calling the FBI about his visit. Mike encouraged them to do so. He had nothing to hide, he was just doing his job. He visited locations where murders had occurred. He went into federal prisons to interview witnesses. He worked on this case for years! Everyone has the right to a lawyer and the right to mount a defense, which includes hiring an investigator and reinterviewing witnesses and going over the crime scene and the investigator's notes.

When Bergrin's appeal was finally submitted to the Newark Federal Court, it included Mike's affidavits and reports. Mike viewed his work as successful. Larry was pleased with his casework, but they both knew the odds that the court would grant hearings on his appeal were slim to none. His work was done and the Bergrin appeal was under review. Mike moved on with his other cases while the appeal was reviewed.

* * *

After Mike's arrest, we realized that EVERY time he interviewed a witness, that individual's next call was to the FBI alerting them of Mike's inquiry. I'm certain that after the umpteenth call to the Newark FBI office, Agent Brokos and her team were not too happy with Michael McMahon. That reaction was unfounded since Mike was simply hired in good faith under the law by a firm paid by the US government. I'm sure the FBI wanted the stain of the Bergrin case to disappear from the record permanently. Mike's poking around, legitimate as it was, only annoyed them, and his in-depth investigation wasn't something they were used to. Larry knew his work would be under the Fed's microscope and he had warned Mike to "dot your i's and cross your t's" on this one. Mike's reports were going to the federal government and there was a possibility he may be called as a witness in the case. He took this very seriously.

Once the appeal was officially filed, Mike never thought about Paul Bergrin again until the day of his arrest on October 28, 2020. The exchange with arresting FBI Agent Sean McCarthy was very telling. Who was McCarthy? I decided to look him up on LinkedIn. His background was plain vanilla. The only high-profile case he had worked on was that of an Orthodox Jewish man in New Jersey who was involved in body-part trafficking. McCarthy's profile indicated that he had worked on fraud and real estate cases and had been assigned to elder abuse cases in the Red Bank, New Jersey, FBI office. He was far from being a seasoned agent. There was no information to corroborate that he had ever worked in the national intelligence division of the FBI. It begged the question: Why was McCarthy anywhere near Mike's case, which was classified as a national security case? This was the first Fox Hunt arrest in history. It made international news. Why did the FBI allow McCarthy to play a role in this case and arrest?

I remembered back when Mike was in the sedan on his way to be processed after his arrest, he had asked McCarthy how he knew about the Bergrin case and McCarthy identified Shawn Brokos as his office mate. He clammed up after seeing the grimace on the female driver's face. You have an agent with no national security experience executing an arrest on a case that is about to make international news involving the CCP. Has McCarthy been handed this role because of some vendetta he had to "get" Mike in retaliation for Brokos? If so, was it McCarthy or was it Brokos in the Newark office, or someone from the Newark US Attorney's office pushing to keep Mike in this case because of Bergrin?

In 2014, for safety concerns surrounding the Bergrin case, Brokos was transferred to the Pittsburgh FBI field office. That didn't stop Paul Bergrin's cousin Ron Bergrin from locating her and showing up at her home. Bergrin's cousin was arrested and jailed but was eventually released after being deemed mentally unfit. Brokos was constantly looking over her shoulder due to the long arm of Paul Bergrin.

Many questions needed answers. How did Mike's case end up in the Brooklyn EDNY with the Newark FBI as lead? What was the reason the FBI New York passed on the case and left it in the hands of Newark? Did the Newark FBI feed inflammatory intel about Mike to the Eastern District of New York to keep the case open to spy on Mike's recorded Bergrin's emails?

I recalled the words McCarthy said in our foyer, "It's not the first time you've been on my board." MY BOARD? Was Mike's name added to the Bergrin white board in Shawn Brokos's office after he visited Bergrin in Brooklyn federal prison? If Agent Brokos was McCarthy's office mate, did her anxiety and fear of retaliation from Bergrin cause McCarthy to influence a decision to "get" Mike in some way? At first, both Brian and Larry were skeptical of this theory. They could not imagine that even vindictive federal agents could stoop to such nefarious intent.

I spent hours combing the internet for anything I could find about any FBI missteps. One case kept popping up, the Trump Russiagate case. I learned that a FISA warrant (Foreign Intelligence Surveillance Act) was the collection of foreign intelligence on domestic soil. More questions needed answers. How did the government obtain FISA warrants? Was there one issued on our family? I needed to learn more. Trump had publicly accused the Feds of spying on him and his team from the moment he came down the golden escalator in 2015. No one believed him, including *60 Minutes* and other media outlets that involved themselves in a continuous dismissal of the facts.

Trump fired FBI head James Comey, but the media bias against him continued with a routine of hosting his enemies to elevate the story. In my unrelenting quest for information, I happened upon an OIG (Office of the Inspector General) report from December 9, 2019. It was a Department of Justice review of four FISA warrants surrounding the FBI Crossfire Hurricane case. This case involved a fake dossier (Steele dossier) created and paid for by Hillary Clinton's DNC that painted Trump as a Russian asset. It was all a lie. The OIG findings were disturbing. The FBI was proven to have lied on requested FISA warrant applications to spy on members of Trump's team. A FISA warrant is to be used only on people who have potential ties to international terrorism. It is not supposed to be used on innocent Americans. After 9/11, the Patriot Act was enacted to protect Americans from potential attacks from our foreign adversaries. The impetus for the Patriot Act was for the safety of our country and it was being abused at an alarming rate.

Unfortunately, the FBI went rogue and, at the direction of FBI Director James Comey, went off the rails and spied on American citizens. The data is horrifying and most people will never know it happened to them. In Trump's case, members of his cabinet and potential team members such as Devin Nunes, Kash Patel, and Carter Page had unlawful FISA warrants put on them before or while they were serving under Trump. It was outrageous but the media pushed the fake Steele dossier as fact for years. This was a hint of the media disregarding the facts about one side of the political aisle over the other. If the FBI could do it to the president of the United States, they could most certainly do it to us.

One day in early 2021 we received a very disturbing letter from Microsoft alerting us they had complied with a search warrant issued on December 31, 2018, from the Department of Justice for our emails. The date didn't seem of particular interest at the time. We knew the government must have looked through our emails but seeing it in writing is something I can't describe. The reason for the Microsoft letter was because the warrant was now finally closed. How long had it been open? I learned they have years before they must finally let you know your emails, texts, and iCloud had been spied on. Corporations such as Microsoft and Verizon are obligated to alert the user that they had complied with a warrant. This letter made my head spin. How were they able to get a warrant? Based on our evidence, there was no justifiable reason to give the FBI full access to our lives.

Now we wanted to look closer at the search warrants in discovery. Mike and I went back to Larry's Newark, New Jersey, office and showed him the letter. Since the search warrants are under a protective order, I can't share the details. I will say this: I'd like the judges that signed off on these warrants to know they had been lied to. Trusting the agents and the prosecutors on this case was a huge mistake. We had no recourse to challenge the warrants. The damage was done. This access to Mike's files brought up another concern. Mike had found in their discovery evidence materials related to other cases he had worked on besides the Chinese case. Photographs of sensitive files including a sex abuse case had been included as well as others. This was highly disturbing.

How could this be true? The FBI is supposed to use filter teams to separate evidence not associated with the case in question. Mike had worked on some very sensitive cases, including the Bergrin case. If, as documented, the warrant on Mike's computer was issued on December 31, 2018, the FBI would have had full access to hundreds of pieces of attorney-client privileged communications, not only for the Bergrin case but for all of Mike's other cases.

Larry fired off a letter to the government to inquire if a filter team had been used as required. The response came a few days later, dismissing our concerns. That answer did not satisfy Mike. We pushed back with the government but were given no further information. To this day we still have no details on who went through all of Mike's privileged files. Our instinct was proven right. They were fishing through Mike's life looking to create a blueprint of a man who showed a pattern of bending the rules to his favor. I believe they wanted to "get" him on the Bergrin case to discredit his work and to put a definitive end to that case.

Their fishing trip went deep into decades of our lives. They looked at over ten years of our banking records and our credit cards. They saw our son's banking records. If there was a FISA warrant, they also could have recordings of our personal conversations. The government will not share their FISA findings in discovery as they classify that intel as a matter of national security (CIPA materials). The only reason the Trump team found out the truth was due to the OIG investigation. Many of them had no idea that they had been spied on for years. Mike's case was classified as national intelligence, which protected the government from being exposed on how they monitored us. Our outrage grew as the government held us hostage.

We felt completely violated. I had no idea if they had spied on our children. How often was I followed? I had more questions as each day went by. The government took months to deliver a new batch of discovery, which prolonged the torture. Because the case was classified as a matter of national security, they had no obligation to give Mike a speedy trial. They hoped he would cave, go bankrupt, or die before the case went to trial. It was psychological warfare and they were winning.

In June of 2022 the final ruling to Paul Bergrin's appeal for hearings based on "newly discovered evidence," some of which came from Mike's investigative work, was denied.

Based on documents presented by the New Jersey Appellate Court, Larry was now convinced Mike was targeted in the Fox Hunt case because his work on the Bergrin case. Mike refusing to take a plea deal was not part of the government's plan. If Mike had taken a plea, every piece of work he did on the Bergrin case would have been thrown out or at a minimum discredited. That didn't happen. We fought back and dug in our heels. Larry knew he would have to address this matter with the EDNY and file a motion to dismiss based on bias against Mike. It was time to throw our first grenade.

Our first in-person status conference was supposed to be routine. The judge asks the prosecutors where things stand with the defense receiving discovery, the prosecutors pretend they are working on delivering it all in an expedited fashion. Stalling was their favorite thing to do to keep us in a suspended state of hell. This was the first time I had seen all the people in person who did this to us. Previously everything had been on Zoom. Walking into the courthouse in Brooklyn was surreal. My heart was beating so fast and I held onto Mike's hand extra tight. I felt sick to my stomach. As we rounded the corner on the fourth floor, Case Agent Christopher Bruno was standing in front of the court room doors, chatting with someone from the prosecutor's office. Sitting on a bench were US Attorneys Craig Heeren and Matthew Haggans. I seethed inside as I shot all of them the nastiest look I could muster up. I wanted to scream at all of them but I just glared instead.

When the doors to the courtroom opened we all entered. The prosecution team positioned themselves on the right, Larry, Mike, and Genna sat on the left. The codefendants sat at our table but did not interact with our team. When Judge Chen entered from chambers I finally got a look at who would have our lives in her hands. Judge Pamela Chen, appointed by Obama, had a very solid career as a prosecutor in the EDNY. Her background focused on civil rights and sex trafficking cases. For some reason our original judge had been replaced with Judge Chen. At the time I was pleased, as I felt her background in civil rights would help us get a fair trial if it got that far. I was still hoping every single day a hero would fly in and stop all of it. Maybe she would be our hero?

That particular day Craig Heeren had invited law school interns to shadow him to the proceedings. These young lawyers no doubt felt they were in the presence of a very powerful prosecutor; Craig had been promoted to deputy chief of the EDNY national security and cyber division in August of 2020. After we walked through some basic updates the judge asked if we had anything further. That's when Larry stood up and let the judge know we would be filing prosecutorial misconduct motions against the DOJ. The entire prosecution team looked up from what they were doing and looked notably upset. The interns' eyes lit up hearing our accusations. They all must have been shocked to hear these prestigious attorneys were being accused of such an offense. The judge acknowledged it was quite an accusation. Larry assured the judge this was not a decision taken lightly and she claimed to look forward to reading our account. As we adjourned, the prosecutors quickly packed up their things and marched past me sitting in the first row of the gallery. I focused my death stare on Craig but I don't know if he was even aware of it. Hopefully someone did and that's all that mattered. The day's events sent a clear message we were not giving up. Quite the contrary. I'm sure their heads were spinning trying to figure out what was coming their way.

They had no idea what McCarthy had said in the foyer of our home the morning of October 28, 2020, but they were about to find out. This was war.

CHAPTER FOUR

On the steps of the EDNY Brooklyn courthouse, we had officially declared war on the federal government and prepared to file charges of prosecutorial misconduct against them. What happens from here? If this was an episode of *Law & Order* that dramatic cliffhanger would cut to a commercial break selling the latest and greatest candy bar or pine floor cleaner while the viewer anxiously awaited the show's return. Upon the fade up out of commercial, the viewer would find Larry in the courtroom arguing our motions to the judge, intercut with a line-up of fuming chiseled-jawed prosecutors in tailored suits plotting their revenge. Unfortunately, that's not how it goes in real life. It would take several months for our motions to be written and filed. The saying goes, "The process is the punishment," and I can attest to the truthfulness of that phrase. A "process" that is dictated by powerful people who want to break you mentally, physically, and financially. We would have to be patient—a virtue I personally struggled with my entire life. I wanted a quick fix so our family could heal from the government's unwarranted attack on us. That was not an option here. Unlike actual war where you seek out your enemy, strike, and conquer, taking on the Department of Justice is a painstakingly slow process buried in case law with meticulously chosen nuanced words and calculated delays. Every written word counts in fighting to persuade a federal judge to rule in your favor. Our original judge had been switched out to Judge Chen, who had a long and successful career as a prosecutor in the EDNY. We were the visiting team on her home turf. The prosecutors trying this case were the same people she would break bread with at the EDNY annual Christmas parties. I found social media posts of Judge Chen smiling cheek to cheek with Breon Peace, who had recently been named the new head of the EDNY and inherited Mike's case. Peace had previously been a prosecutor in the EDNY during the same years as Judge Chen. If they weren't friends, they were at minimum former colleagues who seemed quite happy to share a selfie. We were the outsiders and the odds heavily weighed against us. We were cautioned that the government would not take accusations of prosecutorial misconduct lightly. At the time I had no idea what that meant but felt we regained a bit of power by finally pushing back.

Motions, the cost of which would be tens of thousands of dollars, were unaffordable to us. Larry was aware of our situation but chose to proceed despite our lack of funds. He saw injustice against a good man, believed in his innocence and wanted to use his legal toolbox to take the government to the mat. Motions are filed for several different reasons. The most important reason to file is to document information, on the record, based on evidence supporting our effort to have the case dismissed. Truth be told, a dismissal rarely happens. Should you be found guilty at trial, the motions are crucial for an appeal to show the judge failed in her rulings backed up with documents on the record.

Our motions would be accusatory of the FBI. Larry strongly believed that, at the very least, we would be granted hearings on these motions. Hearings would give us the opportunity to call witnesses and issue subpoenas and other possible communications. Larry warned us not to get our hopes up but felt it necessary to get our arguments on the record. Initially, the motion is filed by us with the court.

The government responds with a litany of reasons for the court to deny our motion. Lastly, our counsel sends a rebuttal of the government's argument to the court. It outlines why their cause for denial is incorrect. The judge then makes her ruling. This legal process can take six to eight months or longer. Sometimes you see this process go faster in a case involving a politician but for the average defendant it is drawn out—in our case for years. While motions are pending there is no trial date set. We requested a speedy trial but due to this case falling under national security they had no obligation to provide us with such relief. The government relies on these delays as psychological warfare. It works. Ninety-nine percent of defendants take a plea deal due to government pressure, financial hardship, or the presence of overwhelming evidence of guilt. That was never an option with us. We were in for the long haul, but the weight of our enemy was ever present. There is nothing the government loves more than a broken defendant. There would be no days off from the stress, anxiety, and fear we were living with. They had the arsenal of time and patience to destroy Mike. Understand, we are talking about a Department of Justice case overseen by National Intelligence and the attorney general of the United States. That lineup is intimidating and frightening.

From the moment the FBI knocks on your door, your fight or flight instinct kicks in. It starts when you wake up, until nightfall when sleep is interrupted by a powerful demonic entity threatening to tear your entire life apart. Mike and I have not gotten a full night's sleep since his arrest. I always envied his ability to fall asleep quickly. He would be well into his slumber within ninety seconds of his head hitting the pillow. It confounded me that someone who witnessed the unthinkable as a NYPD Detective could sleep peacefully at night. How could you spend your days on the front lines in the Bronx and not take all of that home with you? Fortunately, he was able to separate the job from his home life. We had great communication in our marriage. Mike often shared heroic and dangerous work stories with me but was able to leave the most disturbing elements at the precinct. That ability is one of his attributes that made him so successful at the job. He could experience the most horrific situation with clear eyes and deliver the safest and fairest outcome. That's a great cop. If you were in crisis and Mike was the first to the scene, you were in the greatest of hands. He loved his job and couldn't wait to go to work each day. His work as a private investigator restored the passion he had felt as part of the NYPD. Then his world crashed and burned again with the ultimate betrayal by our own government.

Mike questioned whether all his years of dedication and service had been for nothing. I constantly tried to reassure him his feelings were warranted and this invasion into our lives was only temporary. If you allow these evildoers to ruin even one minute of your life, they win. They DO NOT deserve that power over us. It was very difficult for Mike to accept that he had been targeted by the people he believed were on the same side. Every single day I promised him we would get through this. He was usually the one to reassure me when I struggled, now it was my turn to help him. Life was moving on, but a dark cloud followed us every day.

My work as a content creator for an e-commerce company forced me to focus on other things. Mike did not have that option. Larry would encourage him that he could still work, but that wasn't a reality. Who was going to hire Mike? If he worked as a PI and had to testify at trial, he would be discredited immediately, even though it would be without cause. He had to surrender his New Jersey PI license and he let his New York one expire. He felt he would be a liability to any lawyer open to hiring him. Every single attorney he had worked for reached out and was supportive. More importantly they all believed in his innocence from day one. They assured Mike there was a job waiting for him once this mess was cleaned up. That support made Mike feel better, not so much for future job opportunities, but that these lawyers didn't believe the government's accusations. They had all seen these government tactics in their own practice and knew what we were up against.

I found solace at the gym and I knew it would do the same for Mike. I literally forced him to go. I remembered the words of a dear friend, J. D. Roth, the creator of the TV show *The Biggest Loser*. He shared he never met a mental challenge that a pair of sneakers couldn't help. I knew how true those words were based on my own struggles, so I pushed Mike to rally and fight back against the enemy between his ears. The possibility of going to prison for a crime you did not commit was mentally and physically debilitating. Some days he wouldn't get out of bed. On those days I gently warned him, "You can have one day in bed, but ONLY one." Despite his efforts to exercise and stay busy, his night terrors and panic attacks became regular occurrences. One day when he was driving on the highway to Larry's office he had a panic attack. Luckily, he was able to pull into a parking lot so I could drive. I hope no one ever has to witness someone having a panic attack. You feel totally helpless. I was filled with anger and rage seeing what the government was doing to him. There's nothing worse than the feeling that I didn't have the power to stop it. The pain of watching him lose everything he had worked for his entire life overwhelmed me. His heroic existence as a police officer, his respected role as a private investigator, and most importantly his character as a genuinely caring human being was tarnished by the accusations against him. Our lives would never be the same. I surrendered to the reality that we were encountering the biggest challenge of our lives. A positive outcome would need some serious work on my part.

When the world thinks you are a traitor to your country you are constantly looking over your shoulder. Before you walk outside you peek behind the shades to check the streets for the press or an angry American who wants to harm you. Your daily routines become marred with scanning every person at your gym or local coffee shop to gauge whether they know about the charges against your family. I'm sure the children felt the same way. I was especially concerned about Ann Marie, our youngest daughter, who was a vulnerable high school teenager when this happened. We rarely spoke about it but when she had questions, I assured her it would pass and result in our favor. She claimed that no one ever approached her in school regarding her father's arrest. I don't know if she was telling the truth or just protecting me from it. We were all living under the same roof, living out our daily lives yet miles apart in so many ways. We would never get these years back. The irreversible damage was done and the government couldn't have cared less. I have been consumed with anger and lived with a fire burning in my gut every day since Mike's arrest. On October 28, 2020, I became the leader of our family. There was nothing that would stop me from countering the assault on those I loved the most in the world. I vowed to expose and remedy the injustice that destroyed the sanctity under my roof.

Every morning I would wake up in an investigative mode but there were children to raise and bills to pay. Mike was unable to work as a PI and his business went from his best financial year since he opened his business, to zero in 2021. We were not financially in dire straits but our legal fees would eventually bankrupt us. I would do anything I could to avoid selling our house. Mike and I had worked our entire lives, which allowed us to live comfortably. Now that stability was shaken and in danger of being taken away. Our home was our sanctuary. It gave us stability for our children and my eighty-two-year-old mother who lived with us. I had to remain focused and work through my own anxiety to assure I kept my job. Thanks to dear friends and coworkers, I never missed one day of work. I would let my supervisor know if I needed time off and he would handle it without missing a beat. My work never suffered—quite the opposite, I was actually promoted and given a very welcome bonus for the significant revenue my work brought into the company. Monetarily and psychologically, I had to keep this job at all costs. Even during the quarantine I traveled to Pennsylvania every few weeks for production location shoots. Regardless, from the time I backed out of our driveway, my thoughts never left Mike and the kids. My mind was constantly filled with resonating voices with ideas on how I could stop this nightmare that had been dropped on us.

I was desperate for this to end and save my family from further trauma. The importance of fighting for the truth was my main focus. I told myself, if you stay strong and steadfast in the fight, regardless of how many rounds are to be fought, it will ultimately result in a win. I had to believe that. To say I am competitive doesn't quite capture my drive to win. I was never one to accept losing as an option from very early in my life. I started in the entertainment business at the age of nine, surviving an open call of over seven hundred nine-year-olds for a role in the Broadway show *Annie*. As a young teenager on the soap opera *As the World Turns* I learned to be creative and respect the players and the audience. I set my goal on the importance of building trust with the viewers. I walked out of the studio each day, proud and fulfilled as an artist for the majority of my career. I carried that purpose into every aspect of my life. When Mike was arrested, I had to be strong and begin the fight—not just for myself, but for my entire family. My work was cut out for me.

Mike would get up in the middle of the night, every night. I would wake up without him next to me. Each morning I braced myself for what I might find when I left our bedroom. I often found him sitting on the couch just staring into space. It was excruciatingly difficult for me to see him in such emotional pain. I knew he was lost but also knew the kids would be terribly frightened if they saw him in that condition. This wasn't their father. I would pour us a cup of coffee and give him a pep talk as I paced back and forth in our living room. I prayerfully challenged "Big Ter," my deceased father and beloved football coach, to intercede and put the fight and fire back into Mike. After my pep talk I would quietly read a chapter from *33 Days to Morning Glory* by Michael E. Gaitley out loud to Mike. It is a Catholic retreat guide meant to bring the reader to a closer relationship with the Blessed Mother. You start the book on a Marian feast day and the final day finishes on a feast day finalizing your retreat of consecration to Mary. It's a beautiful book with each chapter approximately a ten-minute read. After our morning routine, I would convince Mike to get dressed and join me for a walk. Depending on his mood, I balanced the dual role of cheerleader and tough love drill sergeant. I never wanted to push him if I felt he didn't want to be pushed and, at the same time, I didn't want to NOT intervene if I saw him slipping into depression.

We would constantly refresh our emails for any updates from our legal team. We probably did that a hundred times a day. If we were the soldiers in this war, the emails were the map of the battle plan. The law of daily updates was excruciating. Trying to get into a manufactured routine of "normalcy" was paramount for survival. If, at the very least, I was able to start Mike's day on a positive note I could retreat to my office and work knowing I had done something to keep him present. I prayed a lot and began saying the Rosary every day. I threw myself on God's mercy and asked for strength and guidance to save my husband. I vowed to listen and take action on anything God put in front of me. I begged for intervention and for angels to protect and guide me. I was struggling but if I took my energy off of Mike I felt I would lose him. The only time I allowed myself to make it personal was when I prayed. I prayed for help, blessed myself, and waited patiently to be shown a path to healing this invasion on my family.

My upbringing is the cornerstone for my beliefs. I had always been a very spiritual person. I grew up in a Catholic household and attended Catholic schools from the first grade until graduating from Immaculate Heart Academy High School in 1987. My parents were devout Catholics. My mother taught biology in St. Luke's High School in Ho-Ho-Kus, New Jersey, the same school where she met my father in 1952, and continued to teach science in the grammar school after the high school closed. We attended Mass every Sunday and our social lives were heavily involved with parish activities. We shared our parish with my aunts, uncles, and cousins. My grandfather Myles Byrne and the entire Byrne family were heavily involved with caretaking and any other needs of the parish for decades. My dad Terry, a tree surgeon, coached little league football. My brother played and my sisters and I were cheerleaders. My foundation of faith was built by my parents and the extended Byrne family. I was unaware at the time that this tremendous gift to me and my siblings was deliberate and intentional. They recognized how valuable a foundation of faith would be in our lives. The seeds were planted by the ones who bore witness to its power.

Mike's family was also very devout. He was number six of nine children, Eileen, Kevin, Vincent, Patricia, Kathleen, Ann Marie, Brian, and Mike grew up in a two-bedroom apartment in the Bronx. During that era, Irish immigrants, who dominated the Bronx, identified themselves by the parish they attended. The McMahon family lived in Our Lady of Refuge parish with countless cousins, aunts, uncles, and grandparents. A move to a bigger home had become long overdue and the growing crime in the Bronx was threatening their safety. With the help and generosity of a down payment from Mike's Aunt Maureen and Uncle Jack Callanan, his dad moved the family to New City, New York. Their new Cape Cod–style home had only one bathroom and attic space, but had additional converted bedrooms that provided ample accommodations compared to the Bronx. When eight-year-old Mike first laid eyes on his new home, a concerned son said to his father, "How will we all fit in that house?" Mike's father just laughed it off, knowing the future had just gotten brighter for his children. The Callanan cousins also lived in New City and were the same age as the McMahons, so extended family was only a short walk away. Catholic school was not an option with eight children, so they all were enrolled in the public school system. Mrs. McMahon immediately joined Saint Augustine parish in New City and brought her dedication and devotion with her. Every Sunday she would dress all the children to go to Mass. No exceptions. As the boys grew and were expected to attend on their own, she would grill them every Sunday about the homily said at Mass to make sure they attended. Mrs. Patricia McMahon was a marvel. When she became pregnant with her ninth child, Stephen, who would be born eighteen years after his oldest sibling Eileen, the doctor warned her this should be her last pregnancy. It was. Patricia managed the family while her husband, Vincent, worked full time in New York City to put food on the table. She never missed a school or sporting event and after Mike's dad died of cancer in November of 1992 she worked as a school crossing guard. On October 28, 1992, only weeks before his father's death, the McMahon family also lost Mike's "Irish twin" sister Ann

Marie to cancer at the age of twenty-four. Ann Marie was only one year and two days Mike's senior and the two were best friends. The loss of two from their family unit was immeasurable. I met Mike only a few weeks after these tragedies in February of 1993. He had already experienced a tremendous amount of trauma before we met. Trauma that was thankfully foreign to me up to that point.

Since the day of his arrest, I continued to point out to Mike the date he was arrested, October 28, coincided with the date his sister Ann Marie passed away. I felt so strongly that his sister would never allow this to happen to him on such a memorable date without there being a greater purpose. It was Ann Marie's way of letting Mike know she was protecting him on this difficult journey. I would reassure him that his sister would never let this end poorly. I truly believed that. I could tell this analogy resonated with Mike. It was a glimmer of something he could hold on to. I would constantly point out anything I saw as a sign, hoping Mike would see these "God winks" as I did. Numbers or sayings on vanity on license plates, flocks of black birds landing on our deck, special songs spontaneously coming on the radio, I believed were ways the other side was sending messages to us that we were protected. Surrendering to my faith had been a constant source of peace in my life and wanted Mike to have the same. Since my dad died in 2013, I have gotten signs from him, including vivid dreams where I can actually feel him hug me. That feeling was indescribable and gave me the peace I desperately needed after his passing.

Mike would do his best to see things through my positive lens, but his faith wasn't as strong as mine. After his sister and father died within weeks of each other in 1992, his faith disappeared along with them. He watched helplessly as they suffered and succumbed to their cancers. His dedication to his family was completely void of self and I know his dad and Ann Marie were aware of his pure heart. Despite all of Mike's attempts to help, he lost both of them anyway. I completely understand why he would feel God abandoned him. When we met I was a very naive twenty-two-year-old. I fell in love with him immediately and from the moment we met I tried to bring happiness into his life. The suffering of the McMahon family was palpable and my desire to fix it overtook me.

The McMahon household was filled with love but there with an overwhelming sense of sadness. I can't imagine how Mrs. McMahon was able to wake up and confront her grief every day. I learned very quickly it was her faith and family that saved her. The church was her solace and constant. The Catholic community embraced her and the entire McMahon family. The parish priest would often visit and sit at her kitchen table sharing a pound cake and coffee. I loved that. It reminded me of my Irish grandmother, Martha, who would host dozens of Byrne family members and local priests at her Jersey City brownstone every holiday. Tea, cake, and conversation accompanied by a haze of cigarette smoke in the dining room was where all the world's problems were up for debate and discussion. This backdrop was a familiar one to me and I loved it. The McMahon house was the gathering place for all the holidays. Every single Sunday Mike's ninety-plus-year-old grandmother, Mary, would visit from the Bronx with his Uncle Jimmy. The kitchen window was always cracked a few inches for the heat from the oven to cool the tiny linoleum-floored family epicenter. Irish music played from a dusty black radio with a metal antenna that looked to be from the nineteen-sixties. When I joined the family, it was just one more folding chair to add to mix. Despite what the family had suffered, every family gathering was filled with laughter and unity.

Mike had resisted allowing faith to play a role in his healing after losing Ann Marie and his father. Our marriage in St. Luke's Catholic Church, just a year after we met, was in deference to me and his mother. He had lost the connection with the Holy Spirit but did recognize that our relationship was not by accident. He felt that Ann Marie brought us together. The night we met in a New Jersey bar, he had made a last-minute decision to go. He had just finished a twenty-four-hour tour and attended his grandmother's ninety-sixth birthday party. He was barely able to keep his eyes open but his brother Vinny pushed him to go out for "one more drink." That opportune sequence of events was as far as I could go to get Mike to recognize God's intervention in our lives. When he got arrested in 2020, I knew faith would get him through this but I had a long road ahead to convince him.

In my previous relationship before Mike, I was told I had a "Cinderella complex." I don't disagree with that assessment. I wanted a White Knight to love and protect me, someone special who would support my creative and opinionated sides. I wasn't in a rush to do so at the age of twenty-two. One thing I knew for sure, I would not find it in Hollywood, where I was living at the time. I made the decision to return to New Jersey after I sought guidance from a wonderful Irish priest at a Catholic church in Beverly Hills, California. I knocked on the door to the rectory completely distraught in the fall of 1992. Father Colm sat with me for hours and strongly suggested I "go home" to my family in New Jersey and escape Hollywood. Mere weeks after I made the decision to go home, I got a call from Douglas Marland, the head writer of *As the World Turns,* asking me to reprise my role as Lily. *As the World Turns* was filmed in Manhattan, a half an hour from my home in New Jersey. The timing did not go unnoticed by me as it was confirmation that I had made the right decision to return to the East Coast. I felt God had intervened that day in California and confirmed His presence by presenting a tremendous gift and opportunity.

My deep connection to the Blessed Mother began early in my life. In the Catholic faith, seeking a path as a nun or a mother was seen in the eyes of God as the ultimate ways to serve Him. The Blessed Mother set an example as to who I would strive to be as a human being. I always wanted to be a wife and mother; the nun option was never in the cards for me. There was no way I could come close to the Blessed Mother's strength and purity, but I trusted that whatever path presented to me was guided by a higher power.

When I moved back to New Jersey in December of 1992, I shared an apartment two blocks from the Byrne homestead in Waldwick with my sister Liz. My dad's younger sister, Aunt Patty, invited me to accompany her on a trip to a Paterson, New Jersey church where a statue of the Blessed Mother was said to be "changing colors." I was immediately intrigued and joined her. When we arrived at the church the approximately three-foot-tall statue of Mary was in a corner under a glass case. Nothing in its design varied from a traditional statue you would see on someone's lawn or in any Catholic church. There was a woven basket on the floor in front of the Blessed Mother to place your intentions. I wrote mine down on a tiny piece of paper with the provided pencil. I asked for her help to meet a good man who would be a great husband and father. I folded up my intention and put it in the basket. My aunt wrote her intention then we both kneeled down to pray. After about ten minutes my aunt nudged my arm, "Do you see it?" she whispered. "The greens and the blues." I opened my eyes but did not see what she was seeing. My aunt Patty is a walking saint who might be the most faithful servant of the Catholic Church that I know. She is the essence of Mother Teresa. She was a nurse, then a midwife who worked with the most vulnerable women and babies in the urban areas of New York City. Of course, the Blessed Mother would give her a beautiful light show. As much as I squinted and focused on the statue, I didn't see anything other than a beautiful lady. I closed my eyes and prayed for the gift of seeing the colors. I remember telling the Blessed Mother in my mind that I didn't need to see the colors as I would never doubt my faith, but I would love to have such a gift. I opened my eyes and watched the most beautiful vibrant pinks and golds emerge from the outline of her veil. I was seeing completely different colors than my aunt who was sitting right next to me. We whispered to each other comparing what we were seeing. It was magnificent. I knew I was witnessing a miracle and tried not to blink too often. Within a few minutes the colors disappeared for me, then a few moments later for my aunt. We walked out of the church with full hearts. A few weeks later on February 6, 1993, I met Mike McMahon. My prayer had been received and answered.

After Mike's arrest, Sunday Mass provided a peaceful and quiet respite to focus and pray. I started to notice a pattern when the priest was speaking the homily. As he started to speak his face would come sharply into focus and everything else around his face and behind him would go blurry. It happened every week. I always paid close attention to the message looking for any answer to our suffering. During the times I was on my knees during Mass I would go into what could only be described as a trance. This had never happened to me before. It was very powerful. Then I realized I would always leave church with a clue or insight into this case that must have been planted as I prayed. I saw these whispers as direct messages from God and took them very seriously. On one particular Sunday, the message was to take a closer look at what happened in the weeks before October 28, 2020. Why was I being pushed to examine the lead-up to all of this? There must be a reason. I prayed on this message to recollect the memories I had suppressed due to the trauma. The information started to flow back to my brain at a rapid pace.

I tend to have vivid dreams, more so in the last few years. I would wake up and immediately call Lisa Brown or my friend Alex Verner, a former *As the World Turns* coworker and one of my best friends, to help analyze the messages from these nocturnal events. I think Alex may have kept all the yellow legal pads filled with my crazy nocturnal adventures. My dreams were a gift, especially when my dad would make a visit. I could actually feel the emotional connection to my father I missed so much. In one dream, he looked to be in his forties, in great health, wearing a full-length wool coat, a silk scarf, and displaying his contagious, devilish smile. It was such a blessing. I was so grateful. I began to look forward to my dreams before I went to bed. Who would visit? Sometimes the dreams were so bizarre I woke up exhausted and perplexed at defining the message. My vivid dreams started to occur every night in early 2020. I believe my subconscious was preparing me for what was coming next.

A dream I had in late August of 2020, just weeks before Mike's arrest, was life changing. I was walking down a narrow hallway in a space I had never seen before. The arched ceilings were so low I could almost touch them. Thick, weathered wooden beams contoured the white plaster walls. It felt like I was in an ancient European church you read about and see sketched in history books. I came upon two wooden doors that opened simultaneously. The doors were made of the same wood as the hallway arches and had heavy, wrought iron handles. As they opened I was welcomed by two men wearing brown robes belted with tasseled ropes. They took me by my hand as I entered a small church. There were approximately ten arched pews in a semicircle, five on each side, facing a small altar. The men led me to a body laid out on a wooden table to the left. As I walked closer to the body on the table, I recognized it to be Jesus. He was dead but looked peaceful and had only a small cloth covering his midsection as He appears on the crucifix. I was speechless. I asked the men if I could touch Him and they nodded yes but did not speak. I touched His arm briefly and even though I was dreaming I was 100 percent conscious of this being a religious moment to absorb as long as I could.

The priests then escorted me in front of the altar and turned me towards the back of the church. They told me to get on my knees in prayer. I found myself being drawn to look up to the ceiling and saw the figure of a man. It was not Jesus. In that moment I felt it was Mary's husband Joseph. He was wearing a green robe and had long hair. He slowly raised the palm of his hand upwards facing towards the ceiling of the church. As he did, I began to levitate. I could feel it happening to my body as I was being lifted off the ground. I remember thinking "This is incredible... just go with it... try and appreciate it while it lasts." I hovered about one foot off the ground for a few moments in what I would call a gentle euphoric state. Joseph was then replaced by the Blessed Mother. She was dressed in white with a gentle smile and watching me levitate. I remember thinking "This is about to go to the next level." I was right. The Blessed Mother levitated me higher off the ground and my euphoria became unexplainable. Maybe this is what people mean when they say they were "filled with the Holy Spirit." I didn't want that feeling to end. I took in every single second of the experience. After a few moments, I saw the Blessed Mother take a deep breath, and then ask me, "Are you ready?" I affirmed, "Yes!" Then she literally FLEW into my heart with such a force, it woke me out of my dead "sleep" and I sat straight up in bed with a DEEP GASPING breath. It felt like I had been drowning and was gasping for air after being resuscitated. I was holding my hand to my heart and could feel it racing like I had just sprinted a mile. I got up and went into the bathroom and said out loud. "What's your message? Please tell me!" I was still in a semiconscious state and I felt like I could communicate with her. All I heard was "You are doing the right thing…" "You are doing the right thing…" What did she mean by that? I had been working on a documentary about unplanned pregnancy, so I thought maybe that was what the message was regarding. As the connection faded I went back to bed with an overwhelming feeling of energy and peace.

The very next day I received a weird letter in the mail. It was addressed to me with my legal name, Mary McMahon. No return address, but postmarked from Ohio. The content of the envelope was a photocopied piece of material of Biblical verses outlining the end of times. Very dark scriptures were included and certain parts about redemption and the Devil were underlined. I put it aside and eventually threw it out. I thought maybe I received the letter because I donated to pro-life charities and was on some target list. To this day I have no idea who sent it but looking back, I wondered if someone was trying to warn me. It was unsettling. First the visitation, now this letter and a few other religious "signs" had been shown to me. I called my friend John Edward, who is a psychic medium. He told me to stop what I was doing and pray the Rosary. He felt something evil was circling me and I needed protection.

September of 2020 was a crazy and unsettling time in the country. The presidential election was coming up between Joe Biden and Donald Trump and everyone was on edge. My daughter was starting her sophomore year in high school, our son Max was working full time, and our oldest, Mikey, was finishing his last year in college in New Jersey. COVID-19 was rampant and a concern second only to who would be the next president. Most Americans were distracted by unprecedented events of modern times. Working from home and social interactions were minimal for everyone and social media was feeding our brains at an unprecedented pace.

One day in September I heard a buzzing sound over my head in our backyard. I looked up and saw a drone hovering above me. Drones had become pretty common as a new pandemic hobby, so I thought it was a bored, nosey neighbor. For a split second I thought it would be funny to moon the drone. I made the wise decision not to do it, thank goodness. The drone hovered for a few minutes then disappeared like a mini spaceship into the clouds. A few days later Mike had his annual chest X-ray appointment for 9/11 related issues in Rockland County, New York, just over the New Jersey border. With COVID-19 protocols in place, Mike was told to wait outside until he was called in for his appointment. The building was a stand-alone radiology facility with a small parking lot. When Mike pulled in, he backed into the parking space, so the front of his car faced the medical building. He immediately noticed two black sedans entering the lot. Mike pegged them as unmarked law enforcement vehicles. He assumed they were following someone, but who? He was the only car in the lot. The unmarked cars left the lot and Mike didn't think any more of it. When he finished his appointment he was told to go to another medical building. It was a short drive down the street to another stand-alone location. As he pulled into this lot the same two cars followed him. He took a bit more interest and deduced that some poor guy had no idea these unmarked cars were looking for him and must be lost. Mike forgot about this incident until a few months after his arrest.

Visitations, scary letters, drones, psychic warnings, and unmarked cars surveilling Mike became testimony to the fact that Mike was being watched in the weeks before his arrest in October of 2020. It would be revealed that in August 2020 when the Blessed Mother visited me, the government was putting together the takedown of Michael McMahon at exactly the same time. I knew the Blessed Mother had filled my heart with the strength to fight the evil trying to destroy us. The message to look back and seek answers there was now more obvious than ever. What clues were still yet to be uncovered? I would soon find out and the intent behind what happened to us was more evil than I could possibly imagine. I just continued to keep an open mind and ask for guidance.

Mike and I had gotten ourselves into a routine. Wake up. Pray. Walk. Gym. Every Sunday we would go to Mass and afterwards walk out feeling better. Mike felt the messages in the homilies always applied to him. We would have great talks about the readings at Mass that were so similar to his own situation. The suffering of Jesus and those who dared to follow Him became more personal than ever for Mike. His faith had been awakened but I knew his complete surrender to the process would be my greatest challenge. I would pray the Rosary in a meditative state and continue to listen to the messages. This pattern of prayer bringing results did not go unnoticed by Mike. He started to thank God for every new gift that came forward to help. God was reaching out to him and he was listening. My own survival was a constant worry as I found myself slowly mentally deteriorating. I would forget things and I didn't feel comfortable driving at times. Thankfully I had several people in my life I constantly relied on.

All the "mothers" in my life, and I had a few, became my lifelines. I had been given an incredible gift in August of 2020 by the woman most feared by the Devil, Mary the Mother of Jesus. She filled my heart with strength and gifted me with the constant reminder of her presence. That strength was going to be continually tested in my darkest times. Then there was my mother Mary Byrne who lived with us; Elizabeth Hubbard, who played my character Lily's adoptive mother on *As the World Turns*; and of course Lisa Brown, our attorney Brian Neary's wife and Lily's biological mom on the show. Collectively they were a strong support system. To be honest Lisa wasn't so much a mother figure to me. She would refer to herself as a "sister, friend" but really she was so much more. Every morning I would call her to give her an update on the facts of the case, then walk to my mother's apartment on our property to vent and brainstorm. This was a daily event.

Lisa and I had a psychic connection. That's the only way I can explain it. She would randomly call me and predict things that more often than not would happen. She would get "messages" while she was doing the dishes or cooking dinner, or occupied with some mundane task. She said that's when the psychic portal of her brain was most receptive. We spent a lot of time analyzing "signs," messages, people, and their behavior. I learned how to be a better actress and writer under her guidance. Her way of teaching was to ask questions and give me the opportunity to seek an answer as opposed to telling me her version of the answer. In the arts there are no wrong answers, just different choices. Some creative choices may be more powerful than others. Your gut and the viewer's response to your choices is your gauge. Our work relationship as "mother and daughter" on the show was electric. She always treated me as a peer even though in 1985 when we started to work together, I was only fifteen years old. No time in our forty-year friendship did it become more valuable than after Mike had been arrested. She would always remind me we had the best lawyers in the world, and to trust they would handle this for Mike. That didn't stop me from walking through each and every case detail with her to get her insight. She had been married to Brian for decades and the legal talk in her home had definitely influenced Lisa's ability to comprehend the case. Lisa was an avid boxer and actually bought Mike boxing gloves and private boxing lessons to help him "fight." He loved the boxing lessons and it most certainly did help.

One day she said, "I want you to stop what you're doing and get a sticky note.... Write 'IT'S GOING TO BE OK' on it and put it on the window in front of your sink, so every time you go to wash your hands or do the dishes you will be reminded." As usual I did as I was instructed by my mentor and put the note on the window. It did help every time I saw the message looking back at me. I certainly needed reminding more often than not that no matter how long this would take, it would eventually be in our rearview mirror.

In the fall of 2021 Lisa visited me at my house and we sat in my backyard with my mom and had a nice visit. She was in great spirits and, as always, the positive jolt I needed to keep fighting. Just a week or so later I noticed my daily calls with Lisa started getting shorter. We used to talk for at least an hour every day, then the calls started to max out at ten minutes or so. Instead of Lisa providing words of wisdom, she seemed distant. I figured it was because she was tired of listening to me and my conspiracy theories and dives into rabbit holes. Then one day she called and told me she had lung cancer. She seemed in shock, "Where did this come from? . . ." Lisa was a lifelong smoker but had quit and been vaping for the last seven years or so. Looking back now I realize it wasn't that she was shocked by the diagnosis but just IN SHOCK. She said she was going to follow up with the doctor and let me know what next steps would be taken. I took the news well as I knew there were groundbreaking treatments for lung cancer. My Aunt Patty had just been deemed cancer free after chemo and months of immune therapy. I shared that optimism with Lisa but I don't think she could see the light I was trying to shed.

About a week or two later Lisa called me and told me, "I don't feel right. . . ." She told me she had fallen in her kitchen and was confused. I told her to immediately go to the hospital. She didn't go until the next day and went to the ER at a hospital in Jersey City, New Jersey. They admitted her and I awaited a report. Her son Buddy was alerted and he planned to fly into New Jersey from California. When she called me from the hospital she was in distress and I could hear Brian talking to her in the background. She was complaining that no one knew what was wrong with her. Lisa wasn't one to sit still or not speak up under any circumstance. She was confused and frustrated that no one seemed to know what was going on. She called me a few times in the middle of the night extremely agitated during her hospital stay. I'm so glad I answered the phone. She wasn't making much sense and kept saying she wanted to go home. I told her to wait until the morning and we would figure out what to do next. Satisfied with that answer, she hung up.

The next morning I got a call from her that she had checked herself out of the hospital. Her instincts told her she was not in a place that would help her so she left. This posed a new problem. If that hospital couldn't diagnose her, where should she go? She had no general practitioner and would go to Brian's doctor as needed. The oncologist was pushing to operate but she was showing signs of distress. Lisa's children Buddy and Victoria were on call and it was all hands on deck to face whatever this was. Lisa continued to seem confused when I spoke to her so I decided to take a trip to her house. When I arrived she was acting very strange. I brought her a grilled cheese and a heating pad, thinking maybe she could eat and get some rest. The visit was very upsetting. She kept asking what time it was and to bring her a digital clock. She told me she was tired but an aide was coming to check her vitals so she had to stay awake. I thought it was good that a healthcare aide was coming and if they noticed an urgent issue they would intervene. The aide came and was only there for a few minutes. I expressed my concern and the aide only asked when Lisa would be seeing the doctor again. To this day it bothers me how dismissive she was. There was no doubt Lisa was out of it and needed help. I could see she was slipping away. I thought maybe it was her fall that was causing the confusion and I expressed that to her family. I know how scary and shocking it can be when someone you love is having a medical emergency. I said my piece and reminded the family I was there for them anytime.

Brian called me the next day and told me Lisa was having surgery. I thought it was for her lung cancer but it was not. Her heart had an apparent blockage that needed to be remedied. Honestly, I only remember bits and pieces of the information I was given. I, too, was in a state of consistent panic about her health. Brian told me she was at Hackensack Medical in New Jersey and could receive visitors. When I arrived at the hospital I saw Brian outside. He told me Lisa had had a PET scan that was done to see if her cancer had spread. I was not told the results. I always respected their privacy but still wanted answers. I brought Lisa a piece of pound cake and blessed oil that had touched the religious relics of Padre Pio. When I walked in she was sitting up surrounded by pillows and barely coherent. I rubbed the oil on her back where her lungs would be then massaged her feet, which were swollen and very cold. I didn't get much more information about her prognosis but I didn't like what I saw. I left that hospital with a sinking feeling that Lisa wouldn't come out of this.

When she got home from the hospital she was confined to the living room couch and on oxygen. I would visit her and feel completely helpless. Again, she would ask every few minutes what time it was. Brian was struggling and there wasn't much I could do to help him. Since Mike wasn't working, he offered one day to drive Lisa and Brian to several doctors' appointments. When Mike came home he gave me a grim report. Lisa needed help in and out of his car. She didn't speak at all during their car ride, but Brian expressed his belief her confused behavior might be neurological. I had no idea what doctors she was seeing nor was anyone obligated to tell me. It's upsetting when you aren't technically family but you are in all the best ways.

A few days later I got a call from Lisa's son Buddy who said his mom had been admitted to the hospital and she had taken a turn for the worse. He said it was time for me to come see her and say "Goodbye." WHAT?! I had a million questions for Buddy but wanted to respect his time and hoped I would make it to the hospital in time. I hung up and broke down to Mike. "She's dying!!" Mike was as confused as I was but knew time was of the essence. We quickly got ready to go and the ride to the hospital was quiet.

When I approached her hospital room, I saw Brian, who welcomed us in the hallway. When I walked in the room, I saw Lisa wearing an oxygen mask and her daughter Victoria in a chair next to her bed. Victoria is an extremely soft-spoken young woman in great contrast to her brother Buddy, who is literally a rock star extrovert like his mom. Lisa raised two wonderful and kind children. I touched Lisa's hand and it was ice cold. She opened her eyes for a moment and looked right at me. She was still with us and I had made it just in time. Her flaming red hair now had three inches of gray roots. It probably upset her that she lay there helpless and her grays had taken over. If you knew Lisa and are reading this you completely understand what I mean. Her breathing was shallow and she only took a breath every ten or fifteen seconds. She was surrounded by her entire immediate family, including her stepchildren, Liam and Aiden, who she had raised since they were in grammar school.

Victoria asked if I wanted to replace her in the chair and spend time with her mom. I felt completely humbled that Victoria and Buddy allowed me the privilege to be with them to say goodbye to their mother. I gratefully took a seat and rubbed Lisa's hand. Her breath intake was now only every thirty to forty seconds or so. I knew her death was imminent but I had no idea how fast she was about to slip away. I watched her take a deep breath then her chest stopped moving. I did not want to be the one to tell the room she had passed so I told Victoria to sit down and replace me. Within a few moments it hit Victoria that her mother had passed away as she turned to the room to inform everyone. We called for a nurse to confirm she had passed and call her time of death.

Lisa had stayed here on the earthly plane just long enough for me to be there. Then she crossed over. The room was heavy with emotion and we were all frozen. A huge colorful bouquet of flowers I had sent her was sitting on the table in the room. I took one rose from the bouquet and put it on her chest. I took one sunflower for myself and left her behind to be with her family.

All of us were in shock to say the least. Brian had arranged a beautiful wake and service at a Catholic church in Jersey City, New Jersey. Lisa wasn't Catholic but she and Brian would attend Mass in Ridgewood, New Jersey, together during their marriage. I know Lisa appreciated the tribute and that it would help Brian heal.

When someone dies unexpectedly it is so different than losing someone who has a peaceful passing. My dad had struggled for years prior to his death so when it happened I was at peace knowing he was no longer suffering. This hit differently for so many reasons. I felt Lisa was trying to communicate and was literally paralyzed by her afflictions. Whatever those afflictions were I may never know. It didn't matter anymore. My dear friend was gone.

Right before she died she called me when I was on location in Pennsylvania. I was in the bathroom on set and my phone rang.

Seeing it was Lisa I had to answer since there hadn't been much communication after one of her hospitalizations. She just kept saying over and over again, "I love you Martha Byrne.... Martha Byrne... I love you...." I said, "I know... I know..." and that was it and we hung up. Looking back now I think she had moments of clarity and used them as she wished. I am forever grateful she called me that day. After that call, her coherent verbal communications with me and others basically stopped. She would struggle to speak and was visibly confused. That call had given me some hope she would come out of all of whatever was happening to her. Deep down I knew exactly what that call was but couldn't accept it at the time.

About a week after she died I had several vivid dreams about Lisa. The first one she was much younger and had long curly red hair. This is how I remember her when we first met. In the dream she was on the streets of New York in full dance attire and kicking her legs in the air like she was on a chorus line. Lisa had a long career in musical theater, even starring as the lead in the Broadway hit *42nd Street*. In the dream she was so happy and dancing with pride on the sidewalks of the theater district. I woke up with a beautiful feeling that Lisa was happy on the other side. Then I had another dream that was beyond this world. Lisa was in my son Max's bedroom, which was across the hall from ours. She was the age she was when she passed away, but healthy. She asked me, "Do you want to feel what heaven feels like?" I of course said, "YES!!" Lisa told me that I could only spend a few moments there then I would have to come back. I understood. At that moment Lisa opened up the ceiling of Max's room and the dark sky filled with millions of the brightest twinkling stars I had ever seen. The sky slowly came down and encompassed Max's room and Lisa and me. I could FEEL all the worry I had in my earthly life disappear from my body. I noted that my concern about my children was gone. How was that possible? That this place Lisa brought me to took away all the human stress and suffering, so much so I didn't even worry about my family. Was she showing me that when the day comes that I get called to heaven, it will be OK? Or was she showing me that she was OK?

Lisa brought me back to reality and I felt all the stress and worry return to my physical body as I was still dreaming. The ceiling closed and I thanked Lisa for showing me heaven. Whatever that visitation was, it gave me some closure and I could rid myself of any guilt I had about her passing.

A few weeks later I was washing dishes and saw the "IT'S GOING TO BE OK" note. I was angry and upset so I took it down, crumbled it up, and threw it out. The next day, feeling like I made a mistake by tossing it, I took a new post it and wrote down the same phrase again. This time I put the sticky note on a window next to my kitchen table. Later that night I started to notice something. First it looked like condensation building up next to the note so I didn't think much of it. As I passed by again, I noticed an image starting to appear from the condensation. First it was a white oval shape about an inch long. I stopped and watched as the white oval slowly expanded downward into a pink, gold, green, and blue trailing image with a veil-like framing around the oval as well. I watched this beautiful image continue to grow as the bottom formed into a multi-colored robe that touched the sticky note. This had NEVER happened before on this window. It was clearly a beautiful image of the Blessed Mother. I took a photograph of it that will never leave my phone. That twenty-four hours of doubt vanished and I surrendered back to the truth, that it WAS all going to be OK. Just as fast as she appeared, she faded away into the darkness of the night behind the glass.

CHAPTER FIVE

One morning in March of 2022 Larry Lustberg's name popped up on our caller ID. Larry didn't usually call unless there was bad news he wanted to deliver personally. Genna was the lawyer doing all the prep for the motions so when she called it was never as jarring. Whenever Larry called, Mike and I became extremely anxious. We sat on the living room couch close together, answered the phone, and put Larry on speaker. The tone of his voice was very different than what we were used to. He started the conversation asking how we were both doing. After more than two years, I wanted to cry and say, "We're both holding on by a thread!!" Instead, we both calmly said, "...Good." Larry informed us that the judge had requested an ex parte from our counsel.

An ex parte is a presentation to the judge to give her an understanding of what counsel's line of defense would be at trial. The reason Judge Chen requested this meeting was to determine if she should allow defense counsel to view what is called CIPA (Classified Information Procedures Act) materials. CIPA materials in discovery, if deemed exculpatory for Mike, would have to be approved by the judge and national security for our attorney to see. To view this material an attorney must have a high-level government security clearance, which very few lawyers have. Larry had clearance due to his work on several federal cases, including the Bergrin case. So, if there was CIPA to review, Larry was already approved to do so. If the judge deemed the material exculpatory in nature after hearing our line of defense, Larry would be permitted to go into the SCIFF (sensitive compartmented information facility), a room with no windows where no notes can be taken and phones are not permitted. Defense counsel would review the material and make a request to the court for what they would like to use at trial. The request isn't a guarantee of approval since the government automatically fights all rulings and more often than not succeeds in their argument. The prosecutors argued privately to the judge that there was no exculpatory evidence useful to Mike and therefore no need for a CIPA review. They asserted that the materials included revealed national security tactics the public should not be privy to. They were first to argue their position under seal, then Judge Chen reviewed the CIPA material herself. After her review the judge was concerned enough that she wanted to hear from our side to determine if she should grant access to us. That's why she ordered the ex parte hearing.

Larry was very excited when this opportunity presented itself. It is so rare to get in front of a judge without the prosecution being present. We had no idea what the prosecutors argued to the judge, but we knew they definitely did not want us to see the CIPA material. That was telling. The PowerPoint we used for the proffer in 2021 with all the evidence of Mike's innocence had never been seen by Judge Chen. Now it was our chance to give her a preview of the facts that proved this case never should have been brought against Mike by the DOJ. If the CIPA material backed up our evidence, that Mike was unwittingly used by the Chinese agents, she would surely grant access to CIPA. If the findings were exculpatory, we could file a motion to dismiss based on those findings. This was very good news. News we desperately needed.

Our prayers seemed to be working. We had a bit of hope for the first time since this began. Maybe our judge was the guardian angel and hero we were praying for who would stop this injustice. The ex parte hearing was put on the calendar for the end of March 2022. Larry and Genna didn't have much time to prepare.

For the first time since his arrest, Mike finally had a glimmer of hope. Actions were in progress to rectify this insanity. Larry and Genna were preparing the prosecutorial misconduct motions along with the ex parte to present to Judge Chen. Our message to the government was clear: We weren't backing down. Our army was small but the truth was on our side. With every batch of discovery received from the government it became demonstrably clear that Mike had been scapegoated. The question was why. If it was because of the Bergrin case our prosecutorial misconduct motions would hit that dead-on and possibly exonerate Mike. If we were right, it would decimate the DOJ's case and expose their bias. With minimal guarantee the judge would rule in our favor and order hearings on our yet-to-be-filed motions, the ex parte could possibly swing her to do so. If the CIPA truly did exonerate Mike, maybe this could end sooner rather than later and our misconduct motions wouldn't even need to be filed at all. The government never gives you any time frame so we just kept moving forward and doing the work. We saw any positive movement as a potential end to this hell.

The fact that a handful of people would decide Mike's fate seemed completely unfair. How was it possible that strangers, with a biased point of view about Mike, were given that life-changing privilege? I sat by in silence unable to scream from the rooftops. It was killing me. I respected our counsel's advice not to speak to the press. Still, I was witnessing my husband die an excruciatingly slow death. I had to do something.

As Larry and Genna worked, I went back to the beginning of this case and reviewed Mike's evidence for the hundredth time. He had done everything by the book. In the opinion of other private investigators, he had gone above and beyond with regard to how he handled this case. So, what was the crime? Everything he did was legal. Parking on a public street for surveillance, legal. Accepting partial cash payment for the job, legal. Running the subject's name though public and private databases, which he was permitted to do, was legal. Mike, along with two hired PIs, notified local police every day of surveillance. Mike executed reports and invoices, even for cash received, for every day he worked on the job. He had a signed retainer from his client, which indemnified Mike if this case led to a legal dispute. The long list of Mike's due diligence records proved he wasn't hiding anything. He never deleted any texts or emails from his phone or computer. Even when he purchased a new phone, he transferred everything onto the new device. If he was working as an agent of the CCP as accused, he was really bad at it.

I thought it would be a good idea to start reaching out to other private investigators. I began with the NJ PIA. Mike had been a member for years and I figured it would be a good place to start. Unfortunately, the NJ PIA chose to suspend Mike from their organization after he had called to issue a warning to their members about how he was targeted. This was hurtful and disappointing to Mike. They failed to recognize he was fighting, not just for himself, but for the entire industry by taking on the federal government. If Mike was found guilty of violating FARA and interstate stalking as they claimed, parking on a public street or working for any foreign client could now be charged as federal crimes. The PI industry along with several other entities, including the press, insurance companies, and lawyers, all of whom rely on private investigators, would be culpable. One of the people who ran the NJ PIA was Nicole Cusanelli. It turned out Nicole was a big fan of *As the World Turns*. She seemed genuinely sympathetic to our situation as she had personally dealt with being falsely accused at one point in her career. She kindly invited me to speak at a NJ PIA dinner meeting. I eagerly accepted the invitation and the opportunity to tell our story to those who needed to hear it the most. Most PIs are former law enforcement and sole proprietors of their businesses.

We wanted to educate and help protect others from having their lives turned upside down.

I drove down by myself to the PI Association meeting in central New Jersey. When I walked in I was greeted by Nicole and James Nanos. As much as I was upset with them for suspending Mike, it was more important to get the word out. I was literally shaking as I sat finishing my penne alla vodka at a table with ten private investigators. Nicole called me up to speak as the coffee was served. As I approached the podium I knew what a pivotal moment this was. I was informed the event was being live streamed on Zoom. I didn't care. What I was about to say was far more important than federal agents at the ready with their pens, hoping I would make some fatal mistake. I had seen overwhelming evidence that Mike was innocent but I was forbidden to speak about it. I could only share what Mike had personally saved from the case, none of the other intel. If the government heard even one piece of sensitive information under the protective order coming out of my mouth I would be in serious trouble and jeopardize Mike's case.

I looked around the room, sizing up the audience of approximately fifty guests, all men. I shared a bit of my background then explained that Mike had been arrested for violating FARA and interstate stalking. Immediately many attendees pulled out their phones. I'm sure the brutal and misinformed *New York Post* article popped up. When I walked through the due diligence efforts Mike had made on the case, I noticed the group sitting up a bit straighter in their chairs, hanging on my every word. My story resonated with everyone in the room because they could see themselves in Mike. When finished, I opened the floor to questions. The first question was about FARA. The gentleman asked how Mike could be charged with violating FARA when he was just doing his job? According to the guidelines of FARA, third-party contractors, such as private investigators, are exempt from registering. I agreed with the man, he was correct. I reiterated Mike was still arrested for violating FARA without the FBI having justification to do so. The laws of this country were broken by the FBI and DOJ when they arrested Mike, not the other way around. This silenced the crowd, and I watched them process my dire warning. When I was finished speaking, a few of the men stuck around to learn more about the case. Nicole thanked me for coming and offered me the opportunity to speak again. On my way out the door I checked my email and became overwhelmed with emotion and my heart sank. There was an email with an invoice from Gibbons Law Firm for over tens of thousands of dollars. I texted Larry that I needed to speak to him immediately. I found a dark corner of the restaurant and my phone rang; it was Larry. I was distraught and crying with people within earshot, so I had to whisper. I told Larry how concerned I was about Mike and if he saw that bill, I was terrified of how he would handle it. Larry assured me not to worry about the bill for now, the firm just has to do its accounting of his hours. I asked him to start sending all the bills just to me and not to include Mike. He agreed and told me not to worry about it at that moment, we would figure it out at another time. I shared how scared I was that we would be forced to sell our home. Larry calmed my fears and told me not to concern myself about that right now. I pulled myself together and quickly went to my car in the parking lot. I cried alone in my car for a few minutes, then fortified myself for what would come next. I knew speaking publicly was a risk but I had no choice. Once I finished speaking, the gravity of that decision, then seeing the Gibbons Law invoice, hit me hard. I had done the right thing but it was extremely scary. My focus was to exonerate Mike and that was more important than any fear I may have had executing it. It was the first public action that gave Mike a voice that had been silenced. I was his voice from now until this case was over.

I proceeded to do everything I could to get his story out without doing what I really wanted to do: let loose on social media. Holding back from commenting on Twitter and Facebook about what happened was quite a challenge. I was honestly shocked that, since this happened, no one from my social media platforms seemed to know. That was a blessing and there was no need to open a discussion at that point. The people who followed me for decades were kindhearted and supportive people. This was a fact. So it was possible they knew but were being respectful of what our family was going through.

With my first outreach to NJ PIA under my belt, I started to explore the database of PIs nationwide. The PI industry is an eight-billion-dollar-a-year business. Who were the biggest players raking in the top dollars? This case would affect them the most so there was a possibility they would join our fight. I found plenty of large investigative firms across the country and created a spreadsheet of all of them and then started making calls. I rarely got a response but I wanted to be on record that I had made a concerted effort to educate and warn PIs. The warning wasn't just about Chinese criminal tactics but also about DOJ overreach. In the early days I had no idea how badly the FBI and DOJ had screwed up this case. All I knew was that Mike committed no crime and was scapegoated for some reason. I assumed every call I made was being recorded and possibly sent to the FBI. I didn't care. I was telling the truth with the intention of educating PIs and finding help. These larger firms had offices around the world, so it was far from just a domestic concern. If Mike was targeted for purported nefarious acts, these larger firms were no doubt targets also. Larger firms often subcontract PIs which made them even more vulnerable. How were they vetting these subcontracted PIs? Were they doing any vetting at all? Hiring just one unseasoned PI could be the downfall of their entire business.

One of the biggest PI firms in the world is Beau Dietl and Associates based in New York City. Bo was former NYPD and a staple in the city. He was known as a big-mouthed, wise-guy mini-celebrity. At one point he ran for mayor of New York and lost. He's had countless cameos on television shows and films such as *Goodfellas* and *The Wolf of Wall Street*. His personality is brash and 100 percent New York. He has a reserved table at Rao's restaurant which is unheard of for most peasants. Rao's is a tiny Italian restaurant in East Harlem, New York, where the now famous sauce originated. It is a favorite for A-list celebrities and was a mob staple for decades.

After my test run with the NJ PI Association I thought I should try and get Bo Dietl on the phone. There are a few things I know about people like Bo. Anyone who hangs around celebrities and vies for movie cameos is an opportunist. I spent my life around opportunists and the easiest way to bait one is with the possibility of "an opportunity." I knew Bo fell into this category and might let his guard down with me when he reviewed my resume. I was right. When I called his office his secretary was a bit cautious and advised she would get back to me. Within the hour she returned my call and said Bo would be willing to meet with me at his office on Fifth Ave in New York. I told Mike the good news and we planned our trip to the city. Mike would drive and wait for me in the car. He couldn't join me as he had to stay away from any situation where he might misspeak and cause irreversible harm. Having me be his mouthpiece was the only option and I knew how to handle Bo. My goal was to inform him about the work Mike did on the case and hope he would provide some insight. I didn't hold out much hope for his support as this case involved national security and the Chinese government. The fact he was even willing to meet with me was shocking. With so many people turning their backs on Mike, having a high-profile PI like Bo on our side would be great.

As I was riding up in the elevator to his office my mind was racing on how to open the conversation. When the elevator doors opened I saw the sign for Beau Dietl and Associates. I walked through the glass doors and checked in with the secretary. I could hear my heart beating in my ears and was sure the secretary could sense my nervous behavior. The square footage of the space was massive but the countless office cubicles were empty. The rent for such a space on Fifth Ave across from St. Patrick's Cathedral must be outrageous. It was an impressive footprint to say the least and fueled my goal to get Bo on our side. If he had a business of this magnitude, that meant he employed countless PIs who needed to hear my warning. The secretary escorted me into a large conference room. The walls were plastered with pictures and magazine covers of Bo with politicians, clergy, and celebrities. A six-by-four-foot Bo Dietl for Mayor poster hung on the wall. This guy really liked to show off. His personality was the antithesis of Mike's, that was clear.

The first person who walked in was Bo's chairman of operations, Michael Ruggiero. He was over six feet tall wearing a gorgeous dark tailored suit and fancy shoes. He seemed very wary of my presence and you could tell he was not comfortable with my being there. He shook my hand then sat across from me at a conference table with about five feet separating us. We chitchatted for a few minutes then Bo entered. I stood up and shook his hand. His first words went something like this, "They told me I shouldn't talk to you but I wanted to hear from you myself." Looking back now that statement was filled with clues. At the time I just assumed his "people" warned him not to speak to the wife of an accused Chinese agent. He sat next to Ruggiero and waited for me to speak. He had seen the *New York Post* article and that's all he would share. I laid out the case for Bo and explained to him that Mike didn't do anything illegal. I filled Bo in on Mike's incredible history and how horrific it was that this happened to such a hero. Bo didn't ask any questions and his CEO handed me a business card with DC-based defense attorney Mark Zaid's name on the back. I felt he was more sympathetic than when I first arrived. Maybe not. Why would he recommend an attorney who could possibly help us? Either way, my message of warning had been sent and I left after thanking Bo for taking the time. He said to let Mike know how sorry he was this had happened and that he supported him. When I got back to the car Mike was anxious to hear my report. I felt good about the meeting but wasn't sure if was worth our time. I had no idea the unthinkable effects that would later arise from our trip to Fifth Avenue.

After Mike's arrest I expected to see articles alerting the public to patterns of Chinese criminals running amok in New Jersey. If this case was the "first of its kind" involving Chinese repatriation operations, where were the articles to educate people on what to look out for to protect themselves? After speaking to several PI firms and individuals, it was clear I was the only person reaching out to PIs. Most were unaware Mike had been arrested or the circumstances surrounding it.

This reach out was desperately needed and gave Mike and me purpose. I had gotten over the anxiety of speaking publicly about Mike's case by addressing people it affected the most, PIs. Energized by a sense of purpose along with the lack of transparency to the public from the FBI and DOJ, I elevated my research up a few notches.

I began to follow anyone on Twitter who could be a helpful resource on Chinese espionage and the CCP. If your husband has been accused of being an asset for the CCP it makes sense to research and learn anything and everything you can about the CCP. Mike had been following a man named Gordon Chang on Twitter. Gordon was a staple on Fox News and other media outlets as a world-renowned China expert. Mike had heard a podcast with Gordon as a panelist along with a man name Rob O'Donnell. Rob was a retired NYPD detective who served during the same years as Mike. Mike was very impressed with Rob and told me I should follow him on Twitter. Shockingly, I was able to get Gordon Chang's personal phone number and when I called it, his wife answered! She took some information and I never expected to hear from her again. I was wrong. Gordon himself called back and I told him our story. Gordon was sympathetic to our case but wasn't well versed on Chinese Fox Hunt operations. This surprised me. Gordon is one of the most outspoken people regarding the CCP's takeover of the US but wasn't an expert on Fox Hunt? My heart sank a little bit but I was able to get one of the most knowledgeable people in the world regarding the CCP on the phone. That was something! If I could get Gordon on the phone, maybe I could get other high-profile people to do the same!

I noticed Rob was now following me on Twitter, which meant I could privately message him. I wasted no time and sent him Sebastian Rotella's article about Fox Hunt and a short summary of Mike's background and the case. Within an hour Rob tweeted the article and his support of Mike. WOW!! I was just hoping for a phone call and Rob went right to the world's stage and supported Mike! This was the FIRST TIME someone had publicly supported him and we were beyond grateful yet terrified at the same time! Would the comments get ugly? Would I be TAGGED in the post so my followers would learn what happened to us? Mike and I were filled with mixed emotions. Either way, it was the pivot we needed to validate there WERE supportive people out there. I was finally able to connect with Rob via phone and we became fast friends. As it turned out, Rob served in all of the same divisions as Mike but was just one year ahead of him in the academy. We had a very loud voice in our corner, and it felt good.

With our financial situation in flux I started to look into organizations that could help with our legal bills. There are great people out there who recognize that no one should go bankrupt when innocent and they choose to fight back. To fight the government you are looking at a minimum of one million dollars in legal fees. We had done well enough in our lives that we wouldn't qualify for a public defender. This bill was going to grow with no real end in sight. I was steadfast in the belief I could earn more money, but I wouldn't be able to save my husband if he wasn't fully exonerated. We had to fight. The reality is the cost of these cases usually runs into the three-to-four-million-dollar range. The odds of you winning a federal case are less than 2 percent, so we were facing insurmountable odds.

My dear friend, photographer Barry Morgenstein, reached out very early on after Mike's arrest to show his support. Barry had photographed me during my soap opera days and we reconnected after Mike's arrest. Barry suggested I reach out to the Pipe Hitter Foundation. The PHF was started by Eddie and Andrea Gallagher. Eddie was a Navy Seal captain who was falsely arrested for murder while serving in Afghanistan. His story was eerily similar to ours. After learning more about his wife Andrea, I knew I had found a kindred spirit in her. Andrea was a fierce fighter like me and went through the depths of hell to exonerate her husband. Once Eddie was cleared of all charges, the couple started the Pipe Hitter Foundation. PHF helps military and first responders who were falsely accused of crimes. I sent an email to the website with a short summary of our case. The return email stated that I should get a response within a few weeks if they were willing to take on our case. After a few weeks passed, I resolved myself to that fact we weren't chosen. As upsetting as that was, I knew it was a long shot. So many people need assistance, so I believed someone more in need was chosen. If anyone looked up Mike's case and believed what was in the media, it's not a surprise no one wanted to get involved. According to the *New York Post,* and every other news outlet, Mike was a traitor.

I decided to send another email to the Pipe Hitter Foundation thanking them for taking the time to review our case. I wrote that since the deadline had passed, I assumed we were not chosen as a PH family. I reiterated I would never stop fighting against the injustice for our family and praised them for their work. After I sent the email I closed that door and moved on.

I found out through Barry that Rob O'Donnell was a board member of the Pipe Hitter Foundation! I had no idea. Barry had photographed Eddie and Andrea Gallagher for their book cover and Rob O'Donnell for his headshots. When I heard this news I immediately reached out to Rob and let him know I had applied to be a PH family. He followed up with the other PHF board members and got their attention on our case. Within a few weeks we got the incredible news: The Pipe Hitter Foundation had unanimously approved to support our family. I cannot fully express how much that meant to all of us, especially Mike.

With the addition of the Pipe Hitter Foundation and online support from Rob, we felt a bit of a sea change. It killed me that I couldn't tweet about the case but at least there was finally some movement in a positive light. The Pipe Hitter Foundation had a PR team who wanted me to do some press. They were very patient and respectful about when the right time would be to take that step. Larry wanted Mike to stay away from the media but understood we needed financial assistance and publicity could be very helpful. Because I was already in the public eye, it didn't seem harmful to let me speak to the media. Larry's only warning was to make my appearances all about Mike's innocence and stay away from the government smear as much as possible. That was fine because I didn't have a full scope at that time how badly the

FBI and the DOJ actually failed in the case. Until I could prove my theories, they were just that, theories.

I started doing a few radio interviews and podcasts. The early ones were incredibly nerve-racking. I have done thousands of interviews in my career but always with a friendly press talking about pleasant things, like soap operas and charity events. It felt good to defend Mike and let anyone listening know that Mike did nothing illegal. The interviewers would always ask "Why do you think the FBI went after HIM?" I always struggled with that question. I couldn't tell the world we were about to throw a prosecutorial misconduct charge at the DOJ and our belief of the "why" was included. I just focused on the why not as proof Mike would never betray his country. He had only made a few thousand dollars on this job and did everything by the book. I pointed out that the government took legitimate PI work and deemed it criminal just to bring this case down. There were a few talking points I would hit and I got better with each interview.

I was booked almost every day on one show or another and up to that point everything was done remotely. I set up my office like a TV studio and was ready at any given moment to jump on a Zoom call. Then Newsmax asked me to appear live in their studio. This was a big deal. Newsmax had a huge audience but leaned heavily conservative. To me politics was a non-issue as our story wasn't a political one for us and we needed the exposure. I had a big decision to make, if I promoted my appearance on Twitter and Facebook, my followers would be brought into the loop. Newsmax would most certainly pull some strong opinions from the internet but our story held no political affiliation. One of the Pipe Hitter board members Carl Higbie was a host on Newsmax and would be interviewing me. I got to tell the story of the FBI raid on our home and how Mike did nothing illegal. It was great. I was getting better at the interviews and so far, we hadn't gotten any pushback from the government. There was no way they were happy with me but there wasn't much they could do about it either. Nothing I was saying was false. The narrative they had created was starting to crumble, at least in the eyes of the public.

Every single day I never stopped trying to fill in the missing pieces of the case and get needed answers. I decided it was time to make a visit to the two New Jersey police departments involved in the case. Mike had done surveillance of two homes, one in Millburn, New Jersey, and one in Warren, New Jersey. In both towns he notified the local police by phone or in person the specific locations he would be in the area. Mike provided his phone number, make and model of his car, as well as the other two PIs' information who were working with him. He told the departments they were retired cops and were armed. These notifications are a courtesy by PIs to keep everyone safe but are not required by law. So, if a citizen calls the cops to report a suspicious vehicle, the police know it's a PI who is legally allowed to park on a public street. This prevents unnecessary concern for the neighborhood and if there's any real issue the police can drive by or call the PIs if they have questions or concerns. Letting the local police know is the best course of action. If Mike was involved in anything nefarious he would not be notifying the police. It would be like a bank robber calling the cops to let them know their location, they were armed, and about to walk into the bank.

I was curious to know if the FBI shared any information with the departments about Fox Hunt cases being executed in their towns. I assumed if Chinese agents had been plotting harassment and kidnappings, the FBI most certainly would have alerted the local police. While we were coordinating our trip to South Jersey police, I got an email from Rob O'Donnell with an article published on Yahoo News regarding an FBI memo the bureau had circulated internally just one week after Mike's arrest. The article had a link to the memo with details from Mike's case. It read like a checklist of what to look out for when dealing with potential Chinese bad actors. The timing didn't seem by accident. According to the article, this memo was circulated ONLY to the FBI personnel. I made a hard copy to take with me to the police departments to see if they had ever seen anything similar distributed to their departments.

Months had passed since Mike's arrest so I wasn't sure if I would find anyone who had knowledge of his case at either location. If the FBI had spoken to the local police about Chinese agents running around their towns, threatening a resident, it should be noted in their files. With the FBI memo in hand, we were on our way. We had already done an open-source request (OPRA) for both departments. The OPRA report confirmed Mike's notifications on the days of surveillance and one additional incident at one address he surveilled. We were aware of this public record incident report due to our discovery. According to the records local police were called once in the fall of 2018, a year and a half after Mike had done surveillance on the home in April 2017. There weren't any police reports of the subjects being followed by anyone in 2017 through October 2020. This was great news and confirmed there was no recorded evidence of harassment or stalking at either location Mike surveilled.

The first police station we visited was Warren, New Jersey. Like most local police stations the entrance is small and the check-in window is tinted so you cannot see the person clearly on the other side. The woman asked my name and seemed bothered by my presence. I could barely make out her face and hair color. I could tell she was in her mid- to late fifties with curly red hair. That's about all I could distinguish. I asked if I could speak to someone. I didn't even know what I was going to ask if she actually sent someone out to talk to me. I mumbled something about "my husband ... false arrest ... Chinese ... your district ..." ... ugh. I wasn't very clear because I didn't know specifically what I was looking for. I showed her the OPRA report and she disappeared. I could see her shadow looking at me for just a bit too long and I knew what that meant. When you've been on TV as long as I have, you know in an instant if someone recognizes you. I didn't even need to see her face, only her body language to know I hit a home run. Sure enough, she comes to the window and I see a faint smile on her face, "Are you on *Guiding Light*?" "Close, I was Lily on *As the World Turns*." She said, "I KNEW IT!!" She told me to wait a minute and someone would be right out to speak to me.

In the waiting area there was one door in and out where the cops would enter and exit. A patrol cop came out and introduced himself. I rambled off our story and showed him the local report we had about Mike's surveillance in his town. He told me to wait and he would run the address to see if there was anything else of interest. Upon his return he said he had nothing further. I showed him the FBI memo and asked if he had ever seen anything like this. "No." I asked him if he was aware there were Chinese spies running around his district for years. "No." He took my name and number and wished me the best. He told me he would pass my information on to the lieutenant and if he had any questions he would call me. I walked out slightly disturbed that the local cops had no idea about Mike's arrest or Chinese Fox Hunt operations going on in the town. Our next stop was the police station in Millburn, New Jersey. This station was more important because Millburn was where the alleged "stalking" Mike had purportedly engaged in occurred. The allegation was Mike had provided the Chinese agents with a "previously unknown address," according to the government.

Behind the tinted window of this department was a cop, not a civilian. I showed him Mike's notification report and he told me he would show it to one of the detectives. A few moments later, a plain-clothed detective emerged and I told him our story. Whenever I rattle off the details, I can only imagine what these people think. He seemed very genuine and said he didn't have any more information for me. He shared a story about his personal dealings with the FBI. He told me he had worked on a case for a year involving a drug ring in town. He had gathered binders full of evidence and was ready to take it down. He reached out to the FBI and shared his work with the bureau. He didn't hear from them for a while so after six months had passed he decided to reach out for a status report. The FBI informed him they weren't going to pursue the case. He couldn't believe it. The look in this cop's eyes telling me this story really struck me. He was defeated. You could tell a part of him died the day he got the news. All his work was for nothing. Work that would have saved countless lives was just dismissed by the federal bureau, which looked down on the traditional police officer. That was some insight as to how the FBI feels about anyone outside their federal bubble.

I showed him the FBI memo and he assured me he had never seen it. He said the only time the FBI ever calls is if they need assistance on an arrest. There is basically no communication between the local and federal agencies. He wished me luck and I was out the door. The two visits revealed something that infuriated me. The FBI never shared intel with the local police on Operation Fox Hunt. If the FBI was "raised up" on these activities, which I discovered started as early as 2015, why wouldn't they include local law enforcement in their investigations? They claim these operations were a national security risk, yet didn't alert departments to contact the FBI if they saw any odd activity. If they had taken that one small step, Mike's notifications to local police of surveillance would have started a chain of events that would have kept many people safe and put real criminals behind bars. How can we expect the FBI to warn Mike and other private investigators if they didn't even warn the New Jersey law enforcement where these operations were taking place? It begged the question: What else were they hiding?

On the way home my phone rang. It was the lieutenant from Millburn. I provided more details about the operations going on in his town. He informed me he had no idea about Mike's arrest or that wanted fugitives from China were living in his neighborhood. I inquired if he would have liked to have known that information, considering these alleged events happened one block from a school. He strongly replied, "Yes." The lack of interactions and transparency was shocking to me. If the FBI had let the local police know anything, Mike never would have been arrested and my family would not have been exposed to Chinese criminals, individuals the FBI Director Wray called, "an organized criminal syndicate." My drive to expose the full story and the truth got stronger. Now it wasn't just our family, it was every family in America who was left vulnerable due to the FBI failures. How far up the DOJ food chain did it go? I wasn't going to stop until I found out. Now I had more talking points for my interviews with evidence the FBI failed to notify the local police about their citizens being exposed to Chinese harassment campaigns. This was bad. Who was responsible?

Larry and Genna let us know they were ready to present the ex parte to the judge and were looking forward to it. When the day came to present we were very anxious. Mike would not attend the meeting, so we just waited for the phone call from Larry after presenting to the judge. The presentation could not have gone better according to Larry and Genna. The judge asked a few questions then let Larry know she would decide soon whether or not it would be necessary to view any CIPA materials. Genna and Larry felt Judge Chen was going to be a favorable judge in our case. That was music to our ears. To have a fair and favorable judge is like winning the lottery when you are facing the government beast.

With our prosecutorial motions about to be submitted, Larry got a call from *The New York Times*. They were doing a story about Iranian journalist Masih Alinejad. I knew her background because right before Mike's arrest there was a story about an outspoken Iranian journalist who had been targeted to be kidnapped for speaking out against Iran. What stood out to me was that she had been followed by a private investigator. The press never revealed the PI's name, which was upsetting to me. I thought if I could get the name maybe he could help us because the PI was not arrested for following Masih. I knew there must be more to the story, and I was desperate to find out. According to reports, Masih was moved to several safe houses after the FBI informed her she had been targeted. By moving her around it gave the FBI time to build a case against the Iranians who wanted her dead. *The New York Times* had already interviewed the PI and wanted a quote from Larry about Mike's arrest as both cases involved foreign influence on US private investigators. Larry had an idea. If Mike would agree, we would give the *Times* an exclusive interview. It didn't take but a minute for us to agree. This was huge. Larry letting Mike speak was a major power move and we trusted it was the right one. The interview would take place at Gibbons Law offices and Larry and Genna would be present. Larry felt *The New York Times* releasing an article during the prosecutorial motions and CIPA materials consideration, soon to be delivered, may help Mike get hearings and evidence we needed to clear him. The entire Justice Department reads *The New York Times* and this strategic, yet risky, tactic could move the needle in our favor.

I was wary of *The New York Times* but was assured it would be OK. I knew Larry would never risk Mike's freedom if he thought this would be an ambush. It was time to let Mike speak to the world. He was more than ready to do so.

CHAPTER SIX

Mike and I were extremely anxious to sit down with *New York Times* columnist Ben Weiser. Up to this point the media had falsely portrayed Mike as an American citizen who had betrayed his country. The case made international news and the narrative created by the government was now written in stone. Every article had pulled text directly from the sworn criminal complaint rife with inaccuracies and falsehoods. Not one journalist researched Mike's background or investigated his character to query an answer as to why he would do such a treasonous thing, working with a foreign adversary. No fact-checking of the accusations in the criminal complaint by any publication. Were they just lazy or was it because of a much darker possibility? It seemed odd to me that these journalists failed to accurately tell their stories to include details about the alleged victims, Jin Xu and Fang Liu, who were confirmed to be CCP members accused of embezzlement and bribes while living in China. Only one story about the subjects of Mike's surveillance was written in *The Wall Street Journal* on July 29, 2020. The article portrayed Jin Xu and Fang Liu as victims of Chinese civil lawfare executed here in the US. It featured some examples describing how the CCP used our civil judicial system to intimidate alleged criminals from China who had fled to the US. *The Wall Street Journal* article referenced Jin Xu as a former Chinese government official. His resume as a high-ranking member of the CCP seemed to be left on the edit room floor. Why? I believe that the reader would have seen that to be an important piece of the story. No matter how much I searched I couldn't find another article in the United States about civil lawsuits being used as a harassment tactic by the CCP. The article was written by Aruna Viswanatha and Kate O'Keefe. I looked up both writers and added them to my list of potential resources.

On the other hand, the full throttle defamation of Mike was brutal right out of the gate. The writer at the *New York Post* had no problem using the NYPD connection to get clicks but failed to balance the accusations by pointing out his decorated career. Why did every article leave that information out? It certainly would have enhanced the story and made it more shocking that a man with such a pristine record and accomplished work history would turn his back on his country. The reader would question why a man who lived a life of service to his community, was married to a successful actress, just woke up one morning and gave it all up to work for the CCP. It was obviously too risky for the media to include anything positive about Mike. The government held all the cards when it came to the media. I had no idea at that point to what degree the government controlled the media. I was about to find out.

Around that time Mike was scheduled for a personal interview with the *Times* reporter, we had only received a partial dump of government discovery materials. Much of it was encrypted, which deterred us from opening it without consulting an IT specialist. The government proved unwilling to deliver the material in an organized way, which would not only have saved us time but also money. Even with the minimal amount of discovery evidence we were able to open, it became clear this case was based on flimsy subjective evidence and nonsense. It was clear the DOJ had let anyone who was directly involved with this "scheme" flee the country on their watch. They had missed, purposely or mistakenly, countless opportunities to arrest people over their four-year investigation. The FBI had dozens of interactions with the alleged masterminds of the operation and chose to trust those people. The FBI chose not to bring in Mike or any of the other US law enforcement connected to the case. They got in bed with our enemy and our family has paid the tragic price. The FBI gets small bonuses each year to keep cases open. The bonuses never exceed a few thousand dollars. Our lives were invaded by the federal government for a few extra thousand dollars in their paychecks. Even though we had seen enough to know Mike was used by the government to generate "optics" in the case, we had to walk a very thin line with the *Times* interview. We had to be extremely cautious not to share information we had seen that was under the protective order. The government labels these materials sensitive for various reasons. Naturally, the government does not want documents favoring the defense made public. Much of Mike's evidence was his emails and texts, which he could share publicly if he wished. We refrained from doing that because we were still trying to navigate the entire narrative the government was generating. We had no idea how they were authorized to get multiple search warrants to keep the case against Mike open.

Everything we saw thus far only benefited Mike and confirmed his innocence. Because the government declared this material sensitive, we were unable to speak about it under the threat of legal ramifications, the revocation of bail, and potentially the adding of an ankle bracelet. That directive covered everyone under the protective order, including me. I had been granted the opportunity to view discovery material but was under the same restrictions as everyone else. I had seen enough to realize that the government had no substantive evidence against Mike and was convinced this case had been mishandled by the Department of Justice from the beginning. It would be a challenge to withhold this information we had unearthed from the reporter. What we were free to say was that to this date we had seen no evidence that showed Mike was working for the Chinese government. That came as no surprise to us because there was no indication in the government material delivered to us that could be interpreted as guilt.

Our sit-down with the *Times* would serve as a tool to present our perspective and get the truth out to the global audience.

I never wasted one minute sitting by hoping for a miracle. I was, however, increasingly concerned that the government was not going to let up on us unless Mike would agree to a plea deal. The delay to our motions was unnerving even though we filed the paperwork just weeks prior in August of 2022. I'm sure they believed their pressure tactics would work until they read our prosecutorial misconduct motions against them. Our motions read like a John Grisham novel, filled with compelling arguments and blistering accusations directed against people not prone to hearing such things. I continued to investigate anything and everything that seemed of interest and spent hours online doing research. Just days before the interview I discovered something relevant to our case. I couldn't believe I had missed it. It was a bombshell piece of evidence that could lead to Mike's full exoneration! How could I have missed it when it was made public mere months prior to our motions?

I discovered a criminal complaint filed on March 31, 2022, in the Southern District of New York (Manhattan) regarding an indictment of a man named Sun Hoi Ying, aka "Sun Haiying," who was named as the lead CCP asset in an Operation Fox Hunt/Operation Skynet case. The subject Sun Hoi was "at large," presumably in China. The document revealed jaw-dropping information about a Fox Hunt case in New York involving "PI Firms" and a member of "local U.S. law enforcement." No one other than Sun Hoi was named in the complaint, everyone else was anonymous and listed as "victims" or "co-conspirators." The report seemed incredibly similar to Mike's case. The alleged victim(s) in the Manhattan case were accused of embezzlement and bribery in China, as were the subjects Mike followed during the same late 2016–early 2017 time period. In the SDNY Manhattan case in October of 2016, a "PI Firm" was given twelve "targets" by Sun Hoi to investigate, several were on China's Most Wanted list. The complaint alleged the PIs were working at the direction of the Chinese government, having met with Sun Hoi and another Chinese official in 2016. According to the complaint, the PI Firm employees were aggressive at times. In one instance a PI went on the property of one of the targets, knocking on the front door and photographing the subjects. The distressed target called the police in fear. This complaint was an incredible find! Who were these PIs? Why weren't they arrested? Who were the targets they were told to follow? Was it possible these PIs had surveilled the same subjects as Mike? According to open-source documents there just weren't that many Fox Hunt targets in the US. There was a very strong possibility that Jin Xu and Fang Liu were on that list of wanted fugitives. They were highly sought-after subjects of the CCP according to not only our court documents but others. If this was true we needed to find the PIs and add their affidavit to our motions. I needed to put my detective hat on. I knew time was of the essence. I looked for anything I could find from this case in the SDNY. The actions of the PIs in the SDNY were egregious according to the complaint but didn't amount to criminality as they were working in the capacity of their job. Mike's actions towards the subjects of his surveillance were vastly different and covert, yet he was arrested for interstate stalking! Mike was never asked to do anything illegal. He was never on anyone's property or seen by anyone when he conducted surveillance. I had to digest everything I was reading before I looped Larry in on this information.

Based on the SDNY complaint, the operation in which the "PI Firms" were involved ran concurrent to Mike's work on his case in New Jersey. However, not only were the PIs not arrested, they were given anonymity to protect their actions from the public. Was this done purposely by the New York FBI and SDNY? If so, who ordered it to be cloaked in a veil of mystery? When you read the EDNY criminal complaint against Mike side by side with the one out of the SDNY there are obvious similarities. I started to think that the FBI had a Fox Hunt case file with all the intel, pulled evidence, and dispersed it across their field offices in New York, New Jersey, California, and possibly other states. I couldn't prove it but there were too many clues pointing in that direction. This was very upsetting. How could I find out who these private investigators were? I knew the FBI would not release information that would help Mike in any way. Why in March of 2022 did the FBI choose to indict Sun Hoi who was "at large" in China? No one was arrested in that case and no further action seemed to have taken place based on my digging. It looked as if the case had been officially closed, but why? The statute of limitations had not run out. The NY FBI chose to end it. I had to find out why the member of the "US law enforcement" or any of the private investigators weren't arrested. Who was the person who chose not to pursue charges against them? Was it the DC intelligence agencies? Was it the former head of the SDNY Geoffrey Berman, who had been unceremoniously fired by the Attorney General William Barr in June of 2020? Who was the head of the New York FBI when the SDNY case was being investigated? If it had been decided by the NY FBI not to arrest the PIs in the SDNY case, why was the Newark FBI permitted to go after Mike? The answer only bolstered the case of personal bias against Mike. This case had to be added to our prosecutorial misconduct motions. My head was spinning. Was it possible to get the government to reveal names that could possibly help exonerate Mike? I forwarded the SDNY Fox Hunt complaint to Larry and Genna, who immediately prepared and filed the necessary paperwork with Judge Chen. If she granted us hearings based on the addition of the SDNY case to the motion, we could call the SDNY FBI Case Agent Kelsey Palermo as a witness and request the names of the "PI firms" be unmasked. This was an unbelievable find! The *Times* would most certainly be interested in this development as well. I sent Larry the SDNY case with many questions to consider. Larry was blown away and agreed this needed to be addressed with the court immediately! We had filed the motions a few weeks prior, so we wanted to add these findings before the government's response, which could come any day! As Larry and Genna brainstormed about how to file this new evidence, Mike and I mentally prepared to meet with the *Times*.

On September 27, 2022, while we waited in Larry's office, he prepped Mike for the interview by posing multiple questions that might be asked. I could tell Larry was especially anxious about his decision to allow Mike to do the interview. After all, it was the first time in the two years since the arrest that Mike would be personally presenting his side of the story. Ben Weiser entered the Gibbons conference room accompanied by an associate from the *Times*. They introduced themselves, sat down, and immediately began recording the conversation. Weiser is very approachable and has an unassuming demeanor. My research on Weiser revealed that he, like everyone at the *Times*, absolutely hated Donald Trump. His bias in his reporting was clear so I took his pleasant nature with some trepidation but trusted that Larry would not put us in a position that could jeopardize our case. The relationship between lawyers and the press is an important collaboration meant to maintain open communication between both sides. It's a balancing act for both parties but one needs to maintain civility and professionalism. If the press screws over a lawyer, that relationship is dead forever. The same rule applies in reverse.

Overall, the interview went smoothly. Mike had nothing to hide and was open and honest in representing the facts. Mike is a great conversationalist and I could see Weiser was impressed with him but definitely confused by what he was hearing. If the story Mike was telling was to be believed, it meant the government had lied to the American public. How would Weiser expose that in his story yet satisfy the narrative he had read about in the government's complaint? Would he even be able to include it in his story at all? At the end of the interview he asked me a few questions. I got emotional recounting the FBI raid at our home. I could tell he was genuinely moved by the trauma inflicted on our family. After the interview was concluded, he thanked us for the exclusive opportunity we had offered him, we all shook hands, and they left. If he was true to his job and wrote what we said on the record, the article would be positive. We could only hope. Larry and Genna felt it went well and thought Mike handled himself perfectly. We took the calculated risk with the hope that Weiser would frame the *Times*' article in our favor. Would Judge Chen take umbrage with the fact that Mike had spoken to the press? In the almost two years since his arrest, the press had been completely one-sided in their portrayal of the case.

Any media reach out that I previously had done was minor in comparison to the readership scale of *The New York Times*. We presumed the article would most certainly get a reaction from the court. What that reaction might be was pure speculation. We had no insight into when the article would drop but Larry felt it could land around the time the court would be deciding on whether to grant hearings or finally rule on whether to grant us access to CIPA materials. Why was it taking so long for Judge Chen to rule on CIPA?! It had been months! We continued to hold our breath awaiting the procedural timelines that take forever.

The prosecutorial misconduct motions submitted before our interview were brutal against the FBI, specifically Agent Sean McCarthy. Larry was originally reluctant to believe the government had retaliated against Mike due to his work on the Bergrin case. Now, having seen the evidence against Mike, he realized it was more likely than not it was exactly why Mike was targeted and Larry came with receipts. Over forty pages in the motions detailed the FBI's post-arrest statements, actions in our home, and horrific details of Bergrin's misdeeds to show the judge why Mike was a persona non grata to the FBI. The clear distaste for Mike was vicious and unfiltered the moment they stepped into our foyer on that October 2020 morning. It wasn't just our theory, it was confirmed in a Bergrin brief written by Assistant US Attorney Chief, Appeals Division, Mark E. Coyne, on June 22, 2021. Almost a year earlier on August 25, 2020, just weeks before Mike's arrest, New Jersey Judge Madeline Arleo denied Paul Bergrin a hearing based on "newly discovered evidence" (Rule 33 motion). In her brief Judge Arleo conceded that Mike's evidence was a valid argument in Bergrin's favor, meeting the Rule 33 standard, yet she still denied a hearing for Bergrin. This assessment of Mike's evidence being valid from Judge Arleo gave Bergrin some wiggle room to appeal that ruling. I'm sure this did not sit well with US Appellate Attorney Mark Coyne.

He had to dismantle Mike's credibility to prevent Bergrin from winning his next appeal on Judge Arleo's ruling.

In his June 22, 2021, brief, Attorney Coyne cites Mike's arrest in the EDNY, claiming he has "credibility issues" which must be considered. He accuses Mike of possible collusion with a witness, questions the authenticity of his work, (the same piece of evidence Judge Arleo claimed was credible) and accuses Mike of possibly lying on a sworn affidavit. This is the CHIEF of the Appeals Division in Newark, New Jersey! Coyne has a long career in the Newark, New Jersey, justice system and his distaste for Paul Bergrin was most certainly palpable. Coyne also worked hand in hand with Newark FBI. Bergrin was on his fourth appeal and a constant thorn in the side of the entire Newark, New Jersey, DOJ. They totally disregarded that Mike was hired by an attorney to do a job and reimbursed by the government. Mike had not been found guilty of any crime, yet they were so desperate to shut him down in the Bergrin case, Coyne used the charges against Mike in his brief! That was not a coincidence. In a final ruling in April of 2022, the appeals court ultimately held up Judge Arleo's original ruling and denied Paul Bergrin a hearing on the "newly discovered" evidence. This judge did not cite Coyne's assessment that Mike's work should be questioned based on his arrest. He didn't even mention Mike's name in his ruling. I believe the New Jersey Prosecutor's Office and Appellate Division hoped Mike would take a plea deal in the China case to ensure that his work on the Bergrin case was thrown out. The Bergrin case was litigated/investigated by the Newark, New Jersey, FBI office. The Chinese case was handled by the Newark/Red Bank office of the NJ FBI. Why was Mike's name the only one included in the New Jersey court ruling and not the several other investigators involved in that case over the years? Loose-lipped arresting agent Sean McCarthy tipped his hand during Mike's interrogation. He told Mike, "This case sorta started in New Jersey." What did that mean? Was it McCarthy's way of covering himself knowing Mike, a seasoned detective, at some point would question that glaring disparity of a two-state DOJ? Someone made the call to keep the case in NJ FBI and the list of who it potentially could be was coming together.

The dates surrounding Bergrin were notable clues. On April 28th, 2017, the government filed an opposition to a Bergrin motion. This was only a few weeks after Mike's work on the Chinese case had ended. We know Case Agent Christopher Bruno had obtained Mike's information after downloading "Johnny's" cell phone at Newark Airport on April 12, 2017. Was that the day the Newark FBI connected Mike to the Bergrin case then Bruno became the hero and seized an opportunity to discredit him due to this connection to "Johnny"? Did the internal loathing to "get" Mike on the Bergrin case go into high gear once they had this dim connection to a Chinese agent? Is that the reason they didn't contact Mike that day in April 2017 or anytime during their entire four-year investigation? If Bruno read texts between Mike and Johnny, he had Mike's contact info. Why didn't he call Mike that day in April 2017 to interview him? The texts showed that surveillance on Jin Xu had occurred in New Jersey. Did Bruno contact the local police in the towns involved to learn more? If did reach out, Bruno learned the dates, times and locations from Mike and the other PIs documented in multiple notifications about their surveillance. These notifications included names, make and model of their vehicles, and that the PIs were armed. This is a courtesy done by PIs for safety. Did Bruno follow this lead or not?

November 21 and December 11, 2018, are other important dates surrounding Bergrin. His counsel, Gibbons Law, executed two filings on his behalf on those days. The timing would become extremely relevant as I unraveled the "Why Mike?" in this case after learning the government had obtained a search warrant on us the last week of December 2018. What were they really looking for?

Even though the alleged crimes in our case all occurred in New Jersey, the government needed to find a way to pin criminal activity on Mike outside of the Garden State to validate the "interstate stalking" charge. When it comes to venue to take down a case, the government has a bag of tricks to stack the deck in its favor. The federal government has no "stalking" statute. They only have an "interstate stalking" statute. In order to validate a charge of "interstate stalking," the government had to show activities connected to the criminal acts that were purportedly committed outside the state of New Jersey. The government was able to use the Eastern District of New York as the venue for our case based on the coconspirators arriving on a flight to JFK airport in Queens, New York, and a single wire transfer payment to Mike, which came from a Queens, New York, bank in April of 2017. The justice system chooses a specific venue to facilitate a more beneficial outcome for the prosecution. The question that stood out in our minds was: Why did the New Jersey FBI office try this case out of the NY EDNY US Attorney's office and not the NJ US Attorney's office? There seemed to be quite a few cases involving the CCP under New York FBI. Why did ours remain in NJ FBI for the entirety of the investigation?

I'm sure Agent McCarthy regrets a lot of things he said on October 28, 2020. Unfortunately for him, his words are documented forever in our prosecutorial misconduct motions. It was Larry's opinion that the judge would have to consider McCarthy's behavior, and the additional Bergrin evidence to be suspect enough to grant us hearings. We knew the *Times* article would shed some much-needed light on the case and hopefully encourage the judge to listen to more of the information about our allegations.

Larry alerted the court, via a letter to Judge Chen, of our desire to add the SDNY complaint to the prosecutorial misconduct motions. When Larry sent the notification of additional material to the judge, she instructed Larry to address this matter in our final rebuttal after the prosecutors responded to the original filing. This struck me as odd. If the SDNY case was exculpatory evidence for Mike, why didn't she champion that discovery and rule to include it in our original motions to force the prosecution to respond to the SDNY case? If a defendant is supposed to be innocent until proven guilty, and this material could prove Mike did nothing illegal, shouldn't a judge not only accept it but welcome it? I couldn't help but believe the SDNY case was buried and veiled in secrecy for years by the New York FBI in order for the New Jersey FBI to keep Mike's case open. If the New York FBI office knew about the PI firm's actions in the SDNY case during their four-year investigation, why didn't they stop the New Jersey FBI from their unlawful searches against our family? Didn't they have the legal obligation to intervene? Were there interoffice discussions between the New York and New Jersey FBI and National Security on this matter and the NJ FBI pushed to keep Mike in the case? I had no idea how the inner workings of the FBI functioned but something seemed very fishy.

If Case Agent Kelsey Palermo was told to back off from charging the private investigators in the SDNY case, who issued her those instructions? We know how supervisors run these cases and dictate the course of action. Two names I could find who worked at the New York FBI investigating these cases were Charles McGonigal and William Sweeney. They reported directly to FBI Director Christopher Wray. Had McGonigal or Sweeney passed our case over to New York but let it remain in the Newark FBI office because Mike was an investigator on the infamous Bergrin case and New Jersey wanted to take Mike down? I made a chart of everyone I knew who was involved in all the Fox Hunt cases and the agents assigned to each one. Nailing down the online presence of an FBI agent is really tricky. If someone wanted to be a ghost on the internet, who was better able to scrub any trace of their fingerprints than an FBI agent? LinkedIn provided surprising opportunities to mine information for my endeavor. It was shocking how many federal employees, former and active, were on LinkedIn.

Unfortunately, the many rabbit holes I went down in the SDNY case didn't lead to very much. I'm actually shocked that the DOJ even put out the criminal complaint when no one involved had been arrested in the SDNY case. I did notice that most cases involving Chinese espionage, or any criminality really, the perpetrators were more often than not "at large." Clearly the FBI had unfairly picked Mike, the only US citizen involved, to go after. If we could prove that, case closed. There was no way I could allow the truth to be so blatantly ignored. It's strange when you realize how difficult it is to land any punches on the federal government and end up with even a small victory. You most certainly are the underdog when you're put in their crosshairs. They have all the power and an ego backed up by the DC machine that they never hesitate to use. What really came as a shock to me was to learn they have immunity from prosecution regardless of what they do. I couldn't understand how the FBI was able to blatantly lie and get away with it. Up to this point I had seen enough evidence that anything that might help exonerate Mike was either ignored or completely buried, in order to keep the case open. Who are these people who believe they are above the law?

When *The New York Times* article was published on November 14, 2022, more than four months had gone by and there still was no reply from Judge Chen to our June 2022 ex parte request to view CIPA material. Personally, I wasn't too happy with the article. They included some of Mike's and Larry's quotes, which were great. The article featured a large picture of Mike taken under the George Washington Bridge. The majority of the article was about Iranian journalist Masih Alinejad and the private investigator who had followed her. PI James McKeever was named in the article. We finally had a name! He was someone I could actually speak with and get some insight on his experience with New York FBI. According to the article McKeever had been approached by the FBI after his initial surveillance of Masih. They recruited him to assist their team to bring down the Iranian criminals who targeted her. I couldn't believe how differently Mike had been treated by the NJ FBI. Here you had a PI hired to follow a woman targeted by Iranian bad actors who was never charged. Why? The FBI was aware McKeever had been lied to by the Iranians, as had Mike by the Chinese. Yet they made the decision to use McKeever as an asset, something the Newark FBI most certainly should have done with Mike. What was the difference? The Iranian case was run by the New York FBI—not the New Jersey FBI. The New York FBI office often worked with the NYPD and the Joint Terrorism Task Force, a division of the NYPD. The Iranian case involved a kidnapping plot set in place by international criminals. The New Jersey FBI had the opportunity, as the FBI had done in the Masih case with McKeever, to bring Mike into the case in 2016, use him as an asset, and catch Chinese agents. For whatever reason, they made the decision not to utilize him. How could these agencies treat these parallel cases so differently? When I spoke to McKeever he confirmed the FBI approached him to inform him he had been used by Iranian agents. He told me he followed Masih for three months before the FBI reached out. How long did the FBI monitor McKeever? The facts seemed to show that Masih was never in danger and the FBI handled that case properly. I cannot say the same about the Newark FBI in our case. That poor decision not to bring Mike into the case led to numerous criminal acts by Chinese agents that could have been prevented. Even worse, our family was left vulnerable for years due to their lack of transparency to protect an American family. McKeever was fortunate that the New York FBI "used their smarts" and included him in their case. Mike and our entire family weren't so lucky.

I didn't appreciate how the *Times* included excerpts of false accusations from Mike's criminal complaint as part of the article. We had provided Weiser with proof those accusations were false. Doesn't anyone do any fact-checking on their own? That was unfortunate as it unfairly put Mike in a poor light that opened up an online assault on his character. I responded to some of the comments under the article online. The *Times* hadn't really done us any favors but we agreed to be interviewed to bring attention to our case. We later learned the EDNY refused the reporter's request to provide a comment on Mike's case. That spoke volumes. It certainly wasn't their norm. From the beginning the EDNY had shaped the narrative of this case with the press and now *The New York Times* was throwing some doubt on their position. I'm sure that infuriated US Attorney Craig Heeren, the lead prosecutor. What I came to learn, as this case progressed, was the relationship between the government and the media is incestuous. Far worse than I ever imagined. Is that why the article didn't include more favorable facts for Mike? Was information omitted or added in an effort to not paint Mike as an innocent man?

On November 30, 2022, after five long months waiting for an answer, Judge Chen officially ruled in the prosecution's favor to not allow us to view any CIPA materials. Just prior to this ruling, we filed our final rebuttal to the prosecutorial misconduct motions and were expecting her ruling on that as well. For now, it was a "no" ruling on CIPA. The prosecution had successfully argued not to grant us access to the national security materials. I felt her ruling could be seen in two possible ways. One possibility, the court wanted us to accept there was no evidence in CIPA that was exculpatory and would benefit our defense. I found that hard to believe after the discovery I had viewed. Another possibility was that if the materials included anything that inferred Mike's guilt, the government would surely have used it to force Mike to take a plea deal. I was still very naïve at that time and took it as a positive sign that there was nothing that indicated Mike's guilt. I questioned whether that negative decision was due to the SDNY Sun Hoi case. Did that case cross over into ours and the CIPA confirmed it? Was there an even darker connection to both cases and the judge didn't want us to find out?

I decided to search my LinkedIn account for possible leads. I was shocked that active FBI agents would have LinkedIn accounts, including Mike's arresting officer FBI Agent Sean McCarthy. I purposely didn't hide my searches so when I pulled up McCarthy's page, he would most certainly know I was looking at it. It brought me a small amount of joy to stare at his profile picture and know that one day he would have to face me and my children. I began looking up private investigators and those I thought may be of some help. I connected with dozens of PIs and journalists. If there was an article in *The Wall Street Journal* or *The New York Times* that had anything to do with Chinese espionage I would reach out and send off a message to that person. My short LinkedIn bio read "Three-time Emmy Winning Actress, Writer and Producer." I knew that would get some attention and catch a few followers. I connected with former FBI agents who had no idea who I was other than that short bio. I found experts on Chinese operations that were being conducted across the US and abroad and connected with those people as well. I must have sent hundreds of messages to private investigators who probably Googled me, which explained the lack of responses from most but not all.

There were two major hits I got on the site. The first was connecting with *The New York Times* bestselling author, Peter Schweizer. Peter is one of the most respected researchers on fraud and foreign influence in government. When he accepted my LinkedIn request I was blown away. I know these platforms are riddled with fraud and fake accounts so I proceeded with caution. If it was really Peter Schweizer, I may only have one opportunity to send him a message to get his attention. I decided to wait until I came up with something I thought might pique his interest to garner a response.

I was learning so much from my investigative work, some of which was unbelievable information. I connected with Philip Lenczycki from the Daily Caller, a tremendous researcher and investigative journalist on China. I found dozens of fantastic writers who were experts on China who never get the attention they desperately need to fix so many issues. Then there was Safeguard Defenders, a think tank of international contributors going above and beyond to expose China's human rights violations across the globe. So many brilliant people fighting the violations of the CCP became vital resources to map our case. Once I had a template of China's tactics used to target Americans, I went back to Mike's casework with an entirely new perspective. There was no doubt in my mind that the man Mike was surveilling was involved in some shady business dealings here on US soil. Why did the government look the other way when there was obvious criminal activity being carried out by this man and his family? The government painted them as "victims," but all signs pointed in the opposite direction. Based on my findings ours was not a case of harassment of a Chinese dissident and his family for speaking out against the CCP. He and his family members lived quite comfortably here in the United States. They owned millions of dollars in residential real estate, their daughter attended Ivy League schools, yet no one in the family showed any signs of employment. Who were these alleged "victims"?

Based on Mike's findings and court documents I searched for the names of all the parties possibly involved. I found an additional explosive piece of evidence out of California. An immigration attorney named Victoria Chan had been arrested in April of 2017 for a $50 million immigration fraud scheme involving the government's EB-5 program. The EB-5 is a program that allows a foreigner to invest a minimum of $500,000 to get a fast track to a US visa. The stipulation is that the monetary investments had to be used for a project that would employ at least ten Americans. The projects were construction developments including apartment buildings and strip malls. On the surface it appeared to be a great program, started in 1990, that would bring foreign money into the country and create jobs. There was only one problem. Up until 2009, Chinese investors represented a small fraction of the participants. When economic collapse loomed in China, there was an increase to approximately 80 percent of EB-5 investments coming from Chinese citizens looking to get a fast track to America. The program was an easy target for fraud. Often these construction projects would be nonexistent and used to launder money. Victoria Chan had been caught taking millions in funds and defrauding her clients. Many of her clients were in China where Victoria had an office and hired representatives there to woo investors. Two of her clients were Jin Xu and his wife Fang Liu, the alleged "victims" in Mike's case. This was a game changer. Did Victoria Chan have a role in Mike's case? I had to dig deeper.

I read the search warrant complaint against Victoria Chan and noticed that all the participants and victims of Chan were only represented by initials. I noticed one section had three sets of initials, J. X., F. L., and K. L. These parties were accused of fraud in the search warrant, and J. X. and F. L. were on China's 100 Most Wanted List and appeared to be possible perpetrators of fraud, not victims of Chan. These were only allegations but the search warrant was clear as to who the FBI believed was conned and who was not. Were J. X.

and F. L. Jin Xu and Fang Liu? I Googled any article I could find and sure enough Jin Xu and Fang Liu were named in several articles in local news reports on this takedown in April of 2017. They were not charged in the case as of yet but others who were listed in the search warrant were. I couldn't believe what I was reading. As always, I went back to Mike's evidence he had on his computer.

Mike had provided his "client" a pattern of multiple real estate acquisitions totaling in the millions of dollars starting in 2009 in New Jersey. Some of those properties were purchased under LLCs. Jin Xu had multiple real estate acquisitions in the San Francisco area as well as in New Jersey. Mike had run all the names provided to him through his database of public records when he was hired for this case. Notwithstanding some possible errors, this family seemed to own quite a number of residential properties free and clear—they did not have any mortgages on them. The publicly available home address of Jin Xu in New Jersey was purchased by his wife Fang Liu in 2009 for 2.6 million dollars cash. She bought the construction deed from the builder, which minimizes a paper trail. According to court documents Fang Liu had only obtained her fraudulent green card a few days prior to when this home was purchased. How was this possible? You are not allowed to transfer more than $50,000 from overseas. If you do, it triggers an SAR, Suspicious Activity Report. Where did the $2.6 million cash come from? Fang Liu then added husband Jin Xu to the deed of that home, then transferred ownership of the deed to her sister Yan Liu for one dollar. One year later Yan Liu sold the same house for $2.7 million. If these people were claiming to be hiding from the CCP this was an odd way to do it.

It is important to understand that Mike uncovered these details through open-source documents. His client wanted to know about Jin Xu's assets and where he spent his money. If he had stolen money from a construction company in China, as Mike was told, Mike had uncovered quite a pattern of possible money laundering.

The EB-5 program required a $500,000 commitment for each applicant. So, based on those requirements Jin Xu and Fang Liu had to front $1 million cash to be approved for an EB-5 visa. Victoria Chan's complaint said she had fronted $500,000 for Fang Liu. Maybe I'm crazy but would anyone put up $500,000 with the possibility of never getting reimbursed? The Victoria Chan piece of the puzzle was making me look at Mike's case from a different perspective. When I looked further at the search warrant executed against Victoria Chan, I noticed the date: April 5, 2017. I went back to Mike's records. Coincidentally, that was the exact same week Mike was doing surveillance on Jin Xu in New Jersey. If Jin Xu and Fang Liu had been under criminal investigation by the FBI in California for the last few years for EB-5 fraud, how could the FBI in New Jersey claim they were "victims" in the exact same week? Now things were getting really interesting. It begs the question: Did the FBI ever interview Jin Xu and Fang Liu about the California case? If so, when? According to Christopher Wray at the press conference surrounding Mike's arrest, the "victims" had approached the FBI that they were being harassed. When did that occur? While they were under investigation in California? Something wasn't adding up. The intel showed the California federal agencies (USCIS Citizenship and Immigration) had opened their investigation into Victoria Chan in approximately 2013. Did Jin Xu get a clue he was on the radar for immigration fraud and money laundering in California? If Jin Xu was "raised up" on this investigation, would he be inclined to find a way to stop the feds from arresting him and his wife? Is it far-fetched to consider that they created a scenario in the US so they wouldn't be extradited to China or arrested for the EB-5 fraud here in the US? I wasn't sure but I knew the government was covering up something. Why did the FBI and Homeland Security execute this search warrant and not USCIS?

The case in California revealed something extremely important. The alleged "victims" in Mike's case were neither US citizens, nor political dissidents hiding from the Chinese government. Their addresses were public and they were living a lavish life without any evidence that they held down a jobs in the US. Their daughter went to Ivy League schools and lived in multiple million-dollar apartments. I knew there was more to the story. Would I be able to find the evidence in time to help Mike? Who would know the answers to my questions and be willing to speak to me? I felt close to having the answers, but wasn't sure it was the smoking gun I was looking for. I didn't want to waste time on a trail to nowhere but if I didn't follow each and every clue I could and miss something important, I would never forgive myself.

As we rang in 2023, we still didn't have an answer about our prosecutorial misconduct motions. What was taking so long? If the judge granted us hearings it would take weeks if not months to prepare so we could hopefully get the case thrown out before trial, which was set for the end of May 2023. Then on March 23, 2023, seven months after our prosecutorial misconduct motions had been filed, Judge Chen's decision was handed down. I had been praying for relief. Larry and Genna had worked tirelessly to map out the clear bias against Mike backed by case law that proved the motion deserved hearing. Not only was her answer a flat no, Judge Chen stated if we wanted to use bias as part of our defense we could do it at trial. This was quite a blow. Judge Chen knew the burden of proof in a federal trial was on the prosecutors. To open up an accusation of bias against the Department of Justice at trial would be creating a trial within a trial and not wise. As much as we were warned that motions rarely lead to dismissal, this "no" crushed us. There was no doubt now that our case was going to trial. I couldn't wrap my head around it. The government believed they could win this case with the odds overwhelmingly on their side.

A global public war was on the horizon and on the calendar for May of 2023. I just put my head down and prayed even harder for protection. There were a few days I sat alone in church on the verge of a panic attack but focused on trusting God and pushed through it. How was I going to prepare my children for what was about to happen to all of us. The media had been unfriendly up until this point, how would they handle a high-profile trial?

I felt it was time to contact Peter Schweizer. I had no idea what he could do to help us, but I was in a panic. I figured he would not respond but if there was ever a time to reach out it was now. My direct message to him was something like this: "My name is Martha Byrne McMahon. My husband Michael McMahon, a highly decorated retired NYPD detective, was falsely arrested by the FBI on October 28, 2020, regarding Operation Fox Hunt. The man he was hired to follow owns millions of dollars in US residential real estate and is on China's Most Wanted list. How can a wanted fugitive purchase property in our country?"

That was it. I had sent so many messages to so many people about so many topics, I was fried. I assumed I wouldn't hear back but this time I was wrong. Before the end of the day, I got a message back from Peter. He connected me with one of his researchers at the Government Accountability Institute, Jedd McFatter. Little did I know how that one simple message would open up a worldwide investigation into the DOJ's long-standing relationship with the CCP at the expense of America's security.

CHAPTER SEVEN

I HAD REACHED OUT TO DOZENS, if not hundreds, of people since Mike's arrest. I didn't get many solid hits, returned calls, or emails. When Peter Schweizer connected me with Jedd McFatter, director of research at the Government Accountability Institute, I didn't get my hopes up. One thing I knew for sure was that Peter was a highly regarded non-partisan researcher respected by the DC players yet feared by them at the same time. I liked that. As someone who never played politics myself, I felt Peter was a master at walking the line. I went into the call with Jedd as I had with all the others, being truthful and seeking help. I assumed every call would be one and done after the person heard the details. Many people were afraid to speak to me at all but I was never going to give up trying.

While driving, I saw the caller ID on my phone. I had been expecting Jedd's call so I immediately pulled into a train station parking lot to answer. I was close to home but didn't want to miss the call. My first conversation with Jedd lasted over an hour. I gave him a brief breakdown of our story and he shared how he ended up at GAI. Jedd had quite a colorful resume, including attending seminary school and earning a master's degree in the philosophy of religion. I could tell from our first conversation that we shared the same passion for investigating. My story went well beyond the norm for Jedd's prior researching tasks. If what I was saying was true, the government had chosen to ignore patterns of Chinese money laundering and fraud in the United States and went after an American hero instead. I piqued his interest to say the least.

Jedd's current research project was focused on the connection between the fentanyl trade and real estate ownership of Chinese nationals in the US. At that time there had been a smattering of stories regarding Chinese purchasing farmland near military bases. No one was talking about residential or corporate purchases by foreign adversaries. We were both outraged and shocked how Chinese criminals blatantly abused the government's ignorance of the facts or their willingness to allow it to happen. The cases were voluminous and the government lacked the manpower to address these grave national security concerns. Jedd had worked as a subcontractor for the government in his career so he knew the FBI needed more assistance. Could it be possible that the FBI didn't have the resources in California to investigate the allegations against Jin Xu and his wife Fang Liu surrounding the alleged immigration fraud? Of the dozens of people named in the California search warrant, only Victoria Chan had been arrested and released on bail. Something seemed off about the entire Victoria Chan EB-5 fraud case.

In 2015 there was an EB-5 investigation by the Office of the Inspector General involving Alejandro Mayorkas, the USCIS (Citizenship and Immigration) director at that time. The scathing report exposed that Mayorkas had pushed through an EB-5 project for Hillary Clinton's brother Tony Rodham in Virginia along with other improperly vetted projects, some involving Chinese investments. No disciplinary actions were taken against Mayorkas and Rodham's center for his EB-5 project was closed in September 2016, just weeks before Hillary Clinton was to face Donald Trump at the ballot box. Jedd found a query from Iowa Senator Chuck Grassley regarding the Victoria Chan EB-5 case in 2017. That query led to a government memo noting that

Grassley had dozens of questions he wanted answered specifically about Victoria Chan. There was obviously something nefarious going on, but I didn't know if it was connected to our case in any way. Jedd was kind enough to do some research for me looking for clues while he juggled a multitude of other projects for GAI.

I provided Jedd with public real estate documents from our case and what appeared to be money laundering by the subjects at the center of it. One of Jedd's first questions was if there was any connection to Mike's case and Hunter Biden's business dealings with Chinese partners. As far as I knew there was no connection other than the timing of Mike's arrest in October 2020. Hunter Biden's laptop was all over the news in September and October 2020. A letter signed by fifty-one former and active intelligence experts claimed the laptop was Russian disinformation. Joe Biden referred to that letter during his debate with Donald Trump. The "Russian disinformation" narrative worked and many voters had no idea that they had been lied to. The *New York Post* had run with the real story about the laptop and almost immediately was censored on Twitter, Facebook, and Instagram. When Mike was arrested on October 28, 2020, Twitter was still blocking the *New York Post* from posting on the platform. From day one I thought Mike was arrested as one of many calculated distractions from Hunter's laptop. Hunter had well-documented financial relationships with Chinese officials. Press coverage of Mike's arrest focused around China. Why arrest Mike a week before the election? COVID-19 was rampant and, on the FBI's watch, the main players in the case had fled to China, so what purpose did the arrest of a retired NYPD sergeant have other than publicity? The *New York Post* headline had called Mike "China Muscle" so maybe that was a clue. I always believed this was deliberate timing one week before the presidential election. But if so, who ordered it?

As Jedd continued to look further into the subjects of Mike's case, I was getting more anxious as a date for Mike's trial was set, May 2023. I knew if the court was dragging things out in its responses there must be a reason. I was not one to sit around to wait to find out, so I made a plan and went to work.

Rob O'Donnell suggested I attend CPAC in Washington, DC, which took place from March 1–4, 2023. CPAC is a four-day convention for conservatives attended by hundreds of members of the Republican Party, lawmakers, and media. Every day there are multiple panel discussions about everything from government overreach to gender studies in classrooms. The hundreds of CPAC speakers are some of the biggest political players in DC, such as Steve Bannon (political commentator), Kash Patel (former House senior aide, House Intelligence Committee), Byron Donalds (Florida congressman), John Solomon (political writer) Richard Grenell (former director of national intelligence), Matt Gaetz (Florida congressman), Matt Whitaker (former acting attorney general), just to name a few. The closing speaker on day four would be Donald Trump.

Rob had just joined a Pennsylvania radio station as the afternoon drive time conservative host, so he booked a booth on media row to do his broadcast from CPAC. The press was impressive, with large-scale international outlets represented including *Epoch Times* and Newsmax. Rob instructed me to bring handouts of Mike's story with my contact information. Because Rob had attended in the past, he knew there would be countless contacts there who may be of help to us. I booked my room and rallied my sisters Fran and Liz to join me. We would make it a girls' trip and divide and conquer DC.

Leading up to the trip to DC there were major developments in the EDNY. Deputy Chief of National Security and lead prosecutor on our case Craig Heeren had been on the prosecution team for a case involving a man named Tom Barrack. Tom was Donald Trump's inaugural committee chair in 2016. He was charged with violating FARA, obstruction of justice, and making false statements. The case had earmarks similar to Mike's case where the allegations did not match the evidence. Barrack felt he did nothing wrong and was fighting the charges. It should be noted Barrack is a billionaire and able to hire a team of lawyers to mine the discovery in the case 24/7.

I'm sure the EDNY was giddy with the thought of a slam dunk case involving one of Trump's associates. As it turned out, their winning streak took a humiliating nose dive. On November 4, 2022, Barrack was found not guilty of all charges. This was a tremendous loss for the EDNY, which was not used to losing. The media coverage of this loss made international news and Barrack mercilessly trashed the prosecutors and the entire DOJ. This was not the only publicly embarrassing hit the folks in the Brooklyn prosecutor's office faced leading up to our trial.

In September of 2020, just a month before Mike's arrest, NYPD officer Baimadajie Angwang was arrested in the EDNY and incarcerated for wire fraud, making false statements, violating FARA, and obstructing an official proceeding. He was held for six months in federal prison until he was finally able to make bail. The lead prosecutor Matthew Haggans on the Angwang case was also one of the three prosecutors who had been on our case for years.

The complaint against Angwang was compelling but I took the allegations with a grain of salt. There were multiple audio recordings about Taiwan and Chinese relations between Angwang and an unindicted coconspirator, which sounded damning. There was an exchange discussing Angwang as a member of the NYPD and being very appealing to the coconspirator. These recordings were believed to be so damning by the DOJ, Angwang spent months in federal prison without bail. At the time of his arrest, then New York FBI Assistant Director William Sweeney passionately stated Angwang was "the definition of an insider threat" and thanked the NYPD for its "extraordinary partnership on this investigation." This case made international headlines and was considered a major win for our country. A spy who was an active member of the NYPD and a former marine?

Shockingly, in January of 2023 the case against Angwang was dismissed "in the interest of justice" with a whimper. Angwang's lawyer John F. Carman was perplexed and called the press to put a spotlight on this strange turn of events. He accused the feds of "hiding behind CIPA." Carman had been granted access to CIPA in his client's case and said the material consisted of one piece of paper, the contents of which were heavily redacted. The government chose to close the case claiming the danger of revealing intelligence tactics to the public ruled the case should be closed. Translation: The government didn't want to reveal the tactics of the FBI and National Intelligence for some reason. What was so top secret the DOJ was willing to throw this case in the shredder? This did not sit well with Attorney Carman, and he wanted more details from the prosecution. The press was questioning both sides and the DOJ said nothing further. Whatever happened behind closed doors, Haggans had egg on his face and jumped on a DOJ grenade for some cause we may never know. The EDNY's reputation was being put under the hot lights of public scrutiny and things were not looking good for the government due to their losses. How would our case be affected by these developments?

Both the Barrack and Angwang cases were highly public and at the time I thought beneficial to us. If a Democratic-leaning jury could find Barrack, a Donald Trump associate, innocent, Mike should have no problem getting cleared. Mike had plenty of evidence of his innocence on record and was not a political figure. Angwang had what appeared to be sufficiently more evidence that could be used against him, yet the case was dropped. It didn't take long to realize that these embarrassing losses for the EDNY put our case in the sights of our prosecution team to win at any cost. They would have to pull out all the stops to do it.

A few weeks after the Angwang disaster we got a notification from the court that prosecutors Matthew Haggans and Ellen Sise, who had been on our case since the beginning, were being removed due to "scheduling conflicts." That was interesting. Why would these two prosecutors leave the very first Fox Hunt case that was going to trial? Prosecutors love high-profile cases to pad their resumes. Did they choose to leave knowing this case may also result in a loss and so they jumped ship? They were replaced mere weeks before trial with two freshman prosecutors, Arisa Chen and Meredith Arfa. Based on my research, I could not find that these young US attorneys had ever prosecuted a case to trial, yet they were handed a case with hundreds of thousands, if not millions, of pages of discovery to review and were expected to be ready to go to trial within weeks. Something stunk in Brooklyn and it wasn't the East River.

I don't remember ever seeing Ellen Sise and I only had two encounters with Haggans over the years. The first time I saw Haggans he popped out of the Brooklyn courthouse side door for five seconds to grab his food delivery. The next time was at our first status conference in Brooklyn. He looked miserable and it felt like he couldn't get out of there fast enough. Unlike Heeren who pranced around the hallways like he owned the place, Haggans looked like a teenager who got reluctantly dragged to church on Sunday with a raging hangover. Was it because he was under scrutiny due to the Angwang case when I saw him in the courthouse hallway? Or because the recently appointed new head of the EDNY Breon Peace, who inherited these cases, was miffed he had to clean up Haggans and the New York FBI's messes? If Haggans was forced to close the Angwang case unceremoniously and pulled from Mike's case by Peace, was there more unethical behavior we were unaware of behind Mike's investigation by the DOJ? I vowed to find it if so.

This case continued to consume our lives and my mind was constantly reviewing the facts like Einstein's quest to define relativity. I constantly worried that my obsession distracted me from being a fully present mother. I tried as much as I could but there is no doubt I wasn't able to give 100 percent. It was and still is so upsetting. I left *As the World Turns* in 2008 to focus on my family and now precious time was being stolen. I'm blessed with an extended family and friends who generously stepped in anytime we needed help or just a distraction from the hell we were all dealing with as a family. My friends list had shrunk significantly prior to Mike's arrest and became even shorter afterwards. If you want to find out who your real friends are, just have your spouse accused of being a Chinese agent, and that will do it! I had lost a lifelong confidant in Lisa Brown and not had time to properly mourn her. Then my personal life took another major unexpected turn.

I met Elizabeth Hubbard in March of 1985 when I was cast to play her daughter Lily on *As the World Turns*. I replaced actress Lucy Deakins literally overnight and was thrown into the show without much preparation. Elizabeth had quite a lengthy resume including multiple Broadway and television roles prior to being cast as millionaire lady boss Lucinda Walsh on the show. Elizabeth was well known for her previous role as Althea Davis on the daytime soap opera *The Doctors* starting in 1964. Always the trailblazer, Liz was the first woman to receive the Daytime Emmy Award for Lead Actress in 1974. When I booked *As the World Turns* Elizabeth was already on the show playing Lucinda. My mother was thrilled when I was cast to play Liz's daughter as she was a huge fan of *The Doctors* and Liz was her favorite character. Even though my mother and Liz rarely saw each other outside of the studio, my mother held a great amount of respect for her and felt I was protected while under her watch.

Liz wasn't just an actor, she was a single mother with a son, Jeremy, almost my age. Even though Jeremy and I were close in age we didn't socialize, although when we were together or spoke on the phone he affectionately called me "sis." She and Jeremy traveled the world and he had a front row seat to view her greatness and her role as philanthropist. She brought me to events at the UN several times to raise awareness for women refugees around the world. She traveled to Bosnia, Rwanda, Russia, Germany, and countless other nations to educate and draw attention to the great suffering going on everywhere. She took life-threatening risks, which humbled and shocked me. Her knowledge of any subject seemed to have no bounds. It was a gift to be her acting partner and friend. I absorbed every piece of history or human behavior she shared with me. As a young person I was starved to learn about real life and all its messes and triumphs.

As with Lisa Brown, I could fill a book with the stories, both professionally and personally about how influential Liz was in my life. Even though I left *As the World Turns* in 2008, we never stopped communicating. As a matter of fact, I got to know Liz even better after I left the show. She always asked about the kids and Mike. We often met in the city for dinner and I made trips to Connecticut to see her as well.

When I informed Liz about Mike's arrest, she was completely distraught. In all the years I had known her I had never heard that level of concern in her voice. She loved Mike, not just because he loved me, but because he had helped her many times over the years. Whenever she had a challenge with her son Jeremy, she would call Mike for help or advice. As a single mother raising a free-spirited child in Manhattan, there was more than one occasion the law got involved. Liz would always reach out and Mike and I would help. We were most certainly family to each other. Our dinners together would always lead to Liz asking Mike a million questions about being a cop on the New York streets. She hung on every word of his stories of heroism, which were no doubt going into her arsenal of knowledge for future acting roles.

I tried to remain positive when I spoke with her; I didn't want her to worry. At the age of eighty-six, she was slowing down a bit but her brain was still sharp. We spoke often and I would visit her, cherishing each visit as the years went on. I didn't like her being alone when Jeremy was traveling. She claimed she liked to be alone and if she needed someone in an emergency her neighbor was just a phone call away.

On one visit after Mike's arrest, I walked in and she was sitting in her favorite wingback chair with a walker close by. She was always well-dressed, with her hair done and a bit of makeup. I told her she didn't have to get dressed up for me. She glared at me and said, "I do it for myself." I got the message. I tried to help her walk to the next room after she struggled slightly to get up with her walker. I instructed her as I used to do to my father, "Use your right foot…" and she stopped me again, "I know how to walk." I got the message. She was ferociously independent and not a fan of relying on others. I did not take it personally. I just followed her lead. I was happy to be around her and the reality of what was to come was buried deep in my brain. How could this larger-than-life human being ever leave this planet? Every visit was archived in my heart and leaving her was always daunting.

I always spoke to Liz on her birthday, December 22. My birthday was the twenty-third and she would always call me the next day as well. This was our routine for decades. In the winter of 2022 leading up to our birthdays I tried to call and her cell phone number wasn't working. I tried her landline and thankfully she answered. I didn't like the tone of her voice. I can't explain it but something was wrong. After I hung up I had a sinking feeling she wasn't OK. As the holidays approached, as always, I called her on her birthday. I didn't get an answer on either phone. I tried over and over and still no response. Jeremy had recently traveled to South Carolina, so I was worried she was still alone. I thought about calling the police for a wellness check but remembered I had Jeremy's phone number from years prior. I called and it went right to voicemail. I left a distressed message and Jeremy called me back. He told me Liz had fallen and was bleeding out when he found her on the bathroom floor. I was relieved he was there to find her but then my relief was replaced with dread. He said she had surgery for colon cancer, was in recovery, and would be going home as soon as possible. I planned on visiting her as soon as I returned from DC and felt comfortable going to CPAC knowing Liz was in capable hands. I would visit her upon my return as I knew she would want to hear all about my trip.

My sisters Fran and Liz and I headed to DC. I loved spending time with my sisters, so this road trip was a welcome break. We sang Mamas and the Papas and the Osmonds. Singing was always a must on any road trip for the Byrne girls. Not a shy one in the bunch!

As we checked into the hotel I starting seeing some familiar faces. TV hosts, members of Congress, influencers, Riley Gaines (UPenn swimmer who lost her medal to a transgender athlete) and a lot of Trump/MAGA gear! I didn't know where to start, there were so many people to talk to. We found Rob O'Donnell on media row broadcasting live. Steve Bannon's *War Room* was also live and the crowd watching was in the hundreds. As I walked through the crowd,

I spotted Richard Grenell and Byron Donalds. I didn't know where to start! I was able to speak to several people including Matt Gaetz and Matt Whitaker. Gordon Chang was there and it was nice to finally meet him in person. I handed out dozens of fliers and my business cards. I knew it would be a busy few days!

My sisters and I attended an intimate cocktail party at a brownstone for the Log Cabin Republicans, an organization where the majority of the members are gay. We were the only three ladies in attendance and we had a blast! When Richard Grenell walked in I knew I had to speak to him. Rick was the former acting director of National Intelligence during the years Mike was being investigated. I had less than five minutes to speak to him and after hearing my story he seemed genuinely concerned. He said the government has an obligation to warn anyone who has been unknowingly targeted by foreign bad actors. I told him that along with Mike, there were two other former NYPD intelligence detectives and two active federal agents involved in the case and none were notified during the FBI's four-year investigation. He appeared to be dumbfounded by this information. He asked if the federal agents had been given a defense briefing. "No." I found Rick's assistant and gave him a copy of the story. I had no idea if anything would come from it but I prayed it would. One thing I had learned in show business, contacts are everything. Rick was a good one.

Once back at the hotel everyone gathered in the lobby bar. It reminded me of the Daytime Emmy after-parties where all the shenanigans took place into the wee hours. The bar was hopping and we made the rounds. Rob was at a table sitting with Rick Grenell. Rob joined us and I filled him in on my day's adventures. He knew Rick and I was sure Rob would circle back with him if the opportunity arose. The trip was a success on day one!

Over the next few days I saw Rick around every corner. It became ridiculous. I was doing a radio interview in a small booth far away from the main stage and when I was done, sure enough, Rick was the next guest in the chair. He must have thought I was stalking him. Maybe these encounters were God's way of reminding him about our story or he was moments away from calling security. Either way I was hoping my face was becoming familiar.

Overall, it was a great weekend and hearing Trump speak to close it out was definitely the highlight. I knocked on a thousand doors and if even one would opened, it was worth it. I wasn't giving up, especially with the trial haunting our daily existence. I prayed that someone I met would make a call or intervene to stop the trial. Where was our savior? Had I met him or her in the lobby of the Gaylord Convention Center over a charcuterie board and a cheap merlot? Maybe my years of enacting soap opera Friday cliffhangers that were embedded in my brain was clouding my reality. Would someone swoop in on Monday and save the day? There is always a hero in every story and so far I had not found ours. I was planting seeds of grace in hopes of a miracle but we were running out of time.

As the trial approached, I was worried about taking time off from work. I never told my boss the details of what was happening. It didn't affect my work, so the less it was discussed the better. The trial had been put on the calendar to last for three weeks starting at the end of May. I had two weeks of vacation I had yet to take so I started to plan how to manage the third week I needed to be in court. I would have to have a heart-to-heart talk with my boss and request an unpaid week off. He was always a good guy so I was sure it wouldn't be an issue.

Our company had recently hired a CCO and I didn't have to worry about taking time off from work at all. I was fired for the first time in my life. When I inquired why I was fired she hung up on me. I had a feeling it may be coming after the way I was treated in the weeks leading up to it. Honestly, part of me was relieved. I was free to go to court but upset I would lose the much-needed income. I would figure it out. I always did. At least now I could focus on the trial and prepare myself and the kids for what we were about to face. But how do you prepare for something you have never been through before? Would the press come back and follow us again? How do I protect my family when they have already been through so much? It would be a living nightmare but I was convinced Mike was going to be exonerated and it would end with our victory.

I decided to go see Elizabeth in Connecticut to update her on my DC adventure. When I saw her it was very upsetting. She was a bit groggy as she was on medication for her pain. I had never seen her like this. She was fading away and I knew it would be the last time I would see her. I told her from my heart how much I loved her. I thanked her for everything she had done for me. I held her hand and she looked deep into my eyes. She definitely recognized me but the way she was looking at me was as if she was taking in every inch of my entire face like she was making a mental map. She was downloading into her psyche the details of my eyes, then my chin, my ears, and my mouth. She was very peaceful. Then she spoke to me and said, "You can do more. . . ." I knew exactly what she meant. It was not only a compliment that she believed in me, which meant so much, but a rally cry I needed to fight the biggest battle to come for my family.

A few days later Mike and I were invited to Long Beach Island, New Jersey, by his cousins Ray and Terri McCullagh who had a summer home there. They gave us the place to spend a weekend alone before the trial started. It was a welcome invitation for both of us. Long Beach Island is where I feel most at home. My roots were planted there since my father started taking us on vacation "down the shore" in 1976. The weather that weekend was stunning and the beach was empty. Mike and I could take a few days to rest, away from all the responsibilities at home.

The second day there I woke up to the phone ringing. It was Jeremy calling. I already knew what he was going to say before I answered the phone. Liz had passed away. Liz didn't have many family members left and most of Liz's closest friends had passed away. He told me he would be in touch about a service in the future. I hung up the phone and didn't even cry. I knew she had lived her life on her own terms and left this earth at peace at the age of eighty-nine. There was no one I knew who was as fearless as Liz who had overcome so much in her life.

She shared her struggles in her life with me and I was honored she did so. Very few people were given that trust. Now she was gone.

Jeremy called and invited me up to the house to retrieve some items Liz had put aside for me. There was only one thing I wanted but waited to be invited to be respectful of Jeremy. I asked over the phone if he had seen a specific painting of hers. (Liz was an avid painter.) He said he hadn't seen the one I was looking for, which caused me a bit of distress. I hoped he had just overlooked it and asked him not to get rid of any of her paintings until I could come up.

A few weeks later I pulled into her dirt driveway in the Connecticut countryside. It was a surreal experience. Her spirit was not there anymore among the handcrafted rock walks and gardens she designed herself over the years. When I walked in the front room her furniture and other items were being organized. Paintings Liz had done, some framed and finished, some incomplete on unframed canvases, were leaning up against several walls. Her home was filled with hundreds of photos and items all through the house, each one representing a story from her life. Gifts from leaders of a tribe in Africa or a prop from a play or television show. She had an order to where each item was placed and it had been placed there for a reason. Everything had a purpose to bring a thought or start a conversation. She had thousands of books on her shelves that she had acquired through her life. She used to tell me she would find herself drawn to a book, open it, and whatever the contents, it was exactly what she needed to read. She had dozens and dozens of books on World War Two. She shared many stories with me about living in Manhattan as a child during the war. One story she repeated often was about her father instructing her to pull the shades as a war submarine was coming down the Hudson River. I looked that up; it absolutely happened during World War Two.

As Jeremy gathered the clothing items Liz wanted me to have, including some blouses and a Harley-Davidson vintage biker jacket, I started to search for the painting I wanted. She had gifted me a watercolor of flowers in blue, gold, and green tones for a birthday one year, which has a featured spot on my fireplace. I pulled some others to take home but I was desperately looking for just one.

One day during a visit years earlier, I noticed a portrait that stopped me in my tracks. It was unframed on a two-by-two canvas. It was so obviously Liz in the painting but the eyes, nose, and mouth were missing. Her golden hair in layers shaping her oval face and brushing her shoulders was captured perfectly by her paintbrush. I asked her why she never finished it and she said, "I don't like it.… I never finish my self portraits.…" I noted her tone when she said it. It wasn't said as a throwaway line, it was a deep confession of something only she knew. As her friend I rarely saw the rawness of her life's struggles. To me she was a warrior and symbol of power and greatness. I saw how the public adored her, even if she couldn't see herself in the same way. Her honesty in the decades of her work left a permanent mark on millions of people. It pained me to ever see her question her impact on so many.

I searched and searched for the painting, thinking maybe she painted over it as many artists do. Then I found the painting I was looking for. There it was hidden behind others far less interesting, unframed but still in perfect condition. The face was still unfinished but she had kept it. Maybe she left it just for me so I could find it. Liz would do something like that. Maybe she remembered when I first saw the painting I couldn't stop raving about how beautiful it was, how she captured herself perfectly as the world saw her and anyone who knew her would know in an instant it was her. Since I get to write this final chapter of the painting, I believe she heard me and saved it in the state of which I reacted to it. Maybe she thought about painting over it, but remembered my words and it stopped her. The painting may capture our relationship better than any of the hundreds of scenes we did together over the years. I didn't need to see her face or hear a word come from her mouth. There wasn't anything typical about what we shared.

I took the painting home and put it on a special shelf with a battery-operated light to illuminate it. I love seeing it every day when I walk into my living room. I now had her heavenly spirit to help me, another guardian angel there to lift me up each morning, which I desperately needed. I know the last few months of her life were painful and I hoped I had made her final days a bit easier by helping get her home.

I had a dream about Liz soon after her passing. She was wearing a gorgeous white satin nightgown and matching robe as she sipped champagne. She gave me a tour of her new apartment. It was a gigantic three-story Manhattan apartment with staircases going from the first floor living room up to the dining room, then a third staircase from the dining room to the kitchen. The floor-to-ceiling windows exposed the most glorious view of the Hudson River. There is no doubt this was her heaven. She laid down in an oversized indoor hammock and started to sway back and forth as she took in the view.

Just as Lisa Brown before her, Liz visited me to quell my sadness and pain at her passing. My two "mothers" were on the other side to protect me as I faced unknown territory. I am so grateful for these women who shaped my life in so many different ways. I channeled their strength and relied on my confidence. My foundation was solidified by all my "mothers." I had lost two of the most important people in my life but there was no time to grieve. There was much work to be done. I knew I wasn't alone. I was spiritually fortified as I was about to walk through the depths of hell.

CHAPTER EIGHT

One of my favorite movies is *Braveheart,* starring Mel Gibson. Gibson plays Scottish warrior William Wallace in the First War of Scottish Independence against King Edward I of England. The lesson is clear in the film: You don't have to have the largest army to conquer the enemy, just the smartest. You also must be completely committed to fight to the death for your cause. The finale of *Braveheart* is Gibson's character being tortured to death by being disemboweled. The enemy had slaughtered the love of his life and he had succeeded in taking them out. There is no closer equivalent than the instinct to protect the ones closest to you. I was willing to do anything for Mike and our children. There was no doubt who the victor would be at the end of our story. The day those FBI agents violated the sanctity of our home on October 28, 2020, was their biggest mistake.

This fight-to-the-death instinct goes back generations in our families. Mike and I are descendants of true Irish warriors. Mike's grandfather was imprisoned in the famous Dublin jail Kilmainham Gaol for fighting for the IRA (Irish Republican Army). My great-grandfather Daniel Kearon was a prisoner of war after his ship sunk and he was taken by a German U-boat to a concentration camp and survived. The blood of our ancestors runs through both Mike and me. Not to mention that both sides of our family were prolific boxers, my grandfather Myles Byrne and Mike's cousin, Golden Gloves champion James Tunney. Irish people aren't afraid to fight and, in fact, thrive on battles on and off the front lines.

The political thread of fighters on my mother's side is rich with scandal and greatness. The Tumulty name was notorious in the Democratic Party in Jersey City, New Jersey. One relative, Joseph Tumulty, was governor of New Jersey and secretary to President Woodrow Wilson. His role in the White House was well documented as one of influence and power, much to the second Mrs. Wilson's chagrin. She was so bothered by Joseph's partnership with Wilson that she lobbied successfully to have him removed. My mother's father, Edward Tumulty, was an attorney who graduated from Fordham Law School. Not wanting anything to do with politics, he moved out of Jersey City to avoid getting pulled into the fray. The rite of passage in Jersey City politics was paved with corruption and compromise. My grandfather wasn't wired that way—he loved music and Manhattans, not back-door deals. I don't remember my grandfather Ed, but I most certainly inherited his intuition to smell trouble and have the bravery to go against the establishment.

There is no question we are all mapped with imprinted experiences of those who walked through wars before us. I can attest to the strength of my mother and the fearlessness of my father driving me throughout my life. This is why I was extra sensitive to what my children were learning from me during this time after Mike's arrest. Mike's stance was clear, he did nothing wrong and would never admit to anything he didn't do. I knew if he took a plea deal, two things would happen: Mike would be a dead man walking and our children would forever be disheartened that the good guys couldn't win. How could we encourage our children to always tell the truth, only to watch us cave to the enemy and take the easy way out on the world's stage? What kind of parents would we be if we prided ourselves as people who had blind faith in God yet doubted Him when faced with our biggest challenge? There was no way I was going to fail my children. It was my responsibility and I happily took on the challenge to fight like hell. I knew my children were being woven into every single decision we made and how we reacted to these brutal attacks. Our children would most certainly face terrible challenges in their lives. I wanted to enrich them with as much strength as I could. I had no idea what I was doing but I knew doing nothing wasn't an option.

I had been staying positive with the children as much as I could, even though the trial was coming up. After years of the government presenting no evidence against Mike, I believed we were headed for certain victory. We spent hours trying to figure out how they could put up a case against Mike in front of a jury. Who would believe a man of Mike's background would ever betray his country? His character and service to this country was evidence that he was a man of honor and integrity. The fact that he only made a few thousand dollars on this case made the allegations even more ridiculous. There was no evidence and no motive. We were perplexed at who the government would get to testify against Mike.

The subject of surveillance of Jin Xu, his wife Fang Liu, and sister-in-law Yan Liu had been sued civilly in Essex County, New Jersey, in 2018 for allegedly stealing $30 million from Xinba Construction Company in China. A partial judgement of $15 million had been awarded to the plaintiff (Xinba) in March of 2021. The civil case had hundreds of pages of findings of financial and real estate fraud allegations. Shockingly that case was stayed and sealed in May of 2021 by our lead prosecutor Craig Heeren. A letter dated April 30, 2021, to Judge Petrillo stating the EDNY US Attorney's office would be presenting arguments as to why the case should remain stayed and sealed. That letter was signed by Craig Heeren, and confirmed he along with Matthew Haggans, and Ellen Sise would be attending the oral arguments. To be clear, three federal prosecutors were intervening in a civil case in Essex County, New Jersey, a case that (supposedly) had nothing to do with the alleged charges surrounding Mike's case. The judge agreed to the request of the federal prosecutors. We had no access to the minutes of that hearing to stay the case, but what was their argument? Apparently, it is not unheard of to stay a civil case while a criminal case is being tried. In this case there was already a partial judgement of $15 million. That ruling would help our defense to show the lack of creditability of the subjects of Mike's surveillance. Why stay the case when it seemed to be on the verge of being ruled in favor of plaintiff Xinba Construction Company? There was a lot of evidence in the civil case filings we could use in our defense and we planned on doing so. Unbeknownst to the government we had made copies of all the documents prior to it being sealed.

We read through the allegations and the responses in the civil case. Nowhere in the replies by the defendants did the subjects ever say they had been followed by anyone. Their stance in their response was that the lawsuit was frivolous and brought by the Chinese Communist Party (CCP) to intimidate them. The judge in Essex County disagreed, stating the defendants did not prove to his satisfaction that the CCP was in any way involved in the lawsuit and allowed the case to move forward. This was a huge discovery for us. If a judge ruled there was no proven harassment in a civil court, the federal judge in our case would surely agree. Yet a deputy chief of the EDNY Craig Heeren had stepped in, paused and sealed it. That's when we knew we really had something. The civil lawsuit filed in New Jersey proved there was a civil matter in the US running concurrent to a possible criminal one in China.

If everything we read was true, how could the alleged victims take the stand? They had a long trail of alleged and proven crimes here in the US and China. There was no way they could show up in court. It would be too easy for us to discredit them in front of a jury. No victim, no crime. The DOJ had thrown all their chips behind people who had proven ties to the CCP and a more than questionable pattern of criminality in the United States. Why did the FBI trust them at all? The discovery showed the FBI was having countless interactions over the years with not just the alleged victims, but the perpetrators who allegedly "harassed" the victims. The only person the FBI didn't seem to speak to in the four years of this case was Mike! None of this would be good for the government at trial, yet we were most certainly headed there. Our side was fortified with facts, which we believed would shut down any attempt to convict Mike.

We had Mike's ninety-minute interrogation video, which was extremely beneficial. Mike was used by the Chinese agents and the viewer could observe in real time Mike digesting that realization. We felt incredibly strong in our defense. The burden of proof is on the prosecutors. Our job was to debunk their claims and nullify their accusations. Despite the government's attempt to weigh us down with mountains of discovery—much we couldn't even open—we knew there were items they had yet to provide. We were missing the interviews of the two other PIs involved, Mike Kelly and Eric Gallowitz. Our investigator had spoken to a distraught Gallowitz in 2022. Eric told the investigator he had been interviewed by the FBI right after Mike's arrest, so we knew there was at least one interview missing. He also told our investigator that he called the FBI agent at one point to inquire whether he was under investigation. The agent smugly stated he was "not out of the woods yet." That disgusted me. It was clearly an intimidation tactic to scare Eric and it worked. Eric had done surveillance and run information in databases, just as Mike had done. Eric knew the subject of surveillance was wanted in China and listed on Interpol, an international database of wanted fugitives. Eric had exchanged salty texts with Mike about "scaring" the subjects of surveillance. These former NYPD detectives would never actually harass or scare anyone, but the language from Eric could be viewed as more subjective than Mike's responses to his texts, yet Eric was not arrested for aiding and abetting, only Mike. We had requested any and all interviews immediately so we could properly prepare for the trial. The government's response was that the interviews were not exculpatory to Mike so they had no obligation to turn them over. So, let's review. The government decides whether or not any evidence is exculpatory and has an obligation to turn it over only if they believe it is. We knew the interviews would help Mike and the fact they were keeping them from us spoke volumes. We pushed back on the government hard and demanded they turn them over.

We believed our request for Greg Finning's interview (called a 302) was our most important move. Since the day Greg left our home after the arrest, I prayed he would help us. His self-preservation instincts were apparent but I wanted to believe he would step up. I didn't see Greg much over the three years leading up to the trial. He would text Mike to see if he would be at a certain lacrosse game but was afraid to call him. He would text Mike to have coffee, park around the corner from our house, pull up in his car, and off they would go. He feared the very same people he had worked with as a federal agent. He knew what they were capable of and wanted to avoid being roped into Mike's case at all costs.

For more than a year after the arrest, the government had yet to speak to Greg. This was odd because the FBI had been aware of Greg and Mike's correspondences in 2016 and about this case as early as 2017. In 2016 Greg was an active DEA supervisor in New York who dealt in foreign money laundering and drug trafficking. When Mike got this job in October of 2016, Mike called Greg on his first day of surveillance after learning the subject he was tasked to look into was accused of bribes and embezzlement in China. Greg asked Mike if he knew the subjects were actually here in the States. Mike was not sure of this. Greg mentioned Mike should make sure he's not wasting his time on a wild goose chase. Mike shared the case with Greg as one that may be of interest to him as a possible tip. That was the extent of that discussion.

Based on Mike and Greg's communications seen by the DOJ, they were fully aware there was no request from the alleged Chinese agents for Mike to use Greg for anything. Yet this became one of their key pieces of evidence that Mike asked Greg for information. Mike never asked Greg for anything. If their claims were true, why wasn't Greg interviewed during the FBI four year investigation? Why was Greg finally spoken to more than a year after Mike's arrest? Greg had the highest level of security clearance, so it was a decision by someone to keep Greg out of it. Did they choose not to speak to Greg, so not to "raise up" Mike, one of his closest friends? That excuse falls short if the FBI claimed this case was one of national security concern.

Mike's conversation with Greg, an active federal agent in 2016, could be the best piece of evidence we had to clear Mike. If Mike was involved in an illegal scheme with the CCP, why would he be discussing it with an active DEA agent who was communicating with Mike on a government-issued phone? We needed Greg to get over his fear, but his trepidation was palpable. He had witnessed the inner workings of the feds and it terrified him. So much so that any interaction with Mike was planned with calculated execution. It was very upsetting to me, but I held out hope he would overcome his fear and defend Mike.

We suspected the government had finally called Greg to be interviewed after he went dark for a few months. Sure enough, he had lawyered up, hiring a man named Michael Robotti, a former EDNY US attorney. I wish he had told us he was taking these measures but he had to do what he had to do. We learned Greg had spoken to the government on more than one occasion. We wanted to see those interviews immediately.

The other 302 we demanded to see was from NY FBI Agent Brian O'Rourke. Mike met Brian at the gym in early 2017. He noticed O'Rourke resembled NYPD Commissioner O'Neil. He had never met O'Rourke before but, Mike being Mike, approached him about his resemblance to the commissioner. O'Rourke confirmed that Mike wasn't the first person to make the uncanny connection. Of course, the two had law enforcement friends in common and started telling cop stories. Mike brought up the Chinese case in New Jersey and told O'Rourke the subject was wanted for stealing money in China. O'Rourke asked whether or not the subject had a "Red Notice" on him and Mike wasn't familiar with what that was. (In his interrogation Mike said O'Rourke called it a "red line.") O'Rourke assured Mike it sounded like a typical civil matter and the two went back to their workouts.

Mike told FBI Agent Sean McCarthy about that encounter with O'Rourke the day of his arrest. When our investigator reached out to a now retired O'Rourke over a year later, he said he had not been called by the FBI. Our second call a few months later to O'Rourke was more fruitful. He said a female FBI agent had called him and asked how well he knew Mike. He told her he did not know Mike well and had only spoken to him a few times at the gym. He remembered trading cop stories but didn't remember the specifics. This was very disappointing. Mike remembered details about his "cop story" but O'Rourke kept his memory of their exchange basic.

The FBI agent pressed O'Rourke, asking if Mike had more than one phone. O'Rourke told her he didn't even have Mike's phone number. O'Rourke seemed peeved he had been called by the FBI. Now two federal agents, Finning and O'Rourke, were getting roped into a case for literally no reason. We had to decide if O'Rourke would be a good witness or not for us. He claimed he didn't remember China being discussed in his conversation with Mike. What did Greg say to the government? We had no idea, but we did know that he was a wreck. It's hard for me to accept, but I believe both O'Rourke and Finning instinctively protected themselves, but in doing so, put Mike closer to prison.

Why did the FBI avoid speaking to two federal agents for so many years? The answer was obvious: What they didn't "know" they didn't have to report. It's called plausible deniability. Now that we had confirmation that they had interviewed Finning and O'Rourke, we needed to see these interviews ASAP. They clearly would benefit Mike which is why the prosecution was resisting sending the documents. Larry pushed and we finally received the 302s of Finning, Kelly, and Gallowitz. The accompanying letter from Heeren was snarky and after reading the 302s I now know why. As expected, the interviews of all parties I believed exonerated Mike. They were filled with evidence of Mike's innocence and the support of his former colleagues. There were no recordings provided of these interviews and even without them, the statements were beneficial. This showed how low the government was willing to go. They had held on to these interviews for years and intimidated Mike's lifelong friends to help their case. My hatred and desire to take them down grew with every word I read in those reports.

We had seen plenty from the Chinese side of the investigation to exonerate Mike, but this was the final straw for me. The 302 that was missing was O'Rourke's. This meant it must be a really good one for Mike. We requested it from the government, again! The prosecutors' office claimed it wasn't exculpatory and they wouldn't be sending it. Are you kidding me?! If these three interviews were helpful, what else were they keeping from us?! Was O'Rourke's admission that he was not a friend of Mike's poking a gaping hole in their narrative? Seemed like the FBI really wanted to paint Mike and O'Rourke as friends. We knew O'Rourke had told the FBI on the record that they were not. Was that why they kept it from us? The tactics of the FBI and DOJ felt very dirty. These were not the heroic members of law enforcement I knew and loved since I met Mike. We were in very dark and unfamiliar territory.

I should have known how shifty the FBI was when it came to the 302 after Mike's word-for-word interrogation transcript was vastly different from the 302 written by an FBI agent. The agent who wrote the report off the transcript left out vital statements made by Mike that showed he was innocent and unwittingly used. Thankfully there was a video of the interrogation we could show at trial. Surprisingly, most FBI interviews are not recorded! The 302s are written from notes and memory. The FBI did not have body cams in 2020 which also posed a he said, she said issue, so our encounter the morning of his arrest was open to interpretation. I was starting to get a full grasp of how deceptive the DOJ truly was and it was crushing. If they were working this hard to prevent us from seeing evidence that cleared Mike, what else were they capable of? I was about to find out.

One of my favorite things to do was troll LinkedIn for intel. One finding was Greg Finning's attorney Michael Robotti and prosecutor Craig Heeren, once EDNY cohorts, were still publicly communicating on LinkedIn. They would "like" and comment on each other's posts. I felt that was a major conflict of interest so I would screenshot all of their interactions and mutual connections. LinkedIn was fruitful for me and I successfully connected with some amazing people who were incredibly supportive, but I also found some marks to hone in on. The biggest net I cast was of private investigators. This was two-fold. I was looking for support from the community so I would share our story in the comments on their pages. I hoped the warnings would reach their followers and point out what to look out for if they were approached by a foreign client. It wasn't always pleasant for me to see what the private investigators would post. One example was a podcast I listened to after Mike's *New York Times* article came out. A private investigator named Matthew Spaier said he should have known his client better. This pissed me off. I guarantee not every client that PI worked for was a saint. This particular private investigator had zero law enforcement background but decided he was now an expert. After this happened to Mike, all the PIs he knew, all former cops, said the same thing, "This so easily could have happened to me." I set the guy straight in the comments and he never commented back to me. I did a lot of public defending of Mike on LinkedIn which I knew was also being monitored by the government.

One day on LinkedIn in March of 2023 I saw a photo of a PI standing in front of the New York FBI building in Manhattan. The text over the post was something to the effect of "...Great night at NY FBI with other private investigators...Learned a lot." This was HUGE! I had a million questions about this "meeting" with the FBI. Who was there? Who hosted it? Did they talk about Mike?! The trial was only weeks away, maybe they said something we could use! I needed a guest list. Who could help me? First, I sent a private message to the man who posted it. He didn't get back to me. I scoured the pages of the other PIs in the tri-state area looking for clues. I found a PI who commented under the original post, so I sent him a message. Nothing! This had to be a meeting set up by the FBI due to our upcoming trial. I had been screaming from the rafters that the FBI never warned PIs or innocent

Americans about these dangerous Chinese operations. I made trips to DC handing out my flyers to anyone who would take one. That flyer expressed the same outrage about the FBI's failures.

Soon after that FBI meeting, Rob O'Donnell sent me an alert that was posted on the Federal Director of National Intelligence website. The FBI logo was also featured on the alert. It was a warning to private investigators to be careful not to become pawns in covert Chinese operations. I had given Rick Grenell, former head of National Intelligence, my flyer during CPAC. Did he call the new head of DNI and suggest they issue this warning after hearing my story? Was this another CYA (cover your ass) piece like the FBI meeting with the trial coming up? No one who actually needed to see this warning from National Intelligence would ever see it. PIs weren't on these alerts and unless someone pointed them in the direction to see it, it was pointless. I had done far more to warn PIs than this alert from National Intelligence. Larry thought the alert was good for our case and showed the government warning people was evidence that a problem was an existing one and needed to be addressed! Mike was scapegoated by the DOJ as an example of an unwitting target of Chinese malfeasance. He was sacrificed for their own mistakes surrounding these operations. To me this alert and the FBI meeting was admission they had failed to warn people and put a Band-Aid on a bullet hole. I had to dig further.

I had a contact who could help me find out more about that FBI meeting with PIs in New York. We came up with a plan and sure enough it worked. I found someone who attended the meeting and got some interesting details. The meeting was only attended by approximately sixty private investigators, but the majority were from one PI organization. They were not allowed to use their phones, record the meeting, or take notes. The FBI agents who spoke addressed Mike's case saying he should have known the client was working for the Chinese government. They didn't give any handouts and the PIs were sent on their way. If that wasn't a "cover your ass" meeting, I don't know what was. I was told someone from NJ PIA had been in attendance. I emailed Nicole from NJ PIA and asked if she had attended. Her response was interesting. She wanted to know who told me someone from NJ PIA attended. I told her I couldn't share that information. Then the head of NJ PIA emailed me and asked the same. It was so odd. Maybe the attendees were told not to discuss the meeting by the FBI. If so, doesn't that miss the point to spread the word to PIs about what red flags to look for when contacted by a foreign client? The whole meeting felt pointless except for the FBI to check a box to say they had reached out to private investigators.

Then Mike saw a story on the Twitter feed of a New Jersey radio station. The story included the FBI logo and the heading read: "FBI Issues Alert About Chinese Agents in NJ." The article was an interview with newly appointed Newark FBI Director James Dennehy. It was a piece about the FBI working with local law enforcement in New Jersey. It didn't mention Mike but the language was very interesting. Dennehy said the Chinese will occasionally hire private investigators "who might be unwittingly able to help surveil or to monitor or even be part of the harassment campaign against these victims." This was much softer language than I had ever read about private investigators involved in Fox Hunt cases. I found Dennehy's intent to work closer with local law enforcement may have spawned from my speaking out about the FBI's failures in Mike's case. Unfortunately, what he told the writer was only a tiny part of the bigger picture regarding Fox Hunt. I had been in those New Jersey police stations and spoken to countless PIs. There had been no communication between the FBI and local law enforcement since these Chinese operations started in New Jersey in 2015. I was the one warning people. I decided to reach out to the writer and tell him our story.

I had a lovely chat with the writer and told him I would send some public documents including the declassified internal FBI memo that was released the week after Mike's arrest. I included a summary of our case and the names and numbers of the New Jersey police officers I had spoken with about the Chinese operations in their towns. I informed him that, although Mr. Dennehy was addressing this issue in his article, there were a lot of important facts missing. I asked how the story came about and he told me the FBI had reached out to do the story. Interesting. My goal was to have him amend his story and put in the information I would provide to further educate the readers. I did this with many publications since Mike's arrest, but none ever adjusted their stories. I didn't expect this one to be any different but I wanted it on the record that I had made the effort. With the trial coming up I knew exactly why Dennehy was tasked to do a PR push. The writer asked if I wanted him to call Dennehy back and follow up and I encouraged him to do so. I sent him a lengthy email with a lot of materials to review and then I waited. I checked Twitter every day waiting to see if he would post an updated story.

After a week or so I reached out and inquired why he hadn't amended his story. He said he didn't want to because of his relationship with the FBI. I knew exactly what that meant. I told him I understood his hesitancy and filed it for a later time. This had been a pattern I experienced countless times with the media. I kept every single exchange with every publication and television outlet knowing one day I would expose it all. Today wasn't that day. I had a trial to prepare for.

It's a funny thing how your body processes trauma. You could be going about your day thinking you're fine until you get an alert about something that has been posted on the court docket. Every time an alert came in, Mike and I would get sick to our stomachs. He would open PACER, the site where you can review the filings, but he could never bring himself to read anything. He would walk away from the computer and leave it to me. He became extremely forgetful and was diagnosed with case-specific PTSD, which he was assured would pass once the case was over. I wasn't exactly working at full capacity myself but there was work to be done.

The filings leading up to the trial came in at a rapid pace. Every filing from the government was a shot meant to break us down. When the list of witnesses for the government came in it was voluminous. I recognized many names but others I had to investigate. The list of national security and other federal agents made up the majority of the witnesses. There was one private investigator listed named Kelly Riddle. I looked him up. He had a very impressive resume. How did they find a PI who was willing to go on the stand and testify against Mike? Especially one who seemed to have extensive experience? Larry was glad there would be a PI expert to cross-examine so we tabled our decision to put on our own expert. Again, the burden of proof was on the government, all we needed to do was take each witness out one by one with our cross-examinations.

As we processed this reality we got a call from Larry that the government was going to be accusing Mike of not declaring some cash he received on this case on his 2017 taxes. They were also going to claim he knew he was doing something nefarious by putting some money in our sons' and our joint personal bank accounts other than his business account. Mike was the sole proprietor of his business. He could put his money anywhere he wanted, but that was beside the point. He had documentation to account for every penny earned on this case. What were they planning to lie about this time? They said we paid a credit card bill from one of the accounts a few days after money from this case was deposited in our son's account. I didn't know paying your credit card bill with money you earned was a crime. Of course, it's not but it had to be addressed. Larry said we had to get copies of our tax returns and find that credit card statement from 2017.

My brain went numb. We were doing our best to prepare for trial and then they drop this in our lap. To me, it only proved they had nothing on Mike and were desperate to find anything to make him look guilty. He had not been charged with tax evasion or wire fraud, so this was just something they wanted to use to muddy him up to look bad to the jury. I reached out to our accountant and told him we a needed copy of our tax returns from 2016 through 2018. I desperately tried to find our credit card bills from the accompanying years but was unable to. I called my family members who we had helped financially over the years to see if we had ever wired money to pay their credit card bill. No luck. Somehow the government had obtained these records and was planning to use them at trial.

Our 2016–2020 tax returns were very basic during the years the government had been investigating Mike. We were both semiretired, having both worked our entire lives. I started working as a professional actress at the age of ten and saved enough money to live comfortably. Mike loved being a private investigator but in no way needed the money. It was a part-time job and he often worked pro bono. Our tax returns showed combined income under one hundred thousand dollars a year, sometimes less. What the returns didn't show was that we had savings, no debt, and no mortgage on our home valued at over $1 million. On paper it appeared Mike's PI business McMahon Investigative Group took in approximately $19,000 from this case which was a large portion of his year's business income. It also showed his expenses, including payments to PIs he subcontracted, phone, gas, and office expenses which brought his take-home on this case to be approximately $6,000. Probably less if he deducted other expenses. Mike had detailed invoices of every transaction, including an invoice for $5,000 cash he had received on this case. I looked into how the IRS addresses cash if you are audited. If you can provide itemized documentation for cash received then it is not an issue. The government had scoured our bank accounts, emails, followed us, invaded our privacy unlawfully with false search warrants, and this was going to be their smoking gun? What was the government's angle going to be? I'm glad I didn't know their plan ahead of time because I'm not sure I would have made it to that courtroom. These were evil people and I do not say that lightly. They were desperate and desperate people do outrageous things when backed into a corner. Craig Heeren had to win this case and the removal of two seasoned US attorneys, Matthew Haggans and Ellen Sise, had led to two freshmen female underling attorneys, Irisa Chen and Meredith Arfa, stepping in at the last minute.

These last-minute maneuvers against us by the government were done as psychological warfare. It was revolting that these people were picking over the carcass of our family's wellbeing. They had no idea who they were messing with. With every hit they executed, the more determined I got to conquer them. Even though I wasn't sleeping

I rallied every day like a prize fighter. I would get up and go to the gym every single day and visualize the wind of angels behind me. The time I spent at the gym was so beneficial to keeping my head clear. If I allowed this to break me there was no one there to take my place. I started seeing the end of each day as a victory, having even finished it. I was living hour to hour not knowing what was around the next corner. We were getting down to the wire and had a few pieces of business yet to finish.

There were two people on the witness list we wanted to find and speak to. Codefendant Jason Zhu had put Attorney Liping Shi on his witness list. She was the lawyer who Jason said recommended Mike for this job. Jason's lawyer had already spoken with her and based on that conversation was planning on calling her as his witness. I always wanted to interview her over the years and since Jason was calling her, we sent our investigator to speak to her as well. It was a Hail Mary that turned out to be an explosive find for us. Attorney Shi was very willing to speak to our investigator. She said Jason had come to her in the fall of 2016 claiming he had money stolen from his family business by a man who was located in New Jersey. He needed a licensed PI in New Jersey to work on the case. Attorney Shi said she didn't know of any but had met a lawyer from New Jersey and would get a recommendation. The lawyer recommended Mike and sent her his rates. Attorney Shi wrote up a contract for Jason that included Mike's details. She sent the contract to Jason but never heard from him again. Jason claimed she was too expensive and sought out a Chinese translator instead.

Jason took Mike's information to "Emily" the translator in Queens. This was huge! It proved Mike was not part of the conspiracy with the Chinese agents. He had been recommended by an American lawyer who knew Mike, but who was the lawyer? Attorney Shi couldn't remember the name but said she would look in her records. Another piece of surprising information was that Attorney Shi had NEVER BEEN CONTACTED BY THE FBI UNTIL SHE WAS LISTED AS A WITNESS FOR JASON! How long did the FBI have her name? Was it for years and the FBI knew she was the originator of this case in the US and they didn't want to arrest her? Is it even possible they didn't know about Attorney Shi only weeks before trial? If they had spoken to her as soon as they got her name, the FBI would have known Mike was not part of the Chinese Fox Hunt scheme. Did they purposely avoid Attorney Shi so they could keep the case open on Mike and continue to spy on us? Who else had they conveniently forgotten to speak to?

One person's name kept coming around that kept me up at night, translator "Emily Hsu" aka Lina Xu. Had the government ever spoken to her during their four-year investigation? She was on the witness list from the government, so what was the story? Was Jason's story true that he found "Emily" in a Chinese newspaper? I believed she wasn't arrested because she was a confidential informant for the government. This wasn't just based on a hunch, I had read about a translator in California who had been arrested and pled guilty in a similar case involving Iran. That woman had received money from the Iranian government, deposited it in her business account, then paid for illegal services from that account. If what the government was claiming was true, Jason was paid by and acting on behalf of the CCP. He paid Lina Xu ("Emily") with those funds, she took that money and deposited it into her business account, then wrote a check to Mike from that account. It was the same pattern as the Iranian case yet she was not arrested. "Emily" had lied to Mike about her identity right out of the gate in their very first communication with each other. Her translation business to me was questionable. I found her real name on only one other case in New York where she certified a translation involving over one hundred Chinese plaintiffs.

I went back to "Emily's" communications with Mike. The criminal complaint stated Mike had contact with the coconspirators in 2018. How was that possible? Mike finished his work on the case in spring of 2017. Why were they lying in the complaint about this connection in 2018? What were they talking about? Then I figured out what they were referring to. What I found convinced me even further that Lina was working for the government to possibly entrap Mike.

Mike had last heard from "Emily" in fall of 2016 except for one email dated August 1, 2018. It read:

> Hi Mike,
>
> How are you? Last time I have contacted you was around Sept. 2016 regarding some other cases. One of my clients contacted me this afternoon saying she's looking for two individuals' background record, as follows:
>
> 1. marriage history?
> 2. how many children do they have?
> 3. whether they have any crime record, or ongoing civil or criminal cases against them?
> 4. Are there any debt dispute against them?
> 5. tax returns reports?
>
> The only information my client has is the aforesaid parties' name and SSN.

Noticeably "Emily" never mentioned anything about the case for which she had originally contacted him about in 2016. There were no "cases" only one case. In this 2018 email she never names the client seeking a private investigator but inquires if Mike is able to get tax returns. He writes back he is not legally able to obtain tax returns. That was the last time Mike ever heard from "Emily." We learned from other Fox Hunt cases that Chinese agents would request tax returns on their targets. People have been arrested for attempting to obtain tax returns. Since Mike doesn't break the law, he made it clear to "Emily" that he couldn't obtain returns and then she disappeared. THIS WAS THE CONTACT THE FBI CLAIMED MIKE HAD WITH A COCONSPIRATOR IN 2018! This is another lie from the FBI that appears to be a setup, aka entrapment.

On September 4, 2018, only a few weeks after Mike got that email from "Emily," the alleged "victims" found two men at their front door who placed a threatening note and left. The government was charging Mike with that crime as part of the conspiracy. Did they instruct

"Emily" to send that email in August of 2018 so they could justify a search warrant on us in 2018 and pin Mike in some way to the events in the fall of 2018? It sure felt like that was the case. If I was right, why would "Emily" agree to set Mike up? Did they have something on her they were holding over her head? Or was it something even more disturbing.

When Mike emailed "Emily" in 2016 after he found out Jin Xu and Fang Liu were on China's Most Wanted List he wrote: "I think he should have told us...." She replied: "I see. I think I know what's going on with Jin Xu's case," but didn't elaborate. What did she mean by "I think I know what's going on"? If she was aware of what Fox Hunt was, why didn't she alert Mike to protect Mike and herself? Did she call the FBI when she found out Jin Xu was wanted in China? Or did she already know and used Mike to become a cooperator? There was only one way to find out—go speak to Lina Xu in Queens.

We were one week out from the start of the trial, so time was of the essence. We didn't know if the government was going to call Lina, but she was on their list. I learned the government fills the witness list to intimidate the defendant and ends up only calling a portion of the witnesses at trial. If Lina was going to be called, we wanted to try and find out what she was going to say.

Armed with a casefile on what we knew about "Emily" from Mike's evidence, our investigator headed to Queens. First he tried her office, then her home address, with no success. I told him to wait a few hours to see if she returned. She did not. He went back the next day and not seeing any sign of her, we came to the conclusion that "Emily" was gone. Not finding her in the last three years was a huge mistake. I don't know if she would have even spoken to us, but now we will never know. I had been so successful in getting important evidence on my own, I wish I had trusted my instincts early on and reached out to her. Truth be told, her role in all of this was cloaked in mystery. If we had tried to confront her in the last three years, she could have easily set a trap for us initiated by the government as I believed she had done with Mike in 2018.

"Emily" may have been the key to Mike's freedom all along, but who knows? She was gone. There was no time for regrets but there were many in my heart leading up to trial. I couldn't help it. It was a waste of energy to focus on what "could have been done." It was hard not to torture myself with the "what ifs" or look back on missed opportunities. The time had come to not look back and prepare for the big fight. William Wallace put on his blue and white face paint and worked his warriors up into a frenzy. One of the famous quotes from the movie, which was based on Scottish warrior Sir William Wallace, "We come here with no peaceful intent, but ready for battle, determined to avenge our wrongs and set our country free." We were going to war and about to be publicly disemboweled by the DOJ. My children would have to witness it all. I called on Saint Michael to help defend us in this battle. He would have his work cut out for him for what came next.

CHAPTER NINE

Leading up to the trial the legal battles surrounding this case were debilitating. I tried to keep a positive attitude and trusted God's plan, but it was certainly challenging. Our prosecutorial misconduct motions alleging Mike was specifically targeted were shot down, CIPA materials were shielded from us, and the government was constantly conducting psychological warfare. As the trial approached and the government's witness list shrunk, one person's name remained: Greg Finning. How would they use Greg against Mike? Neither Greg nor Mike could figure it out. Greg had always felt his information helped Mike, so if they were to call him to the stand it could backfire on the prosecution. One thing I knew, we weren't getting any wins, and it was about to get worse.

Our side had put in a list of evidence and potential witnesses we expected to present. We didn't have the obligation to share our defense strategy with the government. They already had a clue based on our proffer and misconduct motions. Before we moved forward to present at trial, there were key pieces to our defense we felt we needed to run past the prosecution. Larry knew these needed to be addressed so the trial wasn't overrun with objections that could interfere with our defense.

One thing I felt was extremely important to present to the jury was testimony of Mike's career as a member of law enforcement and a man of service over the course of his life. To me this would prove to any juror that there was no way Mike would be involved in what he was being accused of. No jury would believe he woke up one day after a lifetime of doing the right thing and decided to work for the greatest enemy of our country for a few thousand dollars. Not only was his life leading up to the trial a map of heroic achievement, but it continued even after his arrest. He prevented a robbery of a ninety-year-old woman at our local bank and an assault on a woman in Grand Central Station. Even though he was unarmed due to turning in his guns after his arrest, he stepped in to help without hesitation. That's who Mike is to his core and the jury needed to get to know "the man."

Another vital piece of our defense was that the thirty-million-dollar civil lawsuit against the alleged victims, Jin Xu, Fang Liu, and Yan Liu filed in 2018. Mike's investigative findings on behalf of his client crossed over into that civil lawsuit brought by Xinba Construction Company. In addition to the named defendants, one of the four LLCs attached to the defendants, JLifetime LLC, was owned by Yan Liu. Mike discovered JLifetime LLC in his investigation back in 2017. There are email exchanges with Mike and his client stating "your money is in JLifetime." There was a connection and we needed to use this civil case as admissible evidence to prove it. The civil lawsuit was a hot-button topic with the government and we had proof.

The information connected to the civil case helped us! Our strong belief was the victims were getting favor from the government to testify in our case. Now that the civil case was paused and sealed, it made our belief even stronger they were involved in a quid pro quo. Why else would victims of alleged harassment, who claimed to be concerned about the CCP, allow themselves to testify in a case that would be covered by worldwide media? To our knowledge the FBI had never given the "victims" the same protection they had provided to Iranian journalist Masih Alinejad. In her case the FBI moved her location to several safe houses, which continues to this day, as her life is still being threatened. Why didn't the FBI do the same for the family in our case if they were genuine targets of the CCP? By testifying, their names and other identifying details would be made public. The "victims" claimed they took measures to remain anonymous but never moved and were easy to find. Their names appeared on public real estate transactions in New Jersey and California. What was the real story? Their responses in the civil lawsuit were very telling and helpful to us. Jin Xu, Fang Liu, and Yan Liu made no statements in the civil lawsuit responses that they were ever followed or surveilled by anyone. They mentioned Jin Xu's father coming from China and the threatening note being put on the door in 2018. If they were trying to prove they were in danger they most certainly would have included being followed and stalked. It would be a risky move by the prosecutors in our case if Jin Xu and his family were to testify. We would most certainly cross-examine them regarding their statements in the civil lawsuit. Knowing this reality, they were still willing to come to Brooklyn, sit on the stand under oath, and help to put Mike in prison. There had to be a reason, maybe more than one.

The third piece of evidence we needed involved the China Initiative. The China Initiative was enacted under the Trump Administration in 2018. Trump appointed Attorney General Jeff Sessions to spearhead the program. Trump clearly wanted to take a hard stance against China. Sessions put together a handpicked team of US attorneys, one in each of five states that were hotspots of Chinese malfeasance. Sessions appointed Richard Donoghue, then head of the EDNY, as one of the five to bring in Chinese cases. The initiative focused on intellectual property theft and Chinese influence in universities. Listed in the document released to the public were bullet point suggestions on how to open cases, including using a possible FARA violation to start a query. If there was a suspicion of a FARA violation, use it as cause to open a case. This tactic as a criminal probe was a new one. It had always been an administrative violation. We believe this is how the FBI was able to open up a case on Mike due to a far-reaching theory by the government that there had been communications between a

Chinese police officer and Mike. (Mike only knew the officer as "Eric Yan," a fact the FBI was completely aware of).

FARA had always been an administrative task for people doing business with foreign governments. Most applicants were lobbyists. Up until Trump's first administration in 2016, FARA violations were rarely charged. It wasn't a criminal violation if you didn't register, just an administrative misstep. FARA violations became newsworthy in 2016 when the FBI went after General Michael Flynn and other potential Trump appointees. They used FARA to open warrants to spy and go fishing into their personal lives. Despite the clear overreach on members of their own party, in 2018 Jeff Sessions instructed the five different head US Attorneys to use FARA to open cases on potential Chinese agents in the China Initiative. Mere suspicion of an unregistered foreign agent to open a case without hard evidence, completely violates the privacy rights of the subject. The DOJ plays the odds that they will find something to charge through incidental capture—that is, combing through every detail of your life hoping to find anything that could be perceived as a crime. We knew the government had gone way overboard in their searches on Mike and there was no there, there! There couldn't be. Mike had never done anything wrong in his personal life or as an NYPD officer. It must have frustrated the FBI agents tasked to create a criminal out of a person who had done so much good.

Exactly what evidence was used to open the case on Mike? We had read the search warrants and knew the answers. It was horrific how these warrants reeked of spin and misinformation. We believed the FBI had violated Mike's civil rights by obtaining illegal search warrants, and possibly a FISA warrant without cause. We wanted to argue that out in court.

Shockingly the prosecutors were successful in arguing to the judge to keep everything we requested out of the trial! We were banned from sharing any of Mike's "good deeds." No details of his accomplishments, heroism, or any story connected to his medals were permitted. No testimony about his commitment to serve others was allowed, including the several times he cheated death by taking on gunfire and running into burning buildings to do so. There were hundreds of incredible stories about Mike we could have shared. The government and the judge agreed his character and heroism was irrelevant. It was heartbreaking. Mike took this news hard. He questioned whether anything he had done up to this point in his life meant anything. If he couldn't properly defend himself with facts, how was he going to be able to beat these people who were intent on conspiring to destroy him?

Being prohibited from bringing in the civil lawsuit was terrible news. I couldn't believe it. That lawsuit went directly to the credibility of the witnesses. It proved there was a civil lane to this case that paralleled Mike's investigation. Why was the government protecting the alleged victims from being questioned about their credibility? It wasn't just the civil case that put their credibility in question. The FBI EB-5 California search warrant from 2017 documented fraud involving their immigration papers, along with evidence of potential money laundering here in the US. How is this not relevant to our case? The judge ruled that none of that information was connected to the charges against Mike. Judge Chen ruled that Mike's findings during his work on this case and the alleged crimes committed by the "victims" in China and the US were irrelevant to Mike's criminal acts of stalking and failure to register as a foreign agent. I had never heard of such a thing. By not allowing the argument that Mike was doing his job as a private investigator, she had completely handcuffed us! The civil lawsuit would show that someone was gathering intel to sue the "victims," which ultimately happened in 2018.

Not only was Mike never asked to do anything illegal (he wouldn't), his client dismissed Mike's suggestion on his last day of surveillance to park in front of the subject's house. Mike used the word "harass" (meaning overt surveillance, which is not illegal) but the client immediately responded, "We can't harass Xu like that lol." They charged Mike with interstate stalking, yet the client's text, "We can't harass Xu like that lol" completely debunked the narrative being proposed by the government. Where was there proof of a conspiracy to harass/stalk this subject? The evidence showed the opposite.

Now the jury would not be able to hear at trial that Jin Xu was liable for $15 million to a construction company or that he and his wife were accused of immigration fraud backed by documentation in the California search warrant. Judge Chen ruled she would permit limited questions about JLifetime LLC and the EB-5 allegations but would shut down questioning if it went too far. The case was feeling more and more like a "Get McMahon" case than a case about protecting national security. If the FBI was so concerned about national security, it would have spoken to the US law enforcement members connected to this case back in 2016. To this day no one from the FBI has ever spoken to Mike about this case. They were silent during their four-year investigation and after his arrest when he offered multiple times to help. How can you claim to care about national security when you don't even speak to Mike, the man who met with Chinese police officer HuJi (aka "Eric Yan")? According to journalist Sebastian Rotella, HuJi was known as the most prolific player in Fox Hunt cases around the world. So many missed opportunities by the FBI—or possibly calculated choices—on their part, which is even more disturbing.

In Mike's desire to help after his arrest, he handed over all of his documents and communications to the government. Were they grateful and asked Mike to cooperate after seeing even more evidence of his innocence? Did they recognize Mike as a valuable asset to understand Chinese tactics on US soil? Quite the opposite. The prosecutors added the materials he provided as evidence against him to bolster their attack in a Brooklyn federal courthouse.

Why did they deny us the use of the China Initiative in our defense? The government had proudly touted the China Initiative cases they had taken down. Not only was Mike's initial arrest documented online but the superseding indictment a few months later was available for all to see. If the government was celebrating this case as one of importance, why couldn't we use it in our defense? We weren't even allowed to say the words "China Initiative." Was there a political reason? Soon after Joe Biden became president in 2021, he dismantled the China Initiative under the claim of racial discrimination against people of Chinese dissent. Was the ruling in our case to prevent us in using the China Initiative a political decision? I found something unsettling when I investigated this further.

When Richard Donoghue was tasked by Jeff Sessions in 2018 to bring in cases in the EDNY, I believe he reviewed cases in the district to elevate to the top of the pile. Mike's case was open and unresolved when Donoghue was handed this assignment and there still hadn't been any arrests. It begged the question: Why not?

There was significant information available to Donoghue to review from EDNY, New York FBI, and Newark FBI, and since the China Initiative was put in place in 2018. "Johnny Zhu," Mike's contact in April of 2017, was allowed to leave the country after he was stopped and interviewed by FBI Agent Christopher Bruno at the airport, despite Bruno knowing he was connected to this case and involved in the alleged "harassment" of Jin Xu. According to writer Sebastian Rotella, Agent Bruno put "Johnny" on the SAME FLIGHT to China as Jin Xu's father, who was allegedly FORCED here against his will. According to the government, "Johnny" was a major participant in this alleged scheme to force the father here. If Agent Bruno knew that, why did he allow "Johnny" to flee. "Johnny" returned to the US seven months later in November 2017 and was interviewed for two days by the FBI. The criminal complaint states that he admitted his participation in the coordinated events surrounding Jin Xu in April of 2017 during that interview, yet he was not arrested. "Johnny" informed the agents how Mike was used in this case. Whatever he told the FBI it did not lead to "Johnny" being arrested or Mike being questioned or arrested. To be clear, if crimes had been committed in New Jersey in April of 2017 and the subjects were actually purportedly in danger, why was no one arrested? After his interview in November of 2017, "Johnny" was free to go off into the United States. Unbeknownst to us, someone had set their sights on Mike after that interview with "Johnny."

It wasn't just "Johnny" who had been interviewed by the FBI. There were multiple Chinese players contacted who were involved which posed another disturbing question. Why did the FBI take the word of "Johnny" and others who were permitted to leave the country without incident, but they never spoke to Mike, the only American? They trusted admitted Chinese agents, who lied to them more often than not but did not speak to highly decorated US law enforcement members, including Mike, his two hired PIs (former NYPD intelligence detectives), and Finning and O'Rourke, two active federal agents. What the hell was going on? Did "Johnny" become an informant under the China Initiative in 2018? We would never know. The FBI allowed "Johnny" to leave the US for good, so we couldn't call him as a witness.

What would Donoghue do? "Johnny" had not been arrested and fled the country. He was left with scraps of Mike's case and another China Initiative case, the seemingly more fruitful one against Angwang, an active NYPD officer. The Angwang case was not a Fox Hunt case but did qualify under the China Initiative and had the New York FBI spearheading it. Donoghue had more challenges with our case. In our case the alleged victims were not political dissidents, they were wanted Chinese fugitives, accused of bribery and embezzlement. There was a thirty-million-dollar civil lawsuit pending against them which included damning information, making them unsympathetic witnesses. Mike was a retired NYPD detective who had committed no crime. How could Donoghue spin it? Or did he? Was it Donoghue pushing the case or someone in the background? The entire intelligence division, especially John Demers and possibly FBI Director Christopher Wray, were determined to make arrests for some reason, the week before the Trump/Biden election. Mike had refused to take a plea, which most certainly put a wrinkle in their plans. What was Donoghue to do now that the case was going to trial? Turned out he didn't have to worry about it. Right after Angwang was arrested in September and Mike in October of 2020, three months later in January of 2021, Donoghue left the government. The years leading up to these arrests and how the investigations were executed became someone else's problem. Or was it?

Jin Xu and wife Fang Liu were served in the civil case in 2018 at their private home in New Jersey. However, the government claimed Mike had provided that same address to the Chinese government in April of 2017, claiming it was not public. In turn, the sharing of the "previously unknown address" led to Jin Xu being harassed. There was only one problem with that accusation by the government. We had a paper trail showing that Jin Xu's address was publicly known since December of 2015. Multiple publicly available real estate transactional documents starting in 2009 contradicted Jin Xu's claim that he was attempting to hide from the Chinese government. Our government was playing whack-a-mole to stay ahead of what Mike had uncovered. They had to keep this information out of the trial.

In May of 2021, by the time the civil lawsuit in New Jersey was sealed and stayed, the plaintiff Xinba Construction Company had moved the case from law firm Dorsey and Whitney to Pillsbury Law Firm. Pillsbury has offices in New York, London, Houston, and Asia with a roster of approximately seven hundred lawyers. An attorney by the name of Michelle Ng moved from Dorsey to Pillsbury and brought the civil lawsuit against Jin Xu with her to Pillsbury. The approximately fifteen-million-dollar partial default judgement against Jin Xu was a testimony to the due diligence of Ng and the team at her previous firm. Then in May of 2021 the stay on the civil case in New Jersey seemingly halted this financial windfall for the new firm, Pillsbury. Attorney Ng must have been upset by this! Why had a civil judge in New Jersey agreed with EDNY Heeren's argument to stay and seal the case? In October of 2021, only a few months after the stay, we discovered a bombshell—Pillsbury had added a new partner, former EDNY head Richard Donoghue.

So, to be clear, when Richard Donoghue was head of the EDNY and appointed to bring in China Initiative cases, he backed the DOJ's assessment that Jin Xu and his family were victims of a Fox Hunt Operation harassment campaign. After leaving government, Donoghue was made partner at the law firm suing the same subjects for $30 million. It sure sounded like a conflict of interest to me! When I shared this discovery with Larry, he said it is very common for people in government to go into private practice, then sometimes even return to government. Lawyers are required to "build a wall" on cases they were privy to while in the DOJ. After what I had witnessed in our case, including Greg Finning's lawyer having a post-EDNY employment connection to lead prosecutor Craig Heeren, I was understandably suspicious of Donoghue's wall. I felt quite strongly this case was discussed prior to him joining Pillsbury.

In an interview Donoghue was asked why he joined Pillsbury. He answered that he knew people from the DOJ who had joined the firm. Who was he referring to? I imagine Donoghue joining as a partner at Pillsbury required a much longer and more thorough vetting process. I had no idea how long he was in talks with Pillsbury prior to joining. I suspect with a strong probability that he was negotiating to be a partner while still working for or communicating with the EDNY. I realized there may be one person who could be able to help us: Attorney Michelle Ng. She was at Doresy and Whitney when Jin Xu had initially been served the lawsuit in 2018 and at Pillsbury in 2021 when the stay was put in place. When we attempted to find out from Attorney Ng how she obtained the address to serve Jin Xu, she refused to help us. That was disappointing. If she could provide the name of the private investigator or the public records she used to find Jin Xu to serve him, it could benefit us tremendously. We had spoken to the process server who told us he got the address from the law firm. Why wouldn't she help us? Was it because of Donoghue? Did he intervene in some way and Attorney Ng was upset her case was possibly headed to the trash bin?

The lack of help from Attorney Ng and Pillsbury confused me. In spring of 2023 Jin Xu, Fang Liu, and Yan Liu were scheduled to testify in Mike's case. If we could discredit them on the stand, it would help Pillsbury win its civil case to the tune of $30 million! We could show the alleged victims had no credibility and help their case to finally be resolved in Pillsbury's favor. If the government succeeded in convicting Mike and the others, it would most certainly be enough for Jin Xu to "prove" he had been harassed by the CCP and the civil case would be thrown out for good. Something didn't add up. Was Ng upset about Donoghue joining the firm and potentially putting his now powerful hand into the civil case to assist his DOJ cronies? Had Donoghue cut a deal with the alleged victims prior to leaving government to squash the civil case in return for their testimony? If the civil case was allowed in, the jury would be given the opportunity to decide if the government was showing favor to the alleged victims in return for their testimony. They had thirty million reasons to lie. The jury should have the opportunity to hear it.

Something was most certainly up with Mr. Donoghue. I thought back to Mike's arrest and the press conference held that day. Someone was missing: Richard Donoghue. I looked deeper into his DOJ career and I saw that not only did Donoghue get transferred to assistant deputy attorney general in DC in August of 2020, Craig Heeren had been promoted to deputy chief of the National Security and Cybercrime Section in the EDNY that same month, just weeks before Mike's arrest. Despite Donoghue's being in DC, where the arrest press conference took place, it was Seth DuCharme, the acting United States attorney in the EDNY, who was patched in via phone to make a statement, not Donoghue. Why wouldn't Donoghue stand proudly next to Christopher Wray and John Demers to celebrate the first Fox Hunt case ever taken down as part of his China Initiative mandate? Why did Donoghue exit in January 2021 only to resurface at Pillsbury where he proudly lists his work on the China Initiative as part of his bio? Would I ever get these answers? The list of mysteries was growing and with no time to resolve them.

We were incredibly frustrated and disgusted with how this case had unfolded. We were not given any rulings in our favor in the last two and a half years, only denials filled with legal mumbo jumbo. Larry kept telling us these responses and denials were now documented for an appeal if we lost at trial. This was supposed to ease our minds but the idea that we would be anything less than victorious was not permitted to enter my psyche. The idea of Mike going to prison made me physically ill. We had to win, there was no other option.

Even with these blows I knew the truth was on our side. It was the one thing that kept me going. The truth had to win in the end, but how far would the government go to suppress it? Were they really willing to risk their careers and my ruthless public shaming to win? How desperate were they to find Mike guilty? We learned from the other codefendants' counsel that their clients had wanted to take plea deals leading up to trial, but the government failed to negotiate. The government is supposed to do everything in their power to prevent a costly trial, yet they would not do so. The DOJ already had a very impressive number of cooperators who had plead guilty in this case. If they added two more to the column that would be a huge feather in the cap of Craig Heeren and the EDNY, yet they refused to negotiate with the two remaining Chinese codefendants. Why?

The government's biggest problem? They knew fairly quickly that Mike would never take a plea deal. Going to trial with Mike alone would most certainly result in a verdict of not guilty. If Mike was the last man standing, he would be able to call codefendant Jason Zhu as a witness to prove Mike had no involvement with this scheme. Case closed. Instead, Jason had to build a defense, as did Zheng, who put the threatening note on the victims' door in the fall of 2018. A "conspiracy" was the only way the government could layer this story to create a presentable narrative to a jury. It was every man was for himself but they were all being tried together under one conspiracy. We questioned whether we should have requested Mike be tried alone. I don't believe Judge Chen would have allowed it based on her overall rulings. Mike was fighting back like hell and had to be tarred and feathered by the government. They needed the remaining two codefendants to help make it happen.

Leading up to the first day of trial we suffered through two days of jury selection. Hundreds of potential jurors filled the courtroom, each plotting a reason to get out of it. It was clear by Craig Heeren's demeanor this process was weighing on him. His goal to fill every seat with someone who may not be favorable to Mike was clear. He dismissed white males from Staten Island, former law enforcement members, and anyone who had a connection to the private investigation industry. In a shocking turn, James McKeever's family member (the PI on the Masih case featured with Mike in *The New York Times* article) was one of the potential jurors. I couldn't believe it when I heard the last name. She said her relative was a PI. Judge Chen was not the judge for jury selection, which was unfortunate. If she had been, maybe she would have heard McKeever's story in the sidebar about her relatives's involvement in the Iranian case and that he was not arrested and worked with the FBI to take the case down. Craig Heeren most certainly heard whatever was said and she was promptly dismissed.

During the jury selection, I prayed the Rosary and asked for a favorable jury to be selected. For the two days this went on, a rookie FBI agent sat right next to me as the judge instructed non-potential jurors to sit in the last row next to each other. We were the only two non-jurors. This young woman wearing an earth-toned beige oversized pantsuit and black flats looked to be in her late twenties. She weighed no more than one hundred and ten pounds, wore no makeup, and I noted her unkempt, unbrushed, shoulder length brown hair. She reluctantly sat next to me and was visibly nervous. I'm sure the heat of anger permeating from my body put off a vibe. She would follow FBI Case Agent Christopher Bruno around right at his heel whenever he made a move. It was obvious she was his errand girl and took orders from him. Now she had the distinct pleasure of being stuck sitting next to me. I always said hello and she never replied back to me. Bruno probably warned her not to engage. Can't show any humanity! As the jury was selected, I wrote feverishly in my notebook, then I would pray tightly holding my Rosary. It was a grueling process to pick the jury.

The defense can eliminate ten jurors. When all was said and done, I can say without doubt that this was not a jury of Mike's peers. Mike was a hero second to none, not only in my book, but in the eyes of the people he had served. It would be nearly impossible to find twelve people who had left such an imprint on society. If a juror showed even a thread that may align with Mike, they were eliminated. I hoped the ones chosen would rely on common sense and exonerate Mike, but I knew the prosecutors had tricks up their sleeves. I had already witnessed plenty of their tactics that revealed the opposite of truth and justice. Whatever was going to happen, the day had finally come to fight in the EDNY ring.

The courthouse was in Brooklyn, quite far from our home in New Jersey. The idea of commuting every day was daunting and our attorneys, who also lived in New Jersey, respectfully requested that we put them up in a hotel near the courthouse. We wanted to do the same ourselves but the thought of paying tens of thousands of dollars to do so wasn't an option. We told Larry we would pay for their hotels and drive ourselves each day. As had happened many times before, guardian angels in the form of family members and friends came to the rescue. They not only paid for our hotel near the courthouse, they paid for Larry and Genna's as well. The hotel costs totaled around $20,000. This was a Godsend to enable us to focus on the trial and stay close to each other. I honestly don't know how we would have survived any of this without our friends and family. We were about to rely on them more than ever as we woke up in the Brooklyn Marriott to face day one of trial.

We knew there would be press coverage of the trial as it had already started the day before. The *Daily News* had a two-page story about the case, again listing false information from the criminal complaint. It was infuriating to me. We had filed countless motions which were publicly available to them and none of those facts made it to print. Why wasn't anyone writing stories about our accusations of prosecutorial misconduct? Or about Chinese fugitives and agents living right under our noses? Was it laziness or a much darker reason the press still wasn't doing their job?

A friend who worked at ABC News asked if I would do an interview outside the courthouse day one of trial. I asked Larry if that was OK and he said no problem. I exchanged text messages and coordinated a place to meet away from the front doors of the courthouse. The hotel was two blocks away so we calculated what time we would need to arrive. This was about to be the most insane ten minutes of our lives. We braced ourselves and walked hand in hand towards the courthouse. As we rounded the corner we saw the press outside waiting. This was not the friendly group we had been used to in the past.

I told Mike to give a thumbs up as he walked in but not to stop and talk. As we approached the building about a dozen members of the press were photographing us and throwing out questions. Mike had a quick response about being happy, the truth would come out, and we both walked into the lobby of the EDNY building. Mike survived his first physical interaction with the press but was shellshocked, I could see it in his eyes. I left him in the lobby and went outside to speak with ABC. I exited the building and went two blocks away to be interviewed. We rolled camera, I defended Mike's position and reiterated that he did nothing illegal, then off I went back into the building.

After I went through security where we all had to hand in our phones, Mike and I stopped in the small snack shop in the lobby. We were enthusiastically met by the manager of the shop. To say he had a big personality would not capture it. He showered Mike and me with compliments as we grabbed some waters and snacks. "Looking sharp!" "What brings you to Brooklyn?" When we told him Mike was the defendant, he looked surprised. "You don't look like you should be here." He shared encounters of celebrity defendants who had popped in his shop over the years. This man had seen some things and shared he had been incarcerated in his past and was grateful to be on the other side of it. His energy and positivity was the perfect way to start our day. I can't explain how much his kindness meant at that moment.

The door to the press room for the EDNY was inside the snack shop, so all the writers had to pass through. A large man with dark hair in his forties overheard us speaking. It was the writer for the *Daily*

News who covered the EDNY and had written the article that I was so upset about. I had angrily emailed him about his story, informing him he had printed false information. Unsurprisingly I never heard back but there we were, now face to face. He said if he printed something false he would fix it and patted himself on the back for not including me in his story like the *New York Post* had done. (Thanks?) I didn't have time to read him the riot act. I told him to read the motions if he wanted more information. He said he didn't have business cards due to budget cuts at the *Daily News*. He wrote his name and number on a piece of paper and I put it in my bag.

As we got to the fourth floor the halls were filled with people ready to go into Judge Chen's courtroom. Many of our friends and family members showed up along with the press and unidentified suited-up men and women. This case was the first of its kind to ever be tried and high-ranking FBI and DOJ members, along with freshman US attorneys didn't want to miss it. Day one is where the prosecutors lay out their case and the defense makes its opening statements. The government has to prove its allegations made in their opening statement through evidence and witnesses. What would they say?! We knew they had no evidence on Mike so how would they spin this to a jury? We were about to find out.

CHAPTER TEN

As we all filed into the courtroom I sat to the left in the middle of the second row. In the front row were codefendant Jason Zhu's relatives, including his son and daughter-in-law. In front, Mike was seated alone on the right side of the defendant's table. On the left side of the defendant table was Larry, Genna, the two codefendants, their counsel and two Chinese interpreters. The table on the right held Craig Heeren in position one, US Attorneys Meredith Afra and Arisa Chen and National Security Attorney Christine Bonomo. At the end of the table with his back to the galley sat FBI Case Agent Christopher Bruno. The jury would be seated to the right, facing the prosecution table. Every seat in the galley was filled except the one to the left of me. Just as the opening statement was about to be delivered, the head of the EDNY Breon Peace entered and maneuvered in next to me. I introduced myself and shook his hand. "I'm Michael McMahon's wife." "Nice to meet you," he said. To this day, I wonder if he had any idea who Michael McMahon was based on his non-reaction.

Judge Chen then invited the jurors to be let in and seated. It's surreal to give such power to people who know nothing about you. Mike was moving uncomfortably in his chair and I could tell something was wrong. He put his head down and I thought he was just composing himself. What I didn't know is that he was on the verge of passing out and was going to stop the proceedings. He said at that moment he heard a voice telling him to look at the blue garbage can in front of him. "Focus on the color blue...keep focusing." He told me he was starting to black out but by focusing on the color blue of the garbage can, he didn't. I can't imagine what he was feeling.

Now that everyone was settled, the government's opening statement began. Surprisingly Craig Heeren didn't take the monumental task of presenting the opening statement of his case to the jury. Someone decided to give this important delivery to freshman US Attorney, Arisa Chen. She was visibly shaking as she spoke. What she said will stay with me forever. The rule is, once she had presented the government's version of events, the prosecution is obligated to prove the allegations with witnesses and evidence.

[Note: The following section will alternate between Chen's statement in *italic text* and my commentary in roman.]

Attorney Chen:

First, defendant Jason Zhu, or Yong Zhu, carried out a Chinese government official's mission to hire an American private investigator to surveil and locate the victim. He hired defendant Michael McMahon.

Defendant Michael McMahon, a former law enforcement officer turned private investigator, agreed to do exactly what Jason Zhu and the Chinese government officials wanted. He physically tailed the victim and his family to find out where the victim lived. He also dug up detailed information about not only the victim and the victim's wife, but also the victim's daughter who lived in California.

The government knew there was no evidence Mike knew his client had any connection to the Chinese government. Mike conducted surveillance on public streets, did not "dig up" evidence, he did searches of public records, which is legal and part of his job as a private investigator.

> *And third, defendant Congying Zheng, using the information and location found by his codefendants went to the victim's home to confront him and threaten the victim, threaten the victim's family, and the safety of his family. By agreeing to do this work for the Chinese government here in the United States, each of the defendants violated American federal laws.*

The government knew that Zheng had no affiliation with Mike or his work on the case in April of 2017. Zheng got the address eighteen months later in September of 2018 from a Chinese gang member, Chaohong Chen, in California. The gang member was not arrested.

> *The victim and his wife were born in China and lived there for much of their lives. Over ten years ago, the victim and his wife came to the United States to be with their daughter, who was already going to school here. As you will hear from the victim, he worked for the government in China until about 2008 when he fell out of favor with the Chinese Communist Party.*

The government knew "the victim and his wife" were members of the CCP while they lived in China and had obtained US Green Cards fraudulently. The "victim" Jin Xu was a high-ranking member of the CCP just before he fled to the US in 2010 after becoming aware he was under investigation for bribery and embezzlement according to Chinese media. The daughter had been sent alone to the US as a preteen to attend school. At the time of the trial she was in her thirties.

> *Once the victim and his wife moved to the United States, the Chinese government's operation to get them to return to China began. And the Chinese government tried different ploys to get what they wanted. Early on the Chinese government issued a public international notice to arrest and return the victim and his wife to China. As spread through media outlets, the Chinese Communist Party accused the victim and his wife of accepting bribes, among other things.*

The US had been actively negotiating with the Chinese government the return of both "victims" to China for years up until and including 2019. According to Chinese publications, multiple US government agencies participated in these talks. These meetings were part of a long-standing cooperation agreement with the US. This agreement was called The Past, Present and Future of United States-China Mutual Legal Assistance.

> *Defendant McMahon was told a vague story that the victim owed money to defendant Zhu and that's why Zhu was looking for him; that's why Zhu wanted surveillance and information on the victim, the victim's wife, the victim's daughter, and other family members.*

The government had documented emails from "Emily" (the translator in Queens) that her client, Jason, had money stolen by the alleged victims. "Emily" was not arrested.

> *But as you will learn, McMahon knew this was not the true reason. His private investigator services were needed. Since almost immediately after he was hired, defendant McMahon found out through the internet that the victim and his wife were publicly wanted by the Chinese government to face criminal allegations.*
>
> *You will also learn that McMahon met with the Chinese official in New Jersey, that he looked the other way as the story about an alleged debt kept changing, and the information he was asked to find became more and more invasive.*

The government knew Mike had been given an alias, "Eric Yan," by a man who identified himself as part of the company who had money stolen from his family business. There is no evidence Mike knew this man was actually HuJi, a Chinese police officer. There is no evidence of anything other than the client's interest in assets including residential property ownership.

> *Now, using a Flushing-based translation company, defendant Zhu and defendant McMahon communicated with each other. They sent each other detailed information about the victim and his family. To get McMahon started, defendant Zhu gave McMahon the victim and his family's birth dates, Social Security numbers, and their New Jersey driver's license numbers.*

> *In turn, defendant McMahon provided defendant Zhu with information about the victims that McMahon had dug up from different databases. Defendant McMahon also sent Zhu detailed reports about what he observed when he sat outside the only address the Chinese government knew at the time, the address of the victim's sister-in-law in Short Hills, New Jersey.*

Mike was a private investigator so using the term "dug up" is misleading the jury. He was legally allowed to run searches. The information provided to Mike from "Emily" not only included the above information about the alleged victims, but also a photograph of a black Mercedes and the license plate of that vehicle. This proved the "victims" were followed by someone else prior to Mike being hired. Mike was never visibly seen outside the address provided by the client.

> *Defendant McMahon also reported back information about the victim's daughter, who had just earned her graduate degree back in 2016. He provided defendant Zhu with the daughter's possible phone number, the university in California where she had just graduated, the address of her dorm, and other addresses where she had lived. McMahon disclosed this information. And as the evidence will show, shortly thereafter, there was an attempt by another coconspirator to surveil the daughter in California. There are messages sent to her through social media as well to harass her.*

Mike did legal searches and all the information about the daughter he found was public record. The "shortly thereafter" events in California in the summer of 2017, the government knew had no connection to Mike. Those events were part of a sting operation involving a rogue Chinese-speaking PI who was working with the FBI as a paid informant. The daughter WAS the subject who was requested to be photographed in that sting but she was never followed or put in any danger. The entire sting was conducted at the direction of the FBI. Where the "coconspirator" got whatever address he provided to the PI, a confidential informant, is unknown. The "harassing" messages through social media were Facebook messages from anonymous senders over a year later in 2018. These messages were sent to the "FRIEND" of the alleged victim, not her directly. This friend was not called as a witness in this case. The messages were not threatening, they merely stated the accusations against her parents in China that had stolen money. Mike's searches revealed her father Jin Xu owned several high end properties in California which aligned with his task to obtain asset information.

> *In April 2017, the operation escalated. The Chinese government was no longer content to just collect information. They were going to create a setup to trick the victim and his wife into revealing their home address. And defendant McMahon agreed to help.*
>
> *A contact that defendant Zhu had introduced McMahon to told McMahon that the victim's eighty-year-old father was going to fly from China to the United States. He said the victim's father would be staying at the Short Hills home; again, the only address that the Chinese government knew at the time, and he wanted McMahon to follow the victim and his family when the father arrived to see if McMahon could find out where the victim lived.*
>
> *As the evidence will show, this operation intended to use the victim's elderly father as bait to draw out the victim so that McMahon could follow the victim and finally locate where the victim lived. And so the scheme was carried out.*

The "contact" "Johnny Zhu" was not introduced to Mike through Jason Zhu. The government knew Mike had no involvement with the plan to bring the "victim's" father from China. Mike knew the father was coming but his text messages revealed he pondered the theory the father may be coming to convince his son to return the stolen money.

> *Chinese government officials sent the victim, and the victim's father, on a fifteen-hour plane ride from China to the United States, escorted by a retired doctor who's employed by the Chinese government. A piece of paper was prepared so that the father's answers to questions at the American border would not raise any suspicion.*

The father flew first class from China and encountered countless members of US law enforcement and customs agents. If he had been forced here against his will he had ample opportunities to alert the authorities. The government knew he and his wife had been in the US together just a few months prior in 2016 to attend their granddaughter's college graduation from Stanford. There was no evidence that the parties accompanying the father were that of a female doctor or a female prosecutor. This was only presented as fact by the government. Both women went sight seeing in New York and shopped at high-end stores while here in the US.

> *As you will learn, at the direction of Chinese government officials, the old man was, in fact, dropped off at the Short Hills home. The elderly father was given one directive, to meet with his son and to convince his son to return to China. Of course, when the victim learned that his eighty-year-old father had arrived in the United States, he did go, in fact, to see his father and bring his father back to his home.*
>
> *In working with his coconspirators, defendant McMahon was ready. McMahon tailed the victim's car for about an hour, following the victim so he could obtain the victim's home address, which was in another town in New Jersey. McMahon provided that information to his coconspirators. And thanks to defendant McMahon, the Chinese government finally learned where the victim lived.*

The government knew the address they claim was "found" by Mike was actually public since December of 2015 as a possible location of the alleged "victims." There is no evidence that it was Mike who was the first person to provide it. They also knew Mike had been followed and tracked by Hognru Jin in April 2017, unbeknownst to Mike at that time. The parents of the "victim" stayed at this same address when they visited in summer 2016 before Mike "found" it in April of 2017.

> *And a year later, that information was used by defendant Zheng and the Chinese government when Zheng walked up to their front door and threatened them—threatened the victim—to go back to China.*

To reiterate, the government knew that information was provided to Zheng by a gang member in California eighteen months AFTER Mike had completed his work on the case. Yet the government included Mike in the actions of others for which he has no connection, a fact the government was well aware of.

For their conduct, the defendants are each charged with four crimes.

First, each defendant is charged with acting as an illegal agent of the Chinese government.

To be charged with a FARA violation you must be aware you are working for a foreign government, know you have to register then deliberately NOT register. There is ZERO evidence Mike had any knowledge there was a connection to the Chinese government. More importantly, private investigators are exempt from having to register as they are subcontracted workers working in the capacity of their field.

Second, each defendant is charged with conspiring or agreeing with someone to act as an illegal foreign agent. Third, each defendant is charged with traveling internationally or traveling between states to harass or intimidate the victim and his family.

There is NO EVIDENCE there was an agreement with ANYONE to work as an illegal foreign agent. The government knew that yet added Mike to this charge.

Now, because defendant McMahon did not personally travel internationally or travel between states, he's charged with aiding and abetting others in doing that criminal conduct.

Translation, he DID NOT engage in interstate stalking so the government added language to charge him with it.

Fourth, and lastly, each defendant is charged with conspiring to engage in the same interstate stalking.

Now, as the government, we bear the burden of proving each defendant's guilt beyond a reasonable doubt.

> *Over the next couple of weeks, the government will present its case in several ways, including through witness testimony, recordings, phone, bank, other records, as well as text and e-mail communications and forensic evidence.*
>
> *First, you will hear from the victim and his family. They will tell you how the Chinese government has targeted them and how it has affected them then and now. You will also hear from some of the defendant's coconspirators, who have pled guilty to their roles in these crimes. These conspirators will bring you inside the criminal conspiracy. More specifically, you will hear from a coconspirator who is directly involved in the April 2017 incident involving the victim's father. That coconspirator was with defendant McMahon, surveilling the victim and his family. And we expect you will hear from that coconspirator how the entire operation worked.*

That coconspirator was FOLLOWING McMahon, not "with" McMahon. The government was aware of text messages confirming that fact. Mike noticed someone following him and he inquires with his contact "Johnny" about a suspicious car. "Johnny" assures Mike "that's my guy." After receiving that response Mike texts the other PI working with him that night. The other PI asks Mike, "Do you trust them?" Mike responds, "No."

> *You will also hear from another coconspirator who went with defendant Zheng to the victim's home to threaten him. Among other things, that coconspirator will explain how defendant Zheng told him that the victim was a former Chinese government official.*
>
> *Now, because they are testifying pursuant to an agreement with the government, you should scrutinize these coconspirators' testimonies and look closely at the other evidence in this case, which will corroborate what they say.*
>
> *That other evidence will include audio recordings, including a recording where a government official from China was caught scheming with others working for her about how to best tail the victim when the victim comes out to meet his elderly father.*

The government has never provided the answer to us as to how this recording was obtained. Only one person on the recording was still in the US and was on the witness list. Mike was not on the recording but he was discussed. The translated audio recording from Chinese to English is a major and controversial piece of evidence.

> *You will see photographs, surveillance photos that defendant McMahon took of the victim and his family. You will see a photograph of defendants McMahon and Zhu arm in arm with a Chinese government official at a Panera Bread in New Jersey.*

The government's narrative was that a meeting in a Panera Bread at lunch time with his client and taking a picture with him in some way implied criminal behavior. The government also had evidence Mike met with his client the day after the meeting in Panera Bread at a law firm in New Jersey where Mike sometimes used an office in the firm to work. The government had obtained the Panera Bread footage but not the law firm security footage. That building is home to hundreds of lawyers, many in criminal defense, and had cameras everywhere. The garage, elevators, and hallways had cameras and yet the FBI never went to obtain footage or speak to the multiple lawyers who were working that day and saw Mike and his clients in the small reception area. They never listed the meeting at the law firm in ANY DOCUMENTS, including the original criminal complaint. They made an effort to keep that vital piece of evidence far away from the case. This meeting at the law firm took place within earshot of multiple defense attorneys in a small reception area.

> *You will see phone records showing that in April 2017, when the victim's father was forced to come to the United States, that defendant McMahon was in frequent communication with his coconspirators to coordinate when and how to follow the victim.*

Again, the government states he was "forced" here but the father never called the police when he arrived. There are no reports from any law enforcement he was in danger when he was here. A few days after his arrival, Jin Xu shipped his father back to China. Jin Xu claimed under oath his "elderly" father had suffered a brain aneurysm just weeks before arriving in the US. (no evidence presented that was true). He was so concerned yet he put his father on a plane back to China alone. The father never alerted security at the airport in Newark he had been a victim of any crime or needed medical attention.

> *You will see bank records showing that McMahon only received payment into his business account for his work once. The records show that wire transfers and deposits for his work tracking the victim were otherwise diverted into his joint account with his wife and his son's student bank account.*

The government had emails between Mike and his client about the bank transfers. When the client was having trouble wiring a payment to Mike's business account he offers alternative personal accounts. Mike is a sole proprietor of his business and can put his money anywhere he likes. Also, these alternative accounts required sharing his home address with the client. If Mike knew he was working with dangerous people there is zero chance he would put his family at risk by sharing such personal information.

> *And importantly, you will see communications, you will see text messages and emails. These messages contain the defendants and coconspirators discussing personal information about the victim and his family. They also detail how to best surveil the victims, and they relay live updates about what's happening. You will see a text message where defendant McMahon proposes that he make his presence known to the victims to harass them.*

The government had an explanation in Mike's own words from his interrogation in 2020 why he used the word "harass" in a text to "Johnny." The government was hanging their entire case on that one word. Proposing this claim to the jury in the opening statement was completely dismissing Mike's explanation to FBI Agent McCarthy and EDNY Investigator John Ross. They also had texts proving it was not Mike but the other PI who suggested overt surveillance. That PI was not arrested. So if the government was relying on "intent," and "aiding and abetting" they had selectively chosen Mike as the sole perpetrator. The government also knew that Mike's surveillance work on this case ended forever only minutes after the proposed "harassment" text was sent and negated by his client in April 2017, "We can't harass Xu like that lol". Mike did not violate any law. He parked on a public street out of view. The government knew he or the other two private investigators were never seen by the alleged "victims."

I cannot express how angry I was when she was finished speaking. The intent was to manipulate the jury to believe their allegations. Now it was clear they had no plans of telling the truth. The government had seen the evidence proving what she was saying was completely misleading and false, yet they just told a jury a damning narrative.

Breon Peace quickly left the courtroom after Attorney Chen's opening statement, walking over me as I sat in stunned silence. Why wouldn't he stay to listen to Larry's opening remarks? Wasn't he the least bit curious to learn who was accused of such heinous acts against this country? Apparently not.

The judge decided to take a fifteen-minute break before Larry was to speak. As we filed out, I was sick to my stomach and became quite vocal in my disgust. "Liars.... How do they get away with lying like that?!... What a bunch of liars.... Disgusting...." I made sure every single person who walked out of the courtroom heard me. The look on Mike's face as he came into the hallway and hugged me broke my heart. The prosecutors just lied to the jury and fed them a desperate, twisted fantasy they made up to win. Our friends and family members were shocked by what they heard. After hearing the truth from our mouths for years, they couldn't believe how they painted Mike as a traitor who sold his soul to the Chinese government. It was vile.

It was so painful to realize and believe our own government would be more than happy to see us all dead. I had just witnessed how coldhearted and vicious they were. I knew they didn't care about my family but to actually hear it was nauseating. Mike was their nemesis and he had a bullseye on his back. It would make their lives a lot easier if Mike jumped off a bridge. There was no way I would give them that satisfaction. It felt like we had been deployed to the front lines of the justice system and we were the ones blindfolded. We had survived to this point and I vowed to cross the victory line bloodied and bruised, we just had to make it there. Now that they had executed their first shot, what could we do to bring the jury back to the truth? It felt like a two-ton cannonball to the gut, thrusting us into a dark hole filled with quicksand. How would Larry save Mike? Would the truth be enough to do it when the other side had long ago thrown anything resembling it to the curb? Watching Larry walk to address the jury was a moment we had been waiting for years. Mike could finally be heard through our most trusted surrogate.

CHAPTER ELEVEN

As OUR FAMILY AND FRIENDS sat on the edge of their seats in the courtroom, Larry addressed the jury.

> Good morning, members of the jury. It's truly my honor to represent Mike McMahon, who's here today not just because he's a hero cop who for years protected the citizens of New York from and investigated the most dangerous of violent crimes earning numerous medals for bravery and sacrifice and ultimately retiring after being seriously injured in the line of duty. I'm really honored to be here to help Mike, who after years of living under the cloud of this indictment hanging over his head finally, finally has the opportunity for the truth to come out that he is totally innocent.
>
> He's innocent of what we call the FARA charges, which is acting as an agent of China in a conspiracy to commit those charges because he had no idea, none, that in performing his normal functions as a private investigator, including surveillance, getting records—you've heard some of this already—that he was working for China, and certainly that he never agreed to do anything like that.
>
> And he's innocent of the allegations of interstate stalking that you've heard about and conspiracy to commit interstate stalking because,

as the government has just told you, he neither traveled interstate nor, more importantly, he never put those whom he was surveilling—and you've heard about that—in any kind of fear. He did not cause, attempt to cause, or reasonably expect to cause substantial emotional distress, as the law requires—and Judge Chen will instruct you as to the law at the end of this case—let alone conspire or agree to do so.

You've heard Ms. Chen just a moment ago say that he proposed being overt with his surveillance so he could harass. You will hear that no one ever agreed to do that. There was no agreement. There was no conspiracy, which is in the essence of conspiracy is agreement.

We don't challenge that he performed surveillance and sought records that were available—that are available to private investigators about the subject of his surveillance, and especially about that subject's assets.

So, given that the facts are really not going to be disputed, what are we all doing here? We're here to determine whether Mike McMahon knew that he was acting as an agent of the government of China. We're here to determine whether Mike knew that he was acting as an agent of the government of China, as well as whether he traveled interstate to engage in stalking by putting people in fear or causing them substantial emotional distress.

So, initially, there will be no evidence, none, that Mike knew that he was working as an agent of China. You're going to hear witnesses, you're going to look at documents, you're going to see emails, you're going to see texts. And you will never see or hear anybody say, I told Michael McMahon that he was working for China. You will never see an email that says Mr. McMahon, you are working for China. You will never see that sort of direct evidence. Rather, all of the evidence will be that Mr. McMahon was told that he was working for a Chinese construction company that was trying to recover millions of dollars that have been embezzled from it.

So, let's look at the circumstantial evidence that the government has just relied on in what they talked to you about.

...that Mr. McMahon met with those who were allegedly the actual agents of China, whether his codefendants, unindicted coconspirators that he—the allegations that he must have known because he met with various people.

...that there were communications, including a wanted poster. You heard about the wanted poster that said that the person he was surveilling was wanted in China.

Did Mike meet with people who were allegedly Chinese agents? Well, he may have. But the question is not who he met with, but whether he knew who they were and what they were about.

And let's assume for purposes of this discussion that the people he met with were, in fact, agents of China. The court will instruct you that his merely knowing them, merely being associated with them, is not enough to prove guilt beyond a reasonable doubt, because in our country, guilt by association is not allowed.

In fact, you will learn that what those people told him over and over and over was not that he was working for China, but that he was working for a construction company that had been the victim of an embezzlement.

You're going to hear about the kinds of things that he did, which investigators always do. They do surveillance, including tailing people. They look at records for people. That's what investigators—he was hired to do that. We don't dispute that. He was hired to do that.

You will learn that he did that working with other people. If you're trying to do something really secret, if you know you're committing a crime, are you going to bring other people? He does. He worked with other investigators who he worked with on the case, also former law enforcement, who worked with him on this case, far from being secretive about it, far from showing criminal intent. You'll see that Mr. McMahon does what investigators do and does it openly.

...he does full reports and Ms. Chen alluded to those reports setting forth his actions in detail. And he keeps those reports. He doesn't provide them to the people he's working with or Chinese people and then destroy them. He keeps them, and he also, in detailed invoices, sets forth exactly what he did. Is this the kind of activity, you will ask yourself during this trial, that a person does if they're trying to hide the fact that they're committing a crime? If they feel like they're illegally working for some foreign government?

...you will see that—and some of this has been discussed already—that he takes the actions he takes in highly public places. You heard about a Panera Bread in Paramus, New Jersey. There are other places where he meets in wide-open, in public, in places where there are cameras with his—with his alleged coconspirators. Again, this is evidence that far from showing guilt absolutely undermines it.

And perhaps most significantly of all, what you are going to learn is that Mr. McMahon in doing the surveillance he did in Short Hills, New Jersey, which you've heard about, and in Warren, New Jersey, where he ultimately goes, informs law enforcement. He calls the police in Millburn, which is where Short Hills is for those of you who have ever been to the Short Hills Mall, and he calls the police in Warren and he tells them: I'm doing surveillance. HE HAS A CONSCIENCE. If he's trying to commit a crime, secretly acting on behalf of the Chinese government, is he going to call the cops and tell them? You will have an opportunity to answer that yourself and to answer the question: Is that what people who are committing crimes do?

Mr. McMahon throughout was open and honest about what he did. He saved his files and he provided them to law enforcement when they asked for them. He voluntarily answered questions about this matter and you will hear about that.

As for stalking, there will be no evidence, none, that the people who he was allegedly stalking ever knew that he was surveilling them, nor were they ever put in fear or harassed or intimidated or caused to suffer substantial emotional distress as a result of the actions of Mr. McMahon: Indeed, he was told not to expose himself, not to make his presence known, and you will hear that he didn't, even when he proposed maybe I should surface. That was vetoed; there was never an agreement to do that.

> So, members of the jury, that's what the evidence in this case is going to show. It's going to show that Michael McMahon, a well-respected private investigator in New Jersey, received a referral for an interesting case and that he did what he always does without ever being informed that he was guilty if he's working for the Chinese Government. Ever. He didn't know that he was involved in a campaign or SKYNET that involved transnational oppression. He really didn't know what any of the others in this case were doing, not only the others who were sitting here with whom he had never actually met until they were all indicted together, but also the other coconspirators that you are going to hear about. He doesn't meet them.
>
> So when you hear and see all this evidence, when you listen to the government's proof and others, when you evaluate it for what it really is as opposed to engaging in unfair and unjustifiable implications that seek—make his normal actions seem somehow sinister, when you look at the government's evidence and decide what it really shows, what you will see is Mike did not know he was working for the Chinese, did not talk to anybody at any time and I'm confident that you will conclude that he's not guilty. And, in fact, this is not necessary. You only have whether he's guilty or not guilty. The evidence in is going to show that Mike McMahon is truly innocent to decide this case and that this prosecution is a true tragedy. For as we all know there's really nothing worse than being accused of something you didn't do, but that's what's happened to Mike McMahon, as you will see. And at the end of the case, I will come back to you and I will ask you for what I think is the certainly called Fox Hunt because [the] only verdict that is consistent with the law and the facts, Mike McMahon should be acquitted.

As Larry finished I surveyed the jurors and couldn't get a read on any of them. I was pleased that after more than two years Mike finally began his defense. We still could not understand how the alleged victims could show their faces. The opening statement by the prosecutors touched on some undeniable facts about their past but fell short of telling the full story of their sullied activities. Would we be able to inform the jury of what we knew or be stopped by the prosecution again?

Larry had done an excellent job mapping out the facts but we had weeks to go to continue to shut down the government's false narrative. Who would they rope into their scheme? We received some interesting news. Government witness, private investigator Kelly Riddle from Texas, was removed from their witness list and would no longer be testifying. That told us that the government was unable to find a private investigator in this country willing to say Mike broke any law. We had to decide whether to bring in our own expert. I made my opinion known to Larry that I felt very strongly that we should. We had a few days to decide on that issue.

On day one, two witnesses were set to testify. First would be Yan Liu (the "victim" Jin Xu's sister-in-law and sister to Fang Liu). Yan Liu was the sole proprietor of JLifetime LLC, the entity that owned both homes surveilled by Mike, one occupied by Yan Liu and the other by the "victims." In 2016 Mike had uncovered an extensive pattern of what appeared to be real estate fraud by Yan Liu, Jin Xu, and wife Fang Liu. Records showed on January 6, 2009 "victim" Fang Liu paid $2.6 million for a construction deed on a New Jersey home. This was only a few days after she had obtained her illegal Green Card. After the purchase, husband Jin Xu was added to the deed. On January 28, 2012, that deed was then purchased for one dollar by Yan Liu, their sister-in-law. In 2015 Yan Liu sold that home for $2.7 million. This was just one of the clues of possible real estate fraud. Judge Chen had warned us she would only allow minimal questions regarding JLifetime LLC. According to documents, it appeared Fang Liu was living in China in 2009, or was she? We knew she had obtained a fraudulent Green Card in 2009. How was she able to purchase a $2.6 million home when she wasn't in the US, or was she? Where did the money come from? What role did JLifetime LLC (Yan Liu) play in the transactions? According to records from the civil lawsuit, allegedly there was a financial transfer from an HSBC bank in China to JLifetime LLC in the EB-5 fraud materials. Something shady was going on but we were very limited on what we could ask.

Through an interpreter Craig Heeren questioned Yan Liu about being visited in New Jersey by people looking for her brother-in-law Jin Xu. She claimed, without evidence, she had been visited twice by two different Chinese men who were trying to find out where Jin Xu was living. The government proceeded to ask about the day in April of 2017 when Jin Xu's father showed up, supposedly unexpectedly, at her door. She claimed to be shocked he was there. Yan Liu immediately called the two phone numbers the father had written on a piece of paper. She was anxious to get him picked up and taken away to the airport hotel by the people who had allegedly "forced" him to the US. In one breath she was saying how upsetting it was the Chinese government had sent an "old man" to the US and the next she couldn't get him off her property fast enough.

She couldn't get in touch with either party and the father stayed overnight at her home. Jin Xu did not want to come get him that night. The next morning on April 6th, 2017 between 9:00 and 10:00 AM she stated she drove Jin Xu's father to the Livingston Mall to meet with his son. She claimed they were being followed to the mall by a non-Chinese person. She couldn't identify the driver and had a vague story about maybe being followed. She testified that since the person was not Chinese she felt more at ease. She dropped the father off to meet Jin Xu then she left. According to her testimony, Jin Xu and his father met in the mall food court. After that meeting Jin Xu drove his father back to Yan Liu's house, not to his own home. When asked if she notified law enforcement of the father's surprising appearance and her being followed, she said "yes." Was Yan Liu referring to the FBI when "law enforcement" was mentioned? There was no police report of this incident that was submitted as evidence. The existing civil lawsuit had no documentation from Yan Liu of this incident or of anyone following her and Jin Xu.

If Jin Xu and his father met in such a public place, where was the surveillance footage from the mall of this meeting? If they are trying to infer Mike was surveilling this meeting, where was the video, photos, and surveillance reports which Mike always did? The mall opened at 10:00 AM, so did she really drop Jin Xu off between nine and 10:00 AM before it opened? The government only presented a recent photo of the mall to the jury, taken years after the alleged meeting in the food court in 2017. Larry called this out because the photo had electric charging stations that were not there in 2017. What was the government up to?

Then the government displayed a picture of Yan Liu taken outdoors on the large screen in the courtroom. They inferred it was taken by Mike the day she claimed she went to the mall on April 6th of 2017 but that was false. Mike didn't take any pictures of her at the mall on April 6th 2017 because he was never at a mall that day or any day. For years the government had Mike's surveillance reports, including the day Yan Liu was supposedly at the mall. His detailed report showed Mike was at a location far away from any New Jersey mall on April 6th. Additionally, the government had cell phone data proving he was nowhere near a mall. Two very important pieces of evidence dispute this entire claim by Yan Liu about a mall meeting on April 6th 2017. One, Mike was not alone doing surveillance on April 6th, Mike Kelly was with him that day. Second, and most importantly, Mike's cell records and documented police notifications show Mike called the local police at 8:30AM the morning of April 6th, alerting them he was doing surveillance. He told the police his location, which was near Yan Liu's home which was in his sightline. NO ONE LEFT THE HOUSE THE MORNING OF APRIL 6th 2017 TO GO TO THE MALL. Yan Liu claimed she left her home that day to drop the father off at the mall, approximately ten minutes from her home, between 9-10AM, then immediately returned. That not is possible since Mike was on record having arrived on site at 8:30AM. Mike texted Mike Kelly a photo displayed in the courtroom at approximately 9:30AM the morning of April 6th. That photo had location data confirming the date it had been taken, six months prior and not at her home or a mall. Yan Liu just committed perjury.

We believe the government created the entire story about Yan Liu taking Jin Xu's father to the mall. If Yan Liu's address was allegedly compromised since 2016, where was the security camera footage if she felt in danger? She claimed she had multiple visits from Chinese people looking for Jin Xu over the years. Why did Jin Xu's home have multiple security cameras when his address was supposedly masked but not hers? Did footage exist but it was hidden as to not incriminate Yan Liu? Why would the government risk one of their witnesses being discredited? They had to. To show interstate stalking you must show a pattern of harassment. If Yan Liu didn't see private investigators Mike or Mike Kelly that day, (she claims she saw a non-Chinese person following her), April 6th is irrelevant to this case regarding this witness. To meet the threshold of interstate stalking the victim has to be put in fear of bodily harm by the perpetrator and there must be a pattern of bad acts. The prosecutors were lying to the jury. Larry immediately objected. I couldn't believe it. It was only day one and the government was already falsifying evidence. When pressed, Yan Liu could not identify where the picture had been taken or by whom. I had anxiously wondered how the government would spin this case and now I knew: They were going to lie.

Yan Liu was then asked about approximately eighteen mailings and packages she received from Wuhan China at her home in 2019. The one package presented at trial came to her home addressed to her husband Xu Bai (Xu Bai never testified at trial and I don't recall ever seeing any statements from Xu Bai). I recall the only package contents presented at trial contained a letter and video allegedly from Jin Xu's sister, attempting to guilt him to go back to China to face the allegations against him. This was odd because if the Chinese government had obtained Jin Xu's address, allegedly from Mike in 2017 but also in the fall of 2018 when the threatening note was put on his door, why would the Chinese government send packages meant for him to his brother-in-law? Why was someone in China sending this package to his sister-in-law's house when they could have easily sent it directly to Jin Xu? Yan Liu claimed to have handed over "some" of the "eighteen mailings" to "law enforcement" (FBI not local police). The rest she wrote "Return to Sender" and mailed back to China at the direction of the FBI. That didn't make any sense. I never heard of the FBI telling someone to send evidence back to the perpetrator. This entire story sounded suspicious.

When Larry cross-examined her and asked if she recognized Mike, she said "no." We prayed she would tell the truth and she did. Now we had the first of three witnesses stating on the record she was not stalked by Mike. Then Larry inquired about JLifetime LLC. "Are you the managing member of something called JLifetime?" Yan Liu's demeanor immediately changed. She was angry and said (in Chinese), "Well I think this is not relevant to this case." We had hit a nerve and the prosecutors were ready to pounce but the judge insisted she answer.

> *Yan Liu:* In the name only. The actual ownership of the company is not mine. It's not me.
>
> *Larry:* So this company is in your name but you don't actually own it?
>
> *Liu:* Yes.
>
> *Larry:* Who actually owns it?
>
> *Liu:* Well I have a contract or agreement with this person, so privately I cannot disclose this information.
>
> Heeren objects.
>
> *Heeren:* Your honor, I'm going to object to relevance at this point.

(Yan Liu admitted fraud and perjured herself under oath in front of an FBI agent, multiple federal prosecutors and the judge. Was I the only one that seemed to notice that? Were the alleged victims given immunity to testify for any previous or future legal violations?)

The judge ordered a sidebar.

Larry explains that JLifetime owns both residences surveilled by Mike. JLifetime LLC purchased the home in December 2015 where Jin Xu resided at the time of surveillance and where he currently resides now in 2023. Xu could be residing at either home, since they were both owned by his family member, Yan Liu aka JLifetime. The government claimed it was Mike who "found" the addresses where Jin Xu was living in April of 2017 (Jin Xu and Fang Liu were also served civilly by a process server at this "previously unknown address" in early 2018).

The judge allowed the question to Yan Liu. She confirmed she owned both residences under JLifetime. The one Jin Xu was living in when Mike did surveillance in 2017 was purchased in December of 2015, a year and a half before Mike "found" it. We were able to inform the jury that in fact both homes in question were owned by the same entity, JLifetime. We prayed the jurors would understand that Jin Xu had evidently not taken any real measures to hide from the Chinese government.

The codefendants' counsel was permitted to question Yan Liu about the one-dollar deed purchase from her sister Fang Liu and brother-in-law Jin Xu. Unfortunately, defense attorney for Jason Zhu, William Tung, misread the deed and asked about an incorrect address. So when Yan Liu said she did not purchase the home he was referring to for a dollar, she wasn't lying. That was incredibly frustrating. We missed an opportunity to inform the jury there was some questionable financial activity by this family. Yan Liu testified she had no job but drove a Lexus SUV and owned millions of dollars in residential properties. I hoped the jury could sense Yan Liu was being deceptive. At the very least, I hoped they would question her statements of being followed and visited by Chinese agents, for which she provided no evidence that it actually happened. Her narrative was the only testimony the jury had before them to believe since we were very limited in what we could ask. Either way she was done testifying. Overall, I put her testimony in the win column for us.

Second was Matthew Maguire from the State Department to present records surrounding visas of the alleged coconspirators from China. This representative DID NOT WORK ON OUR CASE. He was a third-party individual brought in for the sole purpose of reading documents into the record. Due to this action by the government, we would be unable to cross-examine this witness, as he did not work directly on our case. The following visa documents were provided to the representative from the State Department witness specifically to put these individuals on the record as part of this case.

The first business/pleasure (nonimmigrant) visa presented on the large screen in the courtroom was HuJi (aka "Eric Yan"). According to this visa, HuJi visited the US in 2012 under his real name. His initial visa was issued on December 27, 2012. The case notes stated: "Officer with Wuhan Public Security Bureau to attend three-week training at the University of New Haven on forensic investigation practices and U.S. police administration."

University of New Haven's school of forensics is named for and run by world renowned forensic scientist Dr. Henry Lee. Dr. Lee was famous for testifying during the O. J. Simpson trial as a blood splatter expert. HuJi attended this program and was photographed with Dr. Lee presenting him with his course completion certificate.

That photo appeared in an article in Chinese media from the Yangtze River Network on March 16, 2016. The article reports HuJi used advanced English skills to conduct his Fox Hunt Operations. The writer appears to be encouraging others in China to master the English language so they can do the same. When Mike met HuJi (alias "Eric Yan") in the fall of 2016 at Panera Bread, he confirmed this tactic to be correct. Mike said HuJi spoke perfect English and "sounded American" with no trace of a Chinese accent at all.

Three years later, on July 30th, 2015, a new business/pleasure visa was issued to HuJi.

The case notes stated the following:

> "Group of 25 police officers from Wuhan city government going to Harris County, Texas for a three-week police cooperative exchange. They will go study information technology for police officers with Harris County. They all work for different divisions of Wuhan police. Are all clearly police officers. Credible purpose with invite letter. Very strong ties. All using government passport."

What the case notes do not say is that these twenty-five Chinese police officers studied at the University of Houston Law at the invitation of the United States. While HuJi was in Houston he was alleged to have participated in the repatriation of a woman who was in Mexico on vacation. Her husband resided in Houston. Soon after that repatriation in Mexico, HuJi was photographed in China in front of the Interpol building and praised publicly for successfully returning the woman, according to Sebastian Rotella's ProPublica article. Even though HuJi had participated in this supposedly unlawful behavior, he returned to the US in 2016 and was not stopped at the airport. He was free to use the alias of "Eric Yan," set up the events in New Jersey, and meet Mike at Panera Bread and the following day at a Hackensack, New Jersey, law firm.

HuJi's visa was a ten-year visa, expiring on July 28, 2025. He was using our country as a revolving door and the FBI was letting him do it.

The government started adding individuals we were not familiar with as part of the case. They started to create a pyramid of photographs on a five-foot-by-five-foot DIY poster for the jury to review. At the top of the pyramid was a man named Sun Hoi.

> Visa issued for Sun Hoi (Chinese law enforcement) December 2, 2016
>
> Case notes read: 1/4 Wuhan delegation of gov—again, government—an e-car company to meeting with U.S. firm T3 Motion. Official ppts—which is passports—U.S., EU, regional travel.
>
> Sun's employer—"Wuhan Public Security"—there's a typo—"Bureau, Caidian [*sic*] branch."
>
> Visa issued for Xiao Jun (Chinese law enforcement) on December 2nd, 2016
>
> Case notes read: 1/4 Wuhan delegation of gov—which is government—an e-car company to meeting with U.S. firm T3 Motion. Official ppts—which is passports—U.S., EU, regional travel.
>
> Xiao's employer—"The Procuratorate of Wuhan City."

The government makes a point of stating Sun Hoi and Xiao Jun are part of associated cases. The witness explained as follows.

> "Associated cases are other visa applications or records that are associated with a group. So for example, if a family was going to Disney World, each member of that family's application would be associated with the other members on that application."

These "groups" were not going to Disney, Mr. State Department. The national security division and the DOJ failed miserably by not flagging these groups back in 2012, 2015, and 2016. They admitted to the jury that dozens of Chinese government officials came here in 2012, 2016, and 2017 under their real names and listed their Chinese government affiliations. They were forthcoming about where they were going, an EV company, and studying at our universities. The US welcomed them with open arms. If Chinese cops coming to the US in large groups, visiting our universities and an EV company is not a red flag, I don't know what to say. In the courtroom a representative from the State Department was telling a jury this was happening openly with our country's blessing. Would they see what the government was doing here?

These same people we once invited here are now being called coconspirators and the DOJ incorporated Mike into their "crimes." The government claims Mike "should have known" he was dealing with the Chinese government. Yet the same time Mike was supposed to "know" this when he was hired for this case in 2016, our country was hosting these same people and celebrating the partnership with China!

Would the press finally cover this shocking discovery I just witnessed? I looked around the gallery and no one from the press was there. This was a huge revelation! Our government hosted countless Chinese government officials across the country for years. HuJi took a forensics training class with Dr. Henry Lee! Did the FBI ever question Dr. Lee about his relationship with the Chinese government and why he was hosting Chinese police officers? Why and when did the government change their position on these individuals? Was it the China Initiative in 2018 or the Wuhan lab disaster that would expose the truth about the deep ties between the two superpowers?

CHAPTER TWELVE

More landmines were about to obstruct our path. Prior to the start of trial the government had argued to allow the admissibility of additional evidence to the judge. They were desperate to paint Mike as a horrible person and accused him of "consciously avoiding" the idea that he was committing criminal acts. How could he "consciously avoid" crimes when Mike's actions in this case did not break any laws? Have you ever heard of someone "consciously avoiding" a crime but notifying the police they were committing that crime (surveillance)? They also argued to introduce "bad acts" they alleged Mike committed in furtherance of the crimes. They claimed Mike unlawfully accessed DMV records, didn't declare some cash he received in this case on his tax returns, and persuaded DEA Agent Greg Finning to violate federal law. The government argued these "bad acts" showed his willingness to break the law. We felt the additions were prejudicial, false, and not applicable to the charges.

Judge Chen had heard communications the previous day from seven years earlier in the fall of 2016 between Greg and Mike read into the record. The evidence the prosecutors were requesting involved database searches and whether Mike's actions broke any laws. As a

PI, Mike was legally allowed to search the DMV and other databases. Not only because he was a private investigator but because information he found was publicly available. The government knew the DMV search was legal. His contract with the DMV clearly showed that fact. There are multiple non-government databases he could have used to run plates. By running a plate through DMV he was clearly not hiding his actions. DMV does random audits of all private investigators who have access, to make sure users aren't violating the terms. Mike has been audited and never been sanctioned, even after his arrest. Even the DMV didn't see his action in this case as a violation. The alleged query connected to Finning showed no evidence regarding Mike.

Judge Chen shared her ruling prior to the jury being brought in and seated.

> "The government wants to show that in searching the New Jersey DMV database, he violated the terms of his access agreement with respect to that database. And that his request to a DEA agent, Mr. Finning or Agent Finning, prompted or caused Agent Finning to violate his duty with respect to accessing the DHS database.
>
> ...I am going to allow the government to get in the evidence regarding the impropriety or illegality of Mr. McMahon's acts taken in furtherance of the alleged conspiracy. So that's my ruling on the issue."

Judge Chen took Larry's truthful and powerful opening statement about Mike's integrity and flipped it using it as a reason to allow in the database searches as "bad acts" in furtherance of the alleged crimes. She ruled the government should have the opportunity to show, in their narrative, Mike's guilty conscience because they claimed he committed secretive deceptive acts and isn't the man of honor portrayed by our defense. Before her ruling the judge believed the prosecution, as promised, would bring witnesses, including Finning, a DMV expert, and an IRS expert to prove their allegations. If the prosecutors claim that Mike used Finning and accessed the DMV illegally, the judge said "bad acts" should be admissible.

Judge Chen dissected Larry's opening statement to rule on these requests. She could have just said, "After hearing yesterday's testimony regarding the exchanges between Finning and McMahon I rule in favor of the prosecution and allow any acts that may be perceived to further the alleged crimes in this case be admissible." Instead, she took the opportunity, on the record, to allude to Mike's character not being as pristine as Larry had presented to the jury. If the prosecutors convinced the judge Mike's character was flawed, it begged the question: Would a jury believe the government as well? Even after day one when the judge saw the prosecution falsify the photograph of Yan Liu and lie about where it was taken, she ruled in their favor. Her alliance was clear. As a former career prosecutor herself, she may never have encountered an innocent person in the courtroom until Mike. As a prosecutor, if you are conditioned to convict, does that way of thinking just go away when you take to the bench? Judges are supposed to be unbiased when holding people's lives in their hands. The government based its entire case on Mike, so he must be found guilty at any cost. The court allows the opportunity for the prosecution to have the tools they need to prove their case. Deciding what is admissible is up to the judge.

It was very clear after this ruling, Judge Chen had zero interest in Mike's true character or ever considered that he would never break the law. She in effect ruled the government should have the right to destroy him and stand as the sole interpreter of Mike's state of mind. It was a terrifying blow.

We certainly had plenty on our side to fight back but would the judge continue to rule in the prosecution's favor and prevent us from presenting it to the jury? Would we be able to open her mind to the fact that her colleagues in the EDNY, who she had worked with as a prosecutor and now a judge, got this one wrong? Was her alliance to the prosecution or the truth?

My distrust of the judge was evident but I had to toe the line. If Mike were to be found guilty, she had the power to put Mike in prison for whatever amount of time she wanted. To be honest, I got the distinct feeling she did not like police officers. At minimum, her personal experiences with cops as a prosecutor may have been less than positive. She had a very impressive track record fighting for people's civil rights. Prior to trial I saw that as a positive for us, since Mike's civil rights were absolutely violated in this case. I wasn't so confident after her soliloquy she had just put on the record. Either way, we had to accept this decision and move on. Two more witnesses were about to take the stand, husband and wife "victims" Fang Liu and Jin Xu.

Leading up to the testimony of Fang Liu and Jin Xu every member of the defense counsel believed the couple was getting favor from the government for their testimony. There were two main issues the couple were facing in the US which were unresolved at the time of trial.

> NUMBER ONE: The couple had been named in an April 2017 California FBI search warrant involving EB-5 immigration fraud. The warrant accused Fang Liu of falsifying documents to obtain her Green Card and falsely claiming she was never a member of the CCP. Also, the organization used to obtain her Green Card was not recognized by the United States, making her Green Card illegal. Fang Liu used her fraudulent Green Card to obtain one for her husband, Jin Xu. Since Fang Liu's Green Card was fraudulent, Jin Xu's was fraudulent which made their presence in the states illegal. After obtaining a Green Card, next came the fast track to a US visa through the EB-5 immigration program. Fang Liu had to put up $500,000 cash to pay her immigration attorney, Victoria Chan. In this EB-5 case Chan fronted the money for Fang Liu. She was the attorney who had handled both her and Jin Xu's immigration out of her law office in California. Victoria Chan had been arrested in April of 2017 but Fang Liu and Jin Xu inexplicably were never charged. Victoria Chan faced forty years in prison but served only one day. No reason was ever given for that decision. Who in the government at that time allowed that to happen? Who was Victoria Chan and why was she given a pass? There were a lot of unanswered questions surrounding Jin Xu and Fang Liu's involvement in that case.

When pushed, the government confirmed to the judge they were aware Fang Liu had falsified documents. According to Heeren, Fang Liu claimed she didn't prepare those documents and had no idea what she had signed. (Not an acceptable reason to not be charged with a crime. US law says you cannot become a citizen if you have been proven to have falsified immigration documents. You can also be deported.) When Judge Chen pushed Heeren to acknowledge if he accepted her answer as truthful, he said "yes." To be clear, the EDNY was prepared to put the "victims" accused of fraud and in the country illegally on the stand under oath. The California investigation by the FBI surrounding EB-5 fraud was ongoing long before Mike was hired in the fall of 2016. The California EB-5 search warrant was issued the same week Mike was doing surveillance on Jin Xu in New Jersey in April of 2017. Sworn federal documents, one from the Newark, New Jersey, FBI calling Jin Xu and Fang Liu victims and another by CA FBI accusing them of fraud, were filed during the exact same week. These were the people the government was relying on to find Mike guilty and send him to prison.

Their other challenge was one that the government worked overtime to suppress.

NUMBER TWO: The $30 million civil lawsuit filed in April of 2018 in New Jersey against Jin Xu and Fang Liu in which they were accused of theft from Xinba Construction Company was still pending. At the time of trial, a partial default judgment of $15,789,924.27 was granted against them. Inexplicably, in May of 2021 only weeks after that partial ruling, Heeren had stayed and sealed the civil lawsuit in New Jersey, deferring the final judgement. That ruling would have been detrimental to Heeren's narrative that the couple were "victims."

Much to our disappointment, the government had successfully argued that no mention of the civil lawsuit was to be brought in. Judge Chen allowed limited questions regarding JLifetime, a family-owned entity, directly connected to the civil lawsuit against them.

Judge Chen had some questions about perceived possible quid pro quo for the "victims." There was no jury present for the following exchange.

> *Judge Chen:* ...the theory that the defense is pursuing is that the victims could have perceived the government's intervention in the civil case, namely, to ask for the stay, was some kind of a benefit or favor to them such that it could be argued that it colored or influenced or skewed in some way the testimony to be given or anticipated to be given by the victims, John Doe 1 (Jin Xu) and Jane Doe 1 (Fang Liu) and that it might suggest bias.
>
> So what conversations, if any, occurred regarding the government's decision to move to stay the civil lawsuit with those victims?
>
> *Mr. Heeren:* Your Honor, no conversations direct from the government to the victims. Counsel of record did communicate with the victims' attorneys in the civil litigation to find out how to formally file in their case, since we were an intervenor and we shared the papers with counsel, but we had no conversation with any of the victims themselves.
>
> *Judge Chen:* About the government's intention to move to stay or the stay after it had been secured? Those are obviously very different.
>
> *Mr. Heeren:* Correct. I guess I want to be careful to say they obviously knew about the stay—
>
> *Judge Chen:* Right.
>
> *Mr. Heeren:* —but the government never had any discussions with them about doing the stay. The government determined it was in our best interest to make a stay motion and apart from—I'm just trying to think if during preparation it even came up.
>
> *Judge Chen:* Okay. And was there even any conversation—and this is obviously implicit in your answer, but I want to make sure I don't miss anything. Was there ever any explanation to the victims by government counsel as to why it would be in the government's interest to move for the stay of the civil lawsuit, or that it was not uncommon to do this when they are parallel or semiparallel proceedings?

Mr. Heeren: I don't believe we had any conversation with the victims themselves about it. I believe I explained, in general terms, with their lawyers that we're doing this and that we believed it was in our best interest. I just want to be careful because I imagine their lawyers did say something to them about it.

Judge Chen: Right.

Mr. Heeren: One second, your Honor.

(Pause in proceedings.)

Mr. Heeren: I would also say it's entirely possible that law enforcement, the FBI, in the course of their conversations with them might have said something about the fact of the stay. I'm not specifically aware of any conversation about that, but I can't rule it out because they have been in contact throughout the course of this investigation.

Judge Chen: Well, when you were prepping the witnesses on this issue, the victims that is, did they say to you that they've been informed by law enforcement about the requested stay or the intention to request one?

Mr. Heeren: No, I don't believe so. They have talked about the civil litigation more generally. They did not make any statements that I can recall about a stay—about the stay.

Judge Chen: Okay. Well, if—I mean what was I guess their response when they were advised you could be cross-examined about this stay that the government secured?

Mr. Heeren: I'm going to let Ms. Arfa handle that.

Ms. Arfa: I think when asked if they perceived that the stay was a benefit, at least for one of the victims (Fang Liu), the answer was "no I still have to defend this at some point and am still paying money to the attorneys." That was the extent of the discussion.

Judge Chen: Obviously there was never any indication by the government to the victims, either through their lawyers or directly, that the government would at some point seek to dismiss, if the government could do such a thing, that civil lawsuit, and perhaps as has been suggested based on if there are guilty verdicts against the defendants, based on the verdicts in this case.

Ms. Arfa: I'm not aware of any such discussion, no. Just to go on the record as well on it since I did not handle the stay, I did not make any representation of that nature.

Judge Chen: Of any further sort of request for relief from the government with respect to the civil lawsuit?

Mr. Heeren: Correct.

Judge Chen: Okay. It seems to me the probative value of any cross-examination is almost nil because there is really no basis to believe that John Doe or Jane Doe number one perceived that the government was extending a benefit to them in exchange for their testimony or even at all. And Ms. Arfa has just put on the record the fact that at least Jane Doe number one doesn't perceive it as a benefit because it simply forestalls something that they still have to deal with, namely, the civil lawsuit. And the government hasn't made any promises about seeking to intervene later to resolve that civil lawsuit or have it dismissed, if the government could do so.

Now, obviously I think you suggested I think in our earlier discussion that perhaps the verdict in this case could have the benefit of resolving that civil lawsuit. It's not clear to me how that would be so necessarily since the civil lawsuit alleges acts of corruption and this case really only deals with accusations of harassment and acting as a foreign agent for the Chinese government. Really not a direct nexus or I would perceive a basis for moving for the dismissal of a civil lawsuit, which could still have merit. And going back to one of the points I said at the outset of the case is, as far as I'm concerned, the merits or lack thereof regarding the accusations or claims against the victims in this case, are irrelevant and I don't want them introduced really in any form, although obviously they've been alluded to with respect to the Red Notice, but that obviously is unavoidable since that's part of the government's theory as to who is behind these efforts and the connection, if the government can establish one, between the defendants and the Chinese government. But I don't want the jury focusing on what the alleged claims or charges are

> against the victims because that has the great potential for nullification and it is irrelevant to the elements of the government's charges against these defendants.
>
> So the civil lawsuit is to me an unnecessary and potentially confusing and prejudicial issue, which is why I had denied the request earlier when Mr. McMahon made it.

What I noticed in the prosecutor's language when the judge inquired about the quid pro quo was Heeren used the phrases, "I don't believe," "It's entirely possible," "That I can recall," and so forth, to cover himself. Then he passed off a question to Ms. Arfa who had only been working on this case for a few weeks leading up to trial. She answered in a similar nature, "I'm not aware of any such discussion, no." This tactic of non-answering is typical but completely misleading in our case based on the evidence. Mike's entire investigation aligned with the civil case. Heeren was well aware the alleged "harassment" was a key part of Jin Xu and Fang Liu's civil lawsuit defense yet he didn't educate the judge of those facts. Defense counsel's efforts to do so were thwarted at every turn. Undeniably we were shot down, yet again.

As Fang Liu entered the courtroom to take the stand she had a striking resemblance to her sister Yan Liu. She was petite and well-dressed. She never looked at anyone other than the prosecutors as she walked in and took the stand.

There were some notable statements regarding the threatening note that had been put on the door at her home on September 4, 2018. A translator read Fang Liu's response to what happened when two men showed up to her home. Attorney Heeren led the questioning of Fang Liu.

> *Fang Liu:* My husband turn on the security system of our home on his electronic device, and we saw two people who came from the driveway and walkway to our home. And my husband told me to call the FBI right away. So, I called the FBI but it did not go through, so I send them messages.

Heeren: Let me just clarify. When you say your husband turned on the video, was it already recording or did he start recording at that point?

Liu: That system had been working all along, and we can turn it on at any time from electronic device to look at it.

When Fang Liu commented on the videos played in the courtroom, I noticed something interesting. There were multiple angles to review. There was a Nest camera on the corner of the house covering the driveway, an interior camera in the living room facing the back sliding doors and deck, one facing the back of the house on a high angle in a tree approximately twenty-five feet high, and one to the left of the front door in the bushes with an angle aligned to isolate and capture the front door activity only. This camera was oddly positioned, approximately three feet off the ground in the bushes. I had never seen that angle before on any security camera. That camera footage in particular had a reference code tagged on the bottom right, which said RECON YX PC 900. I searched that camera online and found it was a camera often used by the government. It was a motion detector trail camera that hunters sometimes use as well. Fang Liu said she "reviewed the contents of a thumb drive" to prepare to testify. Who put that camera in the bushes knowing it would be the perfect angle to catch the action of the note being placed on the door?

Heeren continued with Fang Liu.

Heeren: I'd now like to talk about your sister, Liu Yan. Did you ever learn that your sister was harassed?

Liu: Yes, I know.

Heeren: What was your understanding of how your sister was harassed?

Liu: My sister told me that she found that someone, an Asian-looking man was jogging around her home and when she drove her car that man was taking a picture of your [her] car and her home.

No evidence was presented that this ever happened.

> *Heeren:* My sister also told me that a stranger claimed to know my husband [Jin Xu], was asking about the address of my husband and also left her a message. She also told me that she found out that someone was looking into the trash, in the recycle bin of her home.

No evidence was presented that this ever happened.

> *Liu:* In 2019, my younger sister kept receiving mail coming from China that lasted for about a half year. There were letters and postcards and a CD-ROM. These letters, postcard, and CD-ROM were sent in the name of my husband's younger sister and also my husband's brother-in-law and also in the names of the relatives of my younger sister in China.
>
> *Heeren:* Who were those letters sent to?
>
> *Liu:* I have not seen those letters myself. My sister talked about them over the phone. I guess the content of them should concern my husband.
>
> *Heeren:* Do you know whether your—did your sister tell you when you spoke whether she had received the letters, setting aside who they were addressed to?
>
> *Liu:* She told me whenever she received the letters.
>
> *Heeren:* About how often did she receive letters?
>
> *Liu:* It would be about once per week or once every two weeks and the maximum amount received was three pieces a day.

To my knowledge only one package was presented at trial to the jury. We pushed to question Fang Liu about the allegations against her and her husband. A sidebar was called regarding the questioning to be permitted about the credibility of the witness.

> *Judge Chen:* ...Now you can ask questions related to credibility but again your argument is, at best, if somehow if they were liars or cheats back in China that goes to their credibility, but I'm not allowing you to go into that because the merits of that or the truth of that you cannot show and it is very prejudicial. If there was a felony conviction that was valid and established, that would be one

thing, but you want to ask about the Chinese government—yes, but Ms. Wong, you may laugh but—

Ms. Wong (Zheng Counsel): But there is—

Judge Chen: No—

Ms. Wong: —they were tried.

Judge Chen: —but in a Chinese system that has no validity here. It does not have sufficient validity that you can then assume that they were properly convicted. I'm not accepting that, that's my point.

I had come to realize that the judge was not permitting the defense to show why the witnesses had credibility issues. She felt the cases against them in China, even though they were found guilty and had property confiscated, were inadmissible due to the validity of the Chinese government. Yet she was allowing the "victims" to testify about events that occurred in China and the US without any evidence to paint a narrative of prejudice to the jury against Mike and the other defendants. How is that fair?

Upon reviewing the civil lawsuit, that we were not permitted to use in this case, I found something interesting. Even though the judge pontificated that this case would hold no bearing regarding the civil lawsuit result, because the "victims" were being charged in a financial crime, she was wrong. The "victims" had claimed in the civil lawsuit that the suit was brought by the CCP to harass them and used the note on the door and the surprise visit of Jin Xu's father from China in this case as evidence of said harassment. If the defendants, including Mike, were found guilty of harassment in a federal court it would "prove" what the "victims" claimed in civil court in New Jersey to be true and the case would have a better chance to be dismissed.

What evidence did Jin Xu and Fang Liu provide in the civil case as evidence regarding the note on the door? Nowhere in that case is it ever mentioned of the FBI being involved in their harassment claims. Wouldn't that bolster their defense to have a federal agency investigating criminal acts against them? They claimed Jin Xu's father was "kidnapped" from China and forced here as evidence in the civil documents. That was quite an unfounded declaration. Jin Xu's parents were both here in 2016 without incident to attend their granddaughter's graduation from Stanford. His father returned to the US alone in April of 2017, also without incident. He had multiple opportunities to alert the authorities if he was the victim of a crime. Another glaring issue is that China has executed exit bans on relatives of wanted fugitives in an effort to force fugitives living abroad to return to China. Why weren't Jin Xu's parents ever stopped from leaving China or when they went through customs if their son was one of China's 100 most wanted? Their narrative didn't add up when looking at the facts. Was there video evidence submitted in the civil case of dangerous men, allegedly sent by the CCP, wandering around Jin Xu's property in the fall of 2018? If the note being placed on the door in September of 2018 was a crime, as they were alleging in our case, why hadn't the FBI released any video to the media, national or local? Did anyone provide the video of the two men on Jin Xu's property to the local police to warn the neighborhood and attempt to identify these allegedly dangerous people? No. What was going on here?

Is it possible the Newark FBI and alleged "victims" both got what they wanted in the fall of 2018? The "victims" got their "evidence" for the civil case that they were being harassed by a note from the CCP, and the FBI had captured video "evidence" they kept for themselves that a "crime" occurred to keep their Fox Hunt investigation open. Were the "victims" and the FBI working together to make this happen? If that was the plan, one part failed. In a response from September 20, 2019, the civil court judge in New Jersey did not find the note as credible proof the note was at the direction of the CCP, had no connection to Xinba Construction Company and allowed the civil suit to continue.

Mike was asked to stand up and Larry directly asked Fang Liu if she had ever seen him. Fang Liu said no she had not. Mike exhaled and sat back down in his chair. We were dealing with people who had thrown the truth in the gutter. We had no idea what they would pull next so every time Larry would ask a witness if they could identify

Mike, it was a crapshoot. Now we had two of the three "stalking victims" who had no idea who Mike McMahon was. How could the government charge Mike with interstate stalking knowing alleged "victims" couldn't identify him? Maybe they were counting on the main "victim," Jin Xu, to lie and say he recognized Mike during his testimony. I had been waiting for over three years to see this man in person. I was shocked he was going to make an appearance. It must have been worth his time.

CHAPTER THIRTEEN

THE ANTICIPATION LEADING UP to Jin Xu's appearance on the stand was intense. Since the day the FBI showed up at our home, we had come to an understanding of who this man was. The question still remained: Why was Jin Xu willing to show his face to the world if he was so concerned about the CCP? There had been other cases of targeted political dissidents including one particular case where CCP operatives overtly sat outside a man's home with signs and a bullhorn. No one was arrested in that case and several similar ones. Why did the US government latch their wagon to Jin Xu's star?

Up until October of 2020, there wasn't much information about Jin Xu available in the US. The July 2020 Wall Street Journal article published almost three years after Mike finished the case only focused on the civil lawsuit against him and his wife. The article never used the term "CCP" in regards to Jin Xu. It referenced him as a Chinese government official in a line or two. So, to be clear, in the fall of 2016 when Mike Googled Jin Xu, only one photo of a *China Daily* PDF of one hundred fugitives wanted for financial crimes came up. That was all the information available in the US internet search engines in the fall of 2016. Remember, we were prevented from using anything from the civil case at trial.

What the US government knew about Jin Xu was another story. Jin Xu had been the head of government in the Huangpi District of Wuhan City in Hubei province, China, and worked on commercial development. Wuhan has a population of approximately eleven million people. He had control over local government departments including the Hankou Bei Management Committee and departments connected to real estate, public security, fire prevention, urban management, and environmental protection. He fled to the US from China in 2010 along with his wife Fang Liu when both were being investigated for embezzlement and bribery.

Public documents on Chinese websites discovered through our investigator revealed the US government had been actively negotiating with the CCP for years to return Jin Xu and Fang Liu to China. The United States has no extradition with China but has a Mutual Legal Assistance Agreement in criminal matters. Those negotiations confirmed they were not political dissidents but subjects of a very serious criminal investigation. Jin Xu was tried on these charges in China and lost and had properties confiscated.

It's odd how much favor our government showed to a man with Jin Xu's track record. For what purpose? How much did NY FBI know about Jin Xu? For some reason NY FBI did not want to attach itself to this case and left it in the hands of Newark FBI. Jin Xu, Fang Liu, and Yan Liu communicated with Newark FBI for years, but never contacted local law enforcement until they were forced to do so in the fall of 2018 the day after the note was put on the door. What would Jin Xu's testimony reveal? We were about to find out.

When Jin Xu entered the courtroom, I wouldn't take my eyes off of him for a second. He was short and slim, approximately fifty years old. His tailored black suit was fitted perfectly to his body to the millimeter. As he walked past me to take the stand I could feel his energy. There was no one calmer in that courtroom than Jin Xu. It wasn't arrogance emulating from him, it was confidence. Jin Xu walked towards the stand passing FBI Case Agent Christopher Bruno sitting in his usual spot at the end of the prosecutor's table. Jin Xu didn't even glance at Bruno—this was Jin Xu's show and it was obvious. Craig Heeren was gathering his papers in a feverish overly caffeinated state. This was the most important day of his case and he was letting everyone know it. Heeren's back was to Mike who was only three feet away from him and Mike was watching Jin Xu with great intent. What would this guy say? He must have seen my interviews, right? Did he think this case would end up with him having to testify? Why was he so calm? Why was no one from the press in the gallery? This man was a high-ranking CCP official from Wuhan. Didn't anyone want to hear what he had to say? I was anxious to hear how far Jin Xu would go to help the prosecution crucify Mike.

There was one piece of information Jin Xu provided regarding the alleged meeting testified to at the Livingston Mall with his father who had flown in from China. Jin Xu said his father came to the US to encourage him to return to China and "not to speak negatively about a certain leader in the U.S. before the China 19th Party Congress commenced."

This statement bolstered Yan Liu's earlier testimony that a man had visited her and allegedly informed her that Jin Xu was no longer just wanted for financial crimes but now it was political as well. Was this an attempt to paint Jin Xu as a political dissent to bolster his US citizenship? Who was this Chinese leader he was referring to?

Then Craig Heeren homed into Jin Xu's recollection of being followed on April 7, 2017, the day after the meeting at the mall with his father.

(Interpreter translated all questions to Jin Xu and vice versa.)

Mr. Heeren: I want to direct your attention now to the next day, Friday, April 7th, 2017. Did you meet with your father on that date?

Jin Xu: Yes, I did.

Heeren: And on April 7th, 2017, did you bring your father anywhere else?

Jin Xu: I brought my father to where I live.

Heeren: Did you notice anything unusual when you were driving to or from meeting your father on April 7th, 2017?

THE INTERPRETER: Can you repeat the date for me.

Heeren: Sure. Let me just repeat the question. Did you notice anything unusual when you were driving to or from meeting with your father on Friday, April 7, 2017?

*Jin Xu:*After I picked up my father and left Liu Yan's home, not long after that I found out there was a car that had been following me so I was suspecting us being stalked. Then I was circling around the communities near Liu Yan's home. As I made circles, that car had been following me so I believe that indeed I was being followed.

And I realized that I could not get rid of this following car, so I stopped my car. And that car that was following me in the direction of above me, that car also stopped and that car was not hiding so we were in a standstill. That standstill lasted for a little while and then that car left. At that moment I brought my father directly home.

Heeren: Do you remember anything about what that car looked like?

Jin Xu: From my impression that car was a gray Honda SUV.

Heeren: How did that experience of being followed make you feel?

Jin Xu: In the beginning when I was being followed, I tried to get rid of that following car as soon as possible. I was feeling afraid in the beginning. However, later on when the standstill happened and that car was not hiding, then I was a bit frightened. I realized that that car was not following me discretely, rather it was a threat. So in the beginning I was panicking but later on I was scared.

Heeren: Did you contact US law enforcement about this incident in April 2017.

Jin Xu: Yes, I reported it to the FBI.

To reiterate, the criminal complaint signed SWORN TO by FBI Case Agent Christopher Bruno read that Mike had witnessed a public meeting of Jin Xu and his father but did NOT say where it occurred in the complaint. We had broken our brains trying to figure out what meeting they were referring to. All of Mike's documents and surveillance reports have no evidence Mike witnessed any meeting between the two. The government was well aware for years that Mike was not at any mall on April 6th, 2017, yet they inferred to the jury he was there during Yan Liu's testimony with the photograph.

The bigger bombshell was Jin Xu's testimony about being chased through his neighborhood by a grey Honda SUV on Friday APRIL 7, 2017. Not only was Mike driving a BLACK SUV during his days of surveillance, he WASN'T WORKING ON APRIL 7, 2017!! He worked the previous day on April 6, 2017, but not on the 7th! The cell site expert placed Mike at his home in Mahwah, New Jersey on the 7th. This was HUGE for us! The other tidbit was there was NO POLICE REPORT or investigation into this alleged chase in Short Hills, New Jersey. No photograph of the car pursing him, no 911 call, no license plate number, nothing. Short Hills, New Jersey, is a VERY WEALTHY town and from my research there was no story on the news about a high-speed car chase. Did the FBI ever try and find any neighborhood Ring camera footage? Or alert the local police about Chinese agents "stalking" one of their residents? No. We saw this as a win. Mike and Mike Kelly followed a black Mercedes from Yan Liu's home on April 6th for approximately thirty minutes to what turned out to be Jin Xu's address, unbeknownst to the two private investigators. Mike Kelly was actually the first person to locate the address that day, not Mike. Mike and Eric Gallowitz also followed the same black Mercedes on April 10th for approximately the same amount of time. Why did Jin Xu confirm with Hereen the Friday April 7th date with the alleged car chase and "stare down" with a faceless someone in a Honda SUV? What appears to have been the purpose of using the 7th was to show an additional "pattern" of stalking. I believe the government did this to infer multiple bad acts on multiple days. Then Heeren moved on to the note being put on the door in September of 2018.

Heeren: After the two men left, what did you do?

Jin Xu: I reported it to the FBI. The FBI asked us to go outside and check what's going on to see what they've done. So I checked the front and the back.... As soon as I opened the door I realized that they had posted a note on the [front] door.

Before I saw this [note] I felt that the threats from the CCP was only a mental threat to me; however, when I saw that note, I realized it had become a physical threat...

Jin Xu had just testified that the April 2017 car chase in Short Hills, New Jersey, made him feel "frightened," "afraid," like he was being "stalked." Jin Xu didn't consider being chased through a residential neighborhood and "stalked" as a physical threat? Jin Xu then went on to testify about his actions following the note placement in September of 2018, eighteen months after Mike finished his work on this case.

Jin Xu: After they came on the first day I reported it to the FBI and the FBI agent told us that they would come again and, if they come again, then you call the local police station and we would alert the local police station to come as soon as possible. Therefore, when they came again as we expected, then we followed the instructions of the FBI. So when he was still there I called the local police in Warren.

Heeren: And after the man left, what did you do?

Jin Xu: In a very short period of time the local police came.

Heeren: Did the FBI also come at some point in time?

Jin Xu: After the local police came, within half an hour the FBI came.

Heeren: Once the FBI came, what, if anything, did you do with them?

Jin Xu: Once they came I showed them the footage of the surveillance camera record.

Jin Xu's answers are filtered through an interpreter but these are the facts. The first day two perpetrators arrived, Jin Xu DOES NOT CALL 911. He is home with his wife and waits until the two men leave. He STILL doesn't call 911, he calls the FBI. The FBI instructs them to call 911 when they RETURN. Based on Jin Xu's testimony he EXPECTED them to return. Why didn't the FBI IMMEDIATELY go to the residence or alert the local police on day one? If they were truly in danger why didn't they protect them? The NEXT DAY one of the perpetrators DOES come back and Fang Liu calls the local police but by the time she calls and they arrive the man is gone. The FBI showed up thirty minutes later, after the local police arrived.

Jin Xu testified, "As soon as I opened the door I realized that they had posted a note on the [front] door." If he was monitoring the men walking around his property on his multiple security cameras on the app on his phone, how come he only discovered the note after they left and he opened the front door? He testified about only hearing the men knocking on the front door. The two men wandered around the property and went to the front door a few times before taping the note to the door. Did he not have access to the surveillance camera in the bushes to witness the activities of the front door? The men were at that door for an extended period of time when they placed the note. Was it possible that the camera in the bushes capturing the note placement was being monitored by the government in real time? Did the FBI know they weren't in any danger? How much did the FBI and Jin Xu know prior to the events of that day? Why didn't the FBI instruct Jin Xu to call the local police on DAY ONE? The perpetrator Zheng claimed he regretted putting the note on the door. There was contradicting information that the gang member in California who had provided him with the address told him to go back. Zheng confirmed to the gang member, who I believe was a confidential informant, that he was going to return to the house and tear down the note. If the FBI even suspected Zheng was going to return, or anyone else for that matter, why didn't they send an unmarked car surveillance team to watch Jin Xu's home? Why didn't they call the local police to send a car to watch the home? Or move Jin Xu and Fang Liu into a hotel for a few days? Mike had several cases while on the NYPD where witnesses were moved to hotels to keep them safe. Was the FBI still monitoring the camera in the bushes? Something wasn't adding up.

Jin Xu went on to testify about a package that arrived at his sister-in-law Yan Liu's home in 2019. He reiterated that the FBI instructed her to send other mailings back to China. (What a joke.) Ironically, these mailings started to arrive soon after the judge in the New Jersey civil lawsuit disregarded the threatening note on the door as credible evidence to dismiss that case. Were the packages a new tactic to prove that Jin Xu was a victim of the CCP? Why wasn't he granted political asylum here in the US if he had claimed the CCP was targeting him for political reasons? No proof had ever been given on record that Jin Xu was wanted as a political dissident. His resume in China was that of a high-ranking member of the CCP who held several powerful positions. It did not appear he was in poor standing with the CCP—quite the opposite. Chinese media claimed he was having marital issues and that's why he resigned from the job he was holding when he fled China for good. What was really going on? Was what he and his wife were accused of in China true? Maybe what was discussed during a sidebar regarding Fang Liu's previous testimony could shed some light on the matter.

> *Judge Chen:* Is the government aware of any part of the prosecution team, the US Attorney's Office, the FBI, helping the victim in terms of her immigration process?
>
> *Ms. Arfa:* We're not.
>
> *Mr. Heeren:* No. The process is they have—as I understand it, that they currently have no status but they are pending here while we do this lawsuit.
>
> *Judge Chen:* When you say "pending here," they are allowed to stay here because of this prosecution?
>
> *Mr. Heeren:* While this prosecution is ongoing. There's been no final determination on their status in the country, as I understand it.
>
> *Mr. Goldberger (codefendant Zheng counsel):* Judge, as I understand it, her husband [Jin Xu] sent a thank you note to the government, some of the agents, in regards to continuing to allow them to process this EB-5 or whatever it is.

Judge Chen: What was the nature of the thank you note, which is, I think, being mischaracterized?

Mr. Heeren: I think there's a note from the daughter that thanks the government for her—related to her green card.

Judge Chen: The daughter's green card?

Mr. Heeren: Right. I don't believe that's accurate.

The government was quite cautious with their words again, "as I understand it," "I don't believe that's accurate." There was evidence these communications took place between the "victims" and the government, specifically FBI Agent Robert Reilly. In my research I found out Agent Reilly was part of the Newark, New Jersey, FBI team. He had a background in media relations from what I could gather. Was it possible he was the point person for Jin Xu, Fang Liu, and Yan Liu once they claimed to be "victims" of "harassment" as early as 2015 or 2016? I wasn't sure but one thing I DID know, the FBI had no place intervening or weighing in on anything involving immigration OR a civil lawsuit against the "victims." Zheng's cocounsel Renee Wong had pointed out an email from Fang Liu to Agent Reilly regarding "following up" on the civil lawsuit. This clearly implies there had been previous discussion on this topic. Now Judge Chen has been presented with circumstantial evidence there was a quid pro quo of some sort. Our arguments to introduce the quid pro quo were dismissed, even though it was Judge Chen who documented concern of the optics.

Now it was Larry's turn at the podium to cross-examine Jin Xu. His first instruction was to have Mike stand up. He asked Jin Xu if he recognized him. He answered, "No." There it was. Now all four "victims", including daughter Xinxi Xu, were unable to identify Mike. The government didn't seem concerned by this but we felt it was enough evidence to the jury he should NEVER be convicted of interstate stalking. None of Mike's actions led to the "victims" being in "fear of bodily harm" which by definition were the parameters to charge an individual with "stalking." Larry continued and all questioning was done through a translator.

Larry: Mr. Xu, in response to the events that occurred in April of 2017, did you change your residence?

Jin Xu: I did not make that change in 2017.

Larry: Okay. And in response to the events that you described earlier today that occurred in September of 2018, did you move from that residence?

Jin Xu: Can you repeat your question again?

Larry: Sure. Let me just backtrack a little bit. You said that the events that occurred in September of 2018, where the two men came to your house, made you feel, whereas before it had been a mental threat, now it was a physical threat.

Jin Xu: Yes.

Larry: And as a result of—and in response to that, did you move from that home in Warren, New Jersey?

Jin Xu: No.

Jin Xu testified the alleged chase in 2017 put him in fear. He just confirmed that he only felt a physical threat in fall of 2018. Renee Wong, defense counsel for defendant Zheng, who put the note on the door, proceeded to cross-examine Jin Xu.

Wong: You testified earlier that something unusual had happened on September 4, 2018; is that correct?

Jin Xu: Yes.

Wong: However, didn't you and your wife meet with FBI agents at your residence only about two weeks before August 21st, 2018?

Jin Xu: I don't remember.

Wong: You don't remember. Do you remember on August 14, 2018, a black sedan driving up to your residence?

Jin Xu: I don't remember the specific timing, however, I do remember there was a black vehicle that was—turned into my home.

Wong: And do you remember if that had occurred in the summer of 2018?

Jin Xu: Around that time it is possible, it would be very possible.

Wong: And did you report that black sedan to the FBI?

Jin Xu: I did report it.

Ms. Wong got on the record that a black sedan had visited Jin Xu approximately two weeks before the note was put on the door on September 4, 2018. Jin Xu claimed he didn't remember the exact timing but confirms he reported the appearance of the black sedan to the FBI.

Wong: Mr. Xu, to your understanding, are you receiving any benefit whatsoever from the government based on your testimony today?

Jin Xu: I don't feel that way. No, I don't.

Wong: Mr. Xu, have you asked for any assistance in regards to immigration from the government in connection with this case?

Jin Xu: I don't remember I said so, and I don't remember I made such a request.

Wong: Mr. Xu, in October of 2019, did you meet with FBI Agent Robert Reilly and provide an EB-5 denial letter for you and your wife?

The government objected and successfully shut down this line of questioning and that was that. Jin Xu left the courtroom and was gone. I couldn't help but wonder again, where was the press? *The New York Times* was supposedly covering this trial but the writer was barely present in court. If this case was the first ever Fox Hunt case to go to trail, wouldn't ANYONE be interested in reporting on it? If Jin Xu and wife Fang Liu were on China's Most Wanted, didn't anyone want to speak to them? Jin Xu was a Wuhan official wanted for embezzlement and bribery! It was shocking to me. What I was hearing in the court room was mind-blowing. Things were about to get crazier.

The next witness was Hongru Jin, a friend of "Johnny's." Unbeknownst to Mike, Hongru Jin had been hired to do surveillance in April of 2017. He was a cooperator for the government and pled guilty to two charges: violating FARA and interstate stalking. He did not speak English and also used an interpreter. We learned during his testimony he was actually on site at Panera Bread during Mike's meeting in 2017 with "Johnny." Hongru Jin stayed far away at a table out of earshot of the conversation. He did not hear the exchange between Mike and "Johnny" at the Panera Bread.

Since "Johnny" fled the country as did coconspirator Tu Lan (supposed Chinese prosecutor), the only person left to testify about Mike's involvement was Hongru Jin. His testimony was vital to convince the jury Mike had engaged in stalking Jin Xu. How could Hongru Jin do that? Mike had no idea who this man was and no communications existed between the two. The only evidence connecting them was the unidentified vehicle Mike saw circling one night and inquired with "Johnny" who it was. "Johnny" had texted back "That's MY guy." It turned out to be Hongru Jin. Not only was Hongru Jin surveilling for Jin Xu, he was also surveilling to keep tabs on Mike.

How could the prosecutors spin this information? If Mike was part of a conspiracy, why was "Johnny" monitoring Mike? What was he worried about? Then Hongru Jin was questioned about a recording that took place at the Embassy Suites on April 3, 2017. When questioned by the prosecutors if Hongru Jin knew who and how this recording had been obtained he said, "No."

It had always been a concern of ours how the recording was obtained. The government would never provide us an answer. They only provided a copy of the audio and the translation done by their internal government translator. We trusted what we had been provided was truthful from translation to text. I did not trust this translation from the moment I was aware it existed but Larry assured me it would be unheard of for the government to be deceptive on such a vital piece of their case.

When asked to identify who was on the recording Hongru Jin confirmed it was "Johnny" and Tu Lan. The exchange between "Johnny" and Tu Lan was witnessed by Hongru Jin, who was with them in the hotel room. Hongru Jin testified that part of the exchange between Tu Lan and "Johnny" was in a dialect of which he only understood

10 percent. This was new information to the defense that he only understood 10 percent of what "Johnny" and Tu Lan were saying! The government was laser focused on the discussion between Tu Lan and "Johnny" regarding how Mike was to be used as part of their clandestine plan. Tu Lan voiced on the recording how she viewed Mike. Mike is an American and she doesn't have much "control," then references Mike being law enforcement. She tells "Johnny" to handle Mike, to be "clear" with Mike and tell him "everything." The day after that meeting in the hotel "Johnny" met with Mike at Panera Bread. The prosecutors lean into the word, "everything," in their translation. They told the jury that "Johnny" must have told Mike "everything" at that meeting in Panera Bread. The exchange was projected on the huge screen in the court room. Heeren is laying out his narrative like he's auditioning for an episode of *Law and Order*. He can't get enough of himself.

Heeren was putting a lot of weight on this recording. There were glaring problems with the recording that were revealed in Hongru Jin's testimony. We learned he could only understand 10 percent in one section of what "Johnny" and Tu Lan were saying. What?! He claimed the dialect in one part was one he could not fully understand. That did not make any sense. Based on questioning, Hongru Jin responded that he understood EXACTLY what was being said in the same dialect a just few sentences later spoken by the same parties, Tu Lan and "Johnny." He totally contradicted himself. What was this game? The prosecutors just used a recording they had in their possession for years but failed to inform the defense the person testifying to its contents under oath could only understand 10 percent of some of it?! Was that even legal?

We were now in the middle of the trial and had to address whatever slick moves Heeren was up to, and they were constant. Hongru Jin was not a bad witness for us but he was a purposely confused one. He would confirm statements made by "Johnny" and Tu Lan but then when it came to one particular section of the conversation, "Tell him everything," claimed it got lost in translation.

Interesting note, Heeren switched translators before Larry cross-examined Hongru Jin. Why did he do that? Was it because the previous one was due for a break or for some other reason?

When Larry pushed Hongru Jin about his previous statement regarding his recollection of Mike's connection to this case, Heeren began to get squirrely and called a sidebar out of earshot of the jury.

> *Mr. Heeren:* So, Your Honor, my only concern is that it's my recollection that Mr. Jin's testimony on direct was that he didn't understand these messages because they were in a different dialect. So, I think asking him to review the transcript at this point for this portion of the recording and asking him to say what it meant, it's leading to some speculation. I'm just concerned about it being confusing.
>
> *Judge Chen:* Well, I'm not sure which portions were in dialect. Are you saying the entire conversation between Tu Lan and Zhu was in dialect?
>
> *Mr. Heeren:* No, the portions that are—and it's indicated in the interpreter's note—
>
> *Judge Chen:* Right, I remember.
>
> *Mr. Heeren:* —the portions that are underlined in that transcript, and we pointed out on direct that, you know, when we played it alongside it, he says that's Hubei dialect.
>
> *Judge Chen:* Let's go back for a minute. The first part of the conversation that was asked about, was that underlined or not?
>
> *Mr. Heeren:* The part—the first time I objected it was. I think there was an earlier portion I didn't object to that, that was in Mandarin.
>
> *Judge Chen:* Let me just say this. I think your objection, though, I think reflects back in some way though to your admission of these as coconspirator statements, and at the time you made that comment on the record about the underlined portion, I actually had a concern about whether you could offer them as coconspirator statements, if in fact your argument is that he didn't understand what they were saying. It's hard to argue that something is a coconspirator

> statement if the person who through whom they are being offered doesn't actually understand them. It's almost like not hearing them in some way.

The judge seemed to have some concerns about the "lost in translation" take the prosecutors were clearly manipulating. Judge Chen had previously intervened twice over concerns about translations between interpreters and witnesses. She made it a point to clarify Chinese interpretations on the record to eliminate any confusion in the transcripts. Judge Chen also stated on the record she understood very little Chinese but spoke out regarding misstatements she recognized and it concerned her enough to intervene. Was she concerned about the statements translated from the recording and was attempting to get the prosecution to address it in this sidebar? Did US Attorney Arisa Chen or Meredith Arfa have any understanding of the Chinese language and dialects? If the judge saw some discrepancies in the way the evidence was being slithered into the case, what obligation, if any, did she have to correct it? What about the interpreters? They most certainly understood what was going on. Did they have any legal obligation to alert the court to clarify statements so the jury would get a clear understanding for deliberations? I don't know.

Larry continued to cross the witness on the recording.

> *Larry:* So, Mr. Jin, I just read you a portion of the transcript, and any first question is—and I can do that again, if you wish—but my question is, the part that I read to you, do you remember hearing that?
>
> *Hongru Jin:* Yes, I remember.
>
> *Larry:* And so what did you understand Johnny Zhu to mean, since you recall hearing it, when he said: If you have a talk with Mike, Mike-Mike will think, Mike will, Mike-Mike will then say that it is you who told me to say so and so. What did you understand that to mean?
>
> *Hongru Jin:* I'm looking at the text right now, but I cannot understand English. First of all, can I listen to what Johnny actually said, that way I can answer more precisely.

Larry: I would have to request the government's assistance if they can play that excerpt, but I'm happy to do that.

Hongru Jin: Thank you.

Judge Chen: So, Ms. Chen, what's the audio that you're going to play? If you can isolate this portion of the conversation in Chinese.

Attorney Chen: I think it's 7:04, Your Honor, beginning at around one minute and thirty-one seconds. And we will end at two minutes and five seconds.

Judge Chen: All right, go ahead.

(Audio played; audio stopped.)

Hongru Jin: Thank you. I listened to that. After I listened to the audio, I felt that when Johnny Zhu mentioned Mike-Mike, it was because earlier Tu Lan said no matter how Mike was like, it would be best for him to fill the instruction and do so. So Johnny Zhu said maybe Mike will not do it as instructed. That's my fault [thought].

Larry: So your thought was, what you understood, was that there was a concern that Mike would not do what—he would not follow that direction; is that correct?

Hongru Jin: Yes.

Larry: Okay. And a little bit later, Tu Lan says this: He is an American, I don't have any control. Do you remember hearing Tu Lan say that?

Hongru Jin: Yes.

Larry: And what did you understand Tu Lan to mean when she said that?

Hongru Jin: It would be the literal meaning, as in the private detective he cannot be controlled or be ordered.

Larry: There's a time when Tu Lan tells Johnny Zhu that Johnny Zhu should tell him, the private investigator, about everything. Do you recall that?

Hongru Jin: I don't remember that. Can you please put the English translate on the screen so that I can look at it?

Larry: Sure. Sure. It says Tu: Tell him clearly. I mean, you need to tell him clearly about everything. Do you see that?

Hongru Jin: Excuse me, maybe difference between the Chinese and English regarding what she said. I need to see further up to help me confirm what she was trying to express. Thank you.

Larry: (To Hongru Jin) Okay, so as you sit here right now, you don't recall that statement?

Hongru Jin: I remember she [Tu Lan] said that, however, I'm not sure whether she said it in Mandarin or in the Hubei dialect, because the audio was very long, I cannot remember exactly.

Hongru Jin is unable to go on the record about this VERY IMPORTANT statement, to tell Mike "everything." This ambiguity caused a major rift in the government's case. If Hongru Jin was unable confirm Tu Lan told "Johnny" to tell Mike "everything" then Heeren's story to the jury that "Johnny" must have told Mike "everything" at the Panera Bread loses any shred of credibility he created. Heeren has to fix it. He questions Hongru Jin again.

Mr. Heeren: Mr. Jin, do you recall that defense counsel asked you about Tu Lan saying I don't have any control over the private investigator?

Hongru Jin: I remember.

Heeren: And looking at the translation it reads: I don't have much control, right?

Hongru Jin: Yes.

Heeren: And then if we could close that part out. Thank you. And scroll down. If you can just blow up: Tell him clearly, please. And a bit earlier Tu Lan says: Tell him clearly, I mean, you need to tell him clearly about everything. Did I read that right?

Hongru Jin: Yes.

Heeren: All right. You can take that exhibit down.

Heeren is asking Hongru Jin if he, Heeren, is READING two lines from the government's English translation properly which is being translated back into Hongru Jin's language and he says, "yes."

Larry asked if Hongru Jin recalls Tu Lan saying, "Tell Mike everything" and Hongru Jin replied, "I don't remember that." Upon hearing the recording he gets flustered. Hongru Jin doesn't speak English and listened to Heeren's version of Tu Lan's statement read through an interpreter. The interpreter translated Heeren's spoken words "did I read that right?" to be translated to prompt Hongru Jin to answer, "Yes." Conveniently, there is no court stenographer who documents the interpreters' interactions in the foreign language. What we do know is that by Heeren reading the text in English and asking, "Did I read that right?" The answer from Hongru Jin was an honest, "Yes." He also had a copy of the transcript available to read in Chinese. The layers of language barriers were deliberate and purposely confusing.

The deception was right there for us to challenge but we were up against insurmountable odds. The Hongru Jin testimony showed Mike was in no way a part of Tu Lan's team. Tu Lan made it clear Mike could not be trusted as he was an American. Tu Lan was adamant the events in 2017 were to be done in secret. "Johnny," who was the leader of the operation, was told by Tu Lan to make sure he was not seen by anyone. Common sense tells a normal person that the Chinese government or anyone working on behalf of the Chinese government would never tell a former NYPD detective their actual goals if they were engaging in criminal activity. If they had, Mike would have immediately called the local police and the FBI. Mike had many former coworkers who became federal agents after leaving the NYPD. Two of these men actually worked in the same field office as Case Agent Christopher Bruno in Red Bank, New Jersey. How could the FBI get this case so wrong? Why did Craig Heeren bring this case up the ladder with the endless missteps he would have to make disappear?

Despite the mouth-dropping events happening in the courtroom, we felt like we were winning. Larry and Genna did an excellent job knocking off the witnesses with ease. Larry would ask minimal questions in his cross-examinations and move on to the next witness for the government. Each day the witness list kept getting shorter. We had Eric Gallowitz on our witness list, who we felt would cover a lot for our side. He would testify not just to the events in 2016 and 2017, in which he participated with Mike in PI work, but also to what private investigators are legally allowed to do. Mike hadn't spoken to Eric since this happened and he felt terrible about anyone getting roped into this nightmare. Our investigator had reached out and spoken to Eric once but that was it. Finning was still on the government witness list with no further information as to why. Judge Chen asked multiple times if the government was planning on calling him and they reassured her they were.

Then a miracle happened. Our former cocounsel Brian Neary was speaking to another lawyer, Paul Brickfield, about Mike's case. They were both lamenting about this horrific injustice. Paul told Brian he remembered recommending Mike to an attorney in Queens about a Chinese case back in 2016. This conversation triggered Paul to look on his phone for any possible evidence that it was connected. To his shock, he found text messages with Attorney Shi Ping about Mike from 2016. She had texted Paul asking if he knew any licensed PIs in New Jersey. He texted back Mike's name and his hourly rates. THIS WAS AMAZING! We had found the person who recommended Mike to Attorney Ping! This would discredit the allegation from the government that Mike was in a conspiracy involving the Chinese government! We knew from Jason that Attorney Ping added Mike's name to the original contract when she was set to represent him to locate Jin Xu. Jason chose not to hire Attorney Ping but took Mike's information to "Emily" the translator. Holy smokes! Larry added Paul Brickfield to our witness list. This must have thrown the government for a loop. Did they know how Paul was connected? Paul was a highly respected defense attorney and a former New Jersey US attorney. The FBI had never spoken to Attorney Ping until she was listed as a witness in our case, only a few weeks before trial. During their first and only interview the FBI had with Attorney Ping she told them she got Mike's name from a New Jersey attorney but couldn't remember who it was. Was this the first time the FBI was aware of her connection to this case? If they had interviewed Attorney Ping over the years, their case against Mike would have stopped dead in its tracks. They would have learned Mike was recommended by a former New Jersey US attorney and was in no way connected to the Chinese government. At least we had found out now and could completely shut down the narrative to the jury. How would the government handle their case being dismantled? If we had learned anything, it was that these people had no moral compass. They had proven over and over again that truth and the law were subjective. Things were about to get even dirtier.

CHAPTER FOURTEEN

In the middle of the trial an article came out about Bo Dietl in the *New York Post* written by investigative reporter Isabel Vincent. The headline read, "Bo Dietl and the curious case of the Chinese 'spy' who bought half his firm." The article went into great detail about Dietl selling 50 percent equity in his company to China Security and Protection Company Ltd. in November of 2015. Two months later in January 2016 in a *LEADERS* magazine article, Bo bragged about the deal and performing surveillance on one of the CCPs most high-profile targets, billionaire Miles Guo, a Chinese Fox Hunt target. Dietl also celebrated this partnership with a new office in Beijing. In 2017 Dietl lied to the FCC on an application to operate radio equipment. He answered, "No," to a question about whether foreigners owned more than 25 percent of his company, when in fact they owned 50 percent. The *Post* confirmed he had met with CCP generals in China but Dietl claimed they had divested from his company. Public documents revealed that was untrue. The most damning piece of information was that he admitted to being hired by a company in China to surveil CCP target Miles Guo but refused to share who it was that hired him.

I couldn't believe it. The article was incredibly beneficial to Mike. Should we call Dietl as a witness? Was it too late? Why didn't he come forward to help us after I sat across from him in his office in 2021! I put myself out there to warn him about these operations. He claimed to be empathetic but all along he was partners with the Chinese government and had surveilled Guo! Why wasn't Dietl arrested and charged with violating FARA? Why was he getting a pass? He publicly stated he knew he was in business with the Chinese government. As a former member of the NYPD, did that connection benefit him in any way? Did he have a relationship with NY FBI? What came to my mind immediately was if he had followed Miles Guo, could it be possible Beau Dietl and Associates was "PI FIRM NUMBER ONE" in the SDNY Fox Hunt case? It would make sense if he was in business with Chinese officials and tasked to tail Miles Guo, why not other Fox Hunt targets in the New York or New Jersey area? Guo owned a mansion in Mahwah, New Jersey. Did Dietl subcontract a PI in New Jersey to follow Guo? If Dietl and Associates was "PI FIRM NUMBER ONE" in the SDNY Fox Hunt case, which had been given dozens of subjects to surveil by Sun Hoi in 2016, were Jin Xu and Fang Liu on that list? Had they provided the preliminary information Mike was given when "Emily" called him in 2016? I had a million more questions, but we were coming to our final days of the trial and I had to file Beau Dietl and Associates for a later time.

We took a major hit when the judge wouldn't allow a portion of Mike's interrogation into evidence. I naively thought we could play the entire interrogation, which showed Mike was unwittingly used in this case. I learned a defendant cannot use their interrogation unless the government approves. The government would not approve. Now the jury would never hear Mike explain exactly what he meant when he texted his client, "what if we harass him, I did that on another case." He had explained to Agent McCarthy in detail what the "other case" was so the FBI had an answer, and since it cleared up the intent of his word, the government suppressed the video. The jury would also not hear McCarthy make the statement that they thought long and hard about who they were going to arrest. So after four years investigating this case they still weren't convinced who were the actual criminals? Did they put everyone's name in a hat and Mike was the unlucky victim? I believe they knew Mike would soon get a letter he had been spied on illegally so the FBI decided to arrest him. If Mike had gotten that letter he would have lost it and demanded answers. By arresting him and believing he most certainly he would take a plea, no one was the wiser. Add this suppression of exculpatory evidence as another example the prosecution hid in an effort to get a conviction at any cost. However, the government is allowed to edit, cut, and paste whatever they'd like to create a story to favor their narrative. How is this fair? Of course, the government picked an out-of-context seven-minute clip from a more than a ninety-minute interrogation. The clip they used came almost near the end of his interview, after Mike had spoken to the federal agents and learned the truth: that he had been used. On the video when EDNY representative John Ross asked Mike what he thought would happen to Jin Xu if he went back to China, Mike says, "I guess prosecute him." We argued that Mike had clearly stated many times leading up to this clip he had been hired for a civil matter. The rule of completion should be applied and allow earlier statements showing Mike's belief (state of mind) this was a civil matter in which one can be prosecuted both civilly and criminally. Judge Chen was brutal to Mike, saying that as a former cop he knows what the word "prosecute" means and denied us adding the earlier statements. I was the only person in the galley when she ruled on that and I said OUT LOUD, "That is NOT FAIR.... That's not fair...." It wasn't only not fair, in many people's opinion her ruling was wrong. She absolutely knew Mike believed he was working on a civil matter. The interrogation clearly shows that when he learned who the people really were who hired him, he understood their real motives were not what he was told. The entire interrogation was great for Mike, so of course it had to be silenced. Shame on all of these people. Everything was backwards. Like every loss we had to let it go. We had some positive witnesses coming and every hit had to be filed so we could stay positive and not completely fall apart.

When Attorney Shi Ping testified, she confirmed Jason Zhu had come to her in the fall of 2016 and claimed he had money stolen from his business. She stated on the record Jason requested a licensed New Jersey private investigator. Ms. Ping confirmed. A New Jersey lawyer recommended Mike and she added his information to her contract. Luckily, she had saved that contract! A copy of Mike's hourly rate was attached but the contract was unsigned. Apparently, Jason was not happy with Attorney Ping's fee, so he never contacted her again. We were so grateful she was willing to testify.

Lawyer Paul Brickfield took the stand next. Paul had nothing but glowing things to say about Mike. He had known Mike for years and recommended him for work all the time. Paul said Mike was an excellent private investigator. It was so nice to finally hear someone say something positive about Mike after the brutal, inaccurate portrayal the government had presented. When Paul was finished testifying for us, the prosecution asked him one ridiculous question, "Do you ever meet with clients and accept cash at the Panera Bread?" He answered, "No."

Then Eric Gallowitz, who was one of the two PIs Mike hired for this case, took the stand. Mike warned me Eric had a tough exterior but his blood ran blue. A true native New Yorker and badass former NYPD detective, he didn't take shit from anyone. His swagger as he took the stand was filled with an air of defiance. I knew the government had been playing mind games with him for years. He had to hire a lawyer and his life had never been the same since Mike's arrest. According to our investigator, Eric had been told by the FBI early on when he asked if he was also under investigation he was told he was, "not out of the woods yet."

Larry questioned Eric and he was visibly nervous and cautious. He knew as well as everyone else in that courtroom the prosecutors were bullies and no one was safe. When the prosecution confronted Eric with some of his salty texts, such as suggesting overt surveillance, "scare them," texting Mike, "bring your gun LOL." Eric had the perfect answers. "I joke around a lot.... I always have my gun on me." When confronted about a text to Mike that read, "SCU Hero," Gallowitz informed the jury the letters stand for Street Crime Unit. (SCU was an elite group of anti-crime NYPD plain clothes cops. Eric and Mike met while working together in Bronx Narcotics.) Eric went on to say Mike performed "heroic acts" when he worked in Street Crime.

With that "heroic" statement Heeren excitedly pulled out a few papers like a kid who just won a stuffed animal on the boardwalk. He told the judge they were CCRB complaints about Mike from when he was on the NYPD from 2000. CCRB is a board that reviews civilian complaints. They are not legal filings. Heeren had pulled two CCRB complaints from the same complainant in an attempt to prove Mike was not such a "hero." Even the judge thought using the complaints was risky since they were not seen as credible accusations. Mike had never been disciplined for anything in his entire career and had no clue what Mr. Heeren was waving around. When Mike reviewed the complaints he remembered what they were about. It involved a gang member soliciting children near a school who complained about Mike. The mother of the gang member was upset because Mike and his team recovered $1,400 in cash. She stormed into the precinct demanding the money and filed a complaint against Mike, who was the supervisor of four other cops named in the complaint. Mike was never disciplined and never lost any vacation time. When Gallowitz was asked about the CCRB complaints he confirmed they are a joke. The jury chuckled at Eric's take. Heeren was so desperate to smear Mike, he mined his entire NYPD history hoping to find some dirt. He had to look all the way back to 2000. Even with that deep dive, the findings showed Mike was a good cop, protecting the public.

I spoke to Eric in the hallway as he left the courtroom. I told him I was disgusted by what they had put him through the last few years. I vowed to never stop until everyone was held accountable for what they had done. I don't know if my words meant anything but they were honest. I knew Mike felt terrible and wanted to speak to Eric but that day was certainly not the time. Eric was collateral damage for the government. To win at all costs they had to disrespect another hero who bravely and heroically served the community. Disgraceful.

After Eric testified, a list of prosecution witnesses took the stand only to read texts and other data into the record. The government never called one person in the federal government who actually worked on the case to testify. NONE! Instead, they called third-party representatives from the government to review and testify to whatever documents had been provided. This meant the defense would not be able to cross-examine any of these people since they had no firsthand knowledge of the case. How can this be legal?! For example, one witness was asked if he had ever been told to query Attorney Shi Ping. The answer was "no." Think about that for a second. You have a possible link to the Chinese government in Attorney Ping but the feds don't query her? If the witness had worked on the case we could have asked, "Why didn't you query Shi Ping?" The answer would be helpful to the defense no matter what the person said. The mere fact the FBI did not look into her association to this case proved the DOJ didn't care about national security or following leads. The only good testimony that came out of these federal witnesses was when they were asked if any knew what "Fox Hunt" or "SKYNET" was they all said, "No." These were active federal agents. The government had drilled into the jury that Mike knew what Fox Hunt and Skynet was in 2016. If these federal employee witnesses and the two federal agents Mike spoke to about this case in 2016 didn't know, how was Mike, a civilian, supposed to know?

The days when the government had documents read into the record were tiresome; some were comical. Such as the day when Craig Heeren and a third-party federal employee read Mike's texts with Eric Gallowitz into the record. The two men would pick which "character" they wanted to play. Their line readings were melodramatic, such as Eric's text, "Bring your gun" (scary line reading for effect). These two wouldn't pass the first round of *America's Got Talent.* As an actor listening to Heeren use inflection to create drama, where none existed, was infuriating and yet another tactic to influence the jury. You can read a line a million different ways but of course Craig made sure every text of Mike and Eric's sounded dirty. This was deliberate to mislead the listener to believe words were crimes.

Every day jurors would stare off into space or fall asleep. It wasn't always the same people sleeping every day. One day I timed a juror sleeping for over thirty minutes during some very important testimony. You are forbidden to wake a juror so I would send a telepathic message to anyone who slept, "WAKE UP! My husband's entire future was on the line! He's looking at years in prison and you are napping?!" Some jurors took notes, some did not. They did seem to be bonding with each other, which we thought was a good thing. One day they came back from a break laughing and smiling. Another day the jurors sent a message to the judge they were having such a good time, they would participate in jury duty again if they could do it together. The judge rolled her eyes at that one. I'm glad they are having so much fun. Mike was barely holding on. This daily assault on him was almost too much to take.

Mikey and Max attended a few times during the trial. I let the children decide if they wanted to come. The boys were adamant they wanted to be there. I could feel the heat of anger coming off of Mikey anytime FBI Agent Bruno walked past us. He muttered the word "evil" just loud enough for him to hear it. Mikey was hoping to be there the day FBI Agent Sean McCarthy was to testify so he could see the weasel who violated our home and family. That day never came. We got word that Agent McCarthy, who had not spent a day in court, was not going to testify. That was odd. How could the arresting officer not testify? He interrogated Mike and was with him for hours the day of the arrest, even offering him his government issued phone to call me and his brother Vinny. Obviously, the government did not want the jury to hear from McCarthy. That was not normal. I think after we accused him of personal bias in our prosecutorial motions the government was not going to let him anywhere near that courtroom. Wise decision.

The day before Greg Finning was supposed to testify for the government, he was called into Brooklyn to be prepped by the prosecutors and FBI Case Agent Christopher Bruno. At that point none of us could still figure out what their plan was. We didn't hear from Greg after that meeting and we were expecting him to take the stand the following day. To our shock, Heeren alerted the court that they would not be calling Greg. What?! After years and years of ignoring and then manipulating Greg, they decided not to call him? What happened in that meeting?? On our way home in the car we called Greg. I told him we heard the government was not going to be calling him. I said now we would definitely need him to testify for us. I strongly believed he would exonerate Mike and possibly be the hero in our story! As I hung up with Greg, I didn't say anything to Mike but I sensed Greg was distant on our call. I'm not sure what the government had said to him but I could tell it wasn't pleasant. If it was adversarial towards him, why was it? What did Greg say in that meeting that ultimately prevented the government from calling him?

By the time we got home there was an email from Larry that Greg was planning on taking the Fifth if we called him to testify. I can't tell you how much that hurt. I could see Mike's disappointment that he would not have a former federal agent and lifelong friend defending him to the jury. Larry and Genna had done an excellent job but we wanted Greg to testify for many reasons. Greg had worked with Mike on the NYPD and been his friend for over thirty years. He would have been a great character witness. Now because of whatever the government said to Greg, he was afraid to testify. The irony is that Greg had worked for years with tremendous success in his career with the federal government. These people were so desperate to win, they were willing to sacrifice Greg, one of their own. A man who served the community while on the NYPD, then the world as a DEA supervisor going after international criminals. Another victim of the DOJ overreach they were willing to throw in the shredder.

Processing this huge loss was devastating but again there was no point in wallowing in self-pity. More witnesses were being called and we needed to prepare. Next on the stand for the government was EDNY Joint Terrorism Task Force Representative John Ross. Ross was present at Mike's interrogation and apparently outside my home the day of the arrest, which until he testified I didn't know. He confirmed he also DID NOT work on the case and only reviewed the facts briefly before the arrest. Again, someone we could not cross-examine. When Larry asked Ross if he felt Mike was "cooperative" in his interrogation he said, "Yes." Sadly the jury would never hear the full hour and a half of that truthful interrogation, only the seven minutes the judge allowed.

For years we were waiting for FBI Case Agent Christopher Bruno to take the stand to defend his case. Up to this point no one who had worked on the case had testified. Were they saving the best and only real witness for last? Bruno sat there every day at the end of the prosecution's table. Some days he would carry boxes for the prosecutors. Other days he would carry that poster filled with a pyramid of pictures of scary looking Chinese men, which included Mike smack in the middle of presumed dangerous Chinese agents. He would just sit there every day as each witness took the stand. His bald head turned red when a witness would perjure themselves and admit to having lied to the FBI (him). Every witness for the government who cooperated perjured themselves multiple times. It had become clear that Mike was literally the only person who had told the truth in this case. Yet, Bruno and Heeren had hedged their bets they could frame their case around an innocent man. If Bruno took the stand and Heeren questioned him it would be a nauseating love fest of ACTUAL coconspirators who chose their egos over the truth. They could cite all their lies as "argument" and continue to punish Mike and our family. It would be hard to take when it happened. But it never did. The prosecution rested having never called the case agent to the stand. Can you imagine? He couldn't take the stand because if he had, then we could question him about his actions. What probable cause did you have to get search warrants on Mike? Why did you trust "Johnny," an admitted Chinese agent and not former and active members of US law enforcement?

Did, during your investigation, you look at Mike's other cases and violate lawyer-client privilege? Why did you let "Johnny" get on the plane back to China with Jin Xu's father in April 2017? You claim the father was "forced" to come to the US by "Johnny's" team which included Tu Lan who you let get away as well. Why didn't you detain "Johnny" at the airport when he was in possession of night vision goggles, which is a federal crime? If "Johnny" committed a crime in April of 2017 as you now allege, why wasn't he arrested when he returned to the US in November of 2017? Why did you let him flee? Was "Johnny" an informant for the FBI? Was translator "Emily" an informant? Why didn't you arrest the gang member in California who provided the address to put the note on the door in the fall of 2018? Why wasn't Attorney Shi Ping ever spoken to until right before trial? Did you ever follow Martha McMahon or the McMahon children? Did Chinese agents ever follow McMahon to his home in New Jersey, thereby putting his family in harm's way on your watch? These questions and so many others would never be answered. We chose not to call Bruno because his track record of lying was a clue he was a risky witness. He had lied for years in this case. There was no doubt he and Heeren would go down fighting.

When all was said and done the government had created a narrative where they took legal PI work and made it appear suspicious if not illegal. According to the government this shows signs of criminality by a licensed PI. These were signs of Mike's criminality presented to the jury.

1. Invoiced his work and documented every hour and dollar
2. Took cash for his job and invoiced that cash
3. Met a client at a Panera Bread (the government claims this is where he is recruited to harass Jin Xu)
4. Met with clients at a law office the day after that Panera Bread meeting with multiple defense attorneys within earshot and security cameras throughout the building documenting it. The government left out this meeting at the law office on the criminal

complaint and many other times. When they do include it they only say it was in a building, not a law office. They had the footage played a thousand times of the Panera Bread meeting, why no footage at the law firm meeting? (We know why.)

5. Notified law enforcement he was armed and doing surveillance every day
6. Hired two former NYPD detectives and they also did surveillance and background checks
7. Spoke to two active federal agents about the case
8. Paid credit card bill with the money he made from this job
9. Put money in other bank accounts that he and wife had access to
10. Did surveillance on a public street
11. Took pictures on a public street
12. Did detailed surveillance reports
13. Invoiced payments to other PIs
14. Did not use encrypted apps, saved every text message and email then transferred all when he purchased a new phone
15. Parked a half a mile away from the main subjects home and was never seen by any of the alleged "victims"

The government lied to the jury and the judge so many times it was hard to keep up. One particularly brazen lie was they told the jury Mike made $19,000 on this case and showed a portion of a spreadsheet with that number on the large screen. When Larry got up to the podium he requested the slide be expanded. What it revealed what was the REAL AMOUNT he walked away with once he paid out his expenses, including to the PIs he had hired. The final number was approximately $11,000 profit. That was even an inflated number at the end of the day. Why was the government doing this? Out of the gate they lied about the photo of Yan Liu, inferring it was taken by Mike the day she allegedly went to the mall. Now they were lying about his finances.

The government had claimed to the judge they would bring witnesses to prove Mike misused the DMV database and an IRS expert to confirm Mike failed to report some money from this case on his taxes. The DMV witness who took the stand was NOT an expert, she only read the documents of Mike's contract into the record so we couldn't cross her about the case. Instead, we presented Mike's original contract, which documented it was perfectly legal for him to run a plate to confirm the information he had been given by his client. No IRS expert ever appeared to testify. Then the promise of testimony of Greg Finning to the judge disappeared. We had to inform the judge Greg was not being called by us as he would be taking the Fifth. The jury had been hearing for weeks that Mike was a tax cheat, abused government databases, used his friends, and was a traitor. The damage was done. They didn't need to bring witnesses, their fairytale had been fulfilled.

I am truly disgusted by government officials in high positions of power such as Craig Heeren and Christopher Bruno. They sent the message to young attorneys and rookie FBI agents who witnessed or participated in this case that what they did was acceptable. Specifically, that convictions overrule exculpatory evidence and if you have to manipulate facts (lie) to do it, no problem. When you cheat to win, that empty victory is more embarrassing than a participation trophy. I'm sure these young and impressionable federal employees didn't dream that their life of service would include perjury and destroying an innocent man. Is that what they were taught in the FBI Academy in Quantico or in law school studying for the bar? I think not. There were so many young faces in that courtroom, witnessing this disgraceful display, or in the case of Attorneys Arfa and Chen, got roped into it late in the game by their superior, Heeren. As someone who mentored young actors my entire life, I took that responsibility seriously. I knew how Elizabeth Hubbard and Lisa Brown took great pride protecting and teaching me to grow into the best of who I could be, not just as an actor but as a person. As a mother it pained me to see the abuse of power and poor leadership being taught to these fledgling minds who will continue to have to make big decisions that could destroy or save lives. I hope this case was a lesson on what not to do for these young people. The saying goes, "People come into your life as a lesson or a blessing." It was up to them to decide which path to follow.

After Larry's fantastic closing argument reminding the jury that the prosecutors failed to prove their case, Heeren got up to the podium for some last licks. Only in federal court does the prosecution get the last word. Heeren continued the lies and added a few more in his final statement which the jury would take with them into deliberations. I was fuming as usual and I just kept shaking my head, "NO," hoping the jury would see me. Would they trust the government and believe this sweaty man before them? Or would they see Mike sitting a few feet away and know he fought this fight because he was strong enough to do it. He was innocent. It was now time to let the jury decide who to believe.

When the judge gave the jury instructions I was not in the courtroom. I was in the hallway with Karen Zraick from *The New York Times* and gave her an interview. I felt it was a good time to do it since all the evidence had been presented. Karen had only been in the courtroom a few times so she missed quite a bit of the case. I wanted to fill her in. When I reentered the courtroom my sister-in-law Eileen was crying. When I asked her why, she told me after hearing the jury instructions she didn't think Mike could win. The instructions made it extremely difficult not to convict all of the defendants since they were all allegedly part of the conspiracy together. Larry had warned us the instructions, as they usually do, favor the prosecution but the final instructions were slightly better than what was originally presented. He had fought successfully to remove some language. The idea that the jury could consider Mike had "consciously avoided" that he was engaging in a crime was ridiculous. How can you avoid a crime when none occurred, despite the government having framed it to appear that way? I was scared to death what could happen next.

Mike's cousin Christine, who had attended several days of the trial, told me there was a basilica a few blocks away from the Brooklyn courthouse. I went by myself and sat in a pew. Daily Mass was just ending with only a few attendees sprinkled throughout this stunning place of worship. As the pastor walked off the altar I stopped him with tears in my eyes. I asked if he had time to speak with me. He said yes and we sat in the front pew. I started to bawl my eyes out. I could barely catch my breath. I told him Mike was an innocent man being torn apart by the justice system just a few blocks away. He had done nothing wrong, that he was a hero who had spent his life committed to others. He asked my name and Mike's name. He proceeded to tell me about the Irish warriors who came to this country and built the church we were sitting in. He said these people were buried on the property. He said they were my ancestors and were with me. Then he pointed to Jesus on the cross. He said, "You know who else was falsely accused? Look what they did to Him." He gave me a beautiful Rosary and prayed for us. He asked me how I felt about the jury. He said he always has concerns about juries being influenced or compromised. I said I wasn't so concerned about that but more so the prosecution making up a story they might believe. He was a kind man. I felt better and filled with God's strength when I left.

The next day, day two of jury deliberations, we got a message to come to the courtroom. We learned one of the jurors had CCP propaganda placed on her door. It contained images of Chinese people being abused and jailed. Judge Chen called the juror in to ask her some questions. She said she did not live in a Chinese neighborhood so she thought it was odd to get this on her door. Two of her neighbors also got the same. Judge Chen asked if she had discussed this with the other jurors and she said she had not. When asked if she felt scared or concerned she said, no because she had neighbors who were cops. We had a decision to make. We could remove her as a juror, request a mistrial or keep her. We ultimately decided to keep her since she said she felt safe because her neighbors were cops. I wonder to this day if the FBI vouchered that evidence and took fingerprints. Did they speak to her neighbors? Was any investigation even opened? I doubt it. I hope to one day find out who did it and at whose direction.

The jury never asked for any read-backs of any witness testimony. That was a good sign to me. I felt like we were successful in negating every piece of evidence presented, every false narrative, with common sense and I believed the end of our nightmare was in sight. We had to break on a Friday for the weekend, which was very upsetting. I was sitting on a bench and Mike was standing. We saw the jurors exiting. A redheaded woman saw us and said to the man with her, "Awkward." Mike heard it too. He said he felt he was going to be found guilty when he heard her say that. It took everything in me not to follow her and tell her she had been lied to. I felt helpless but I didn't give up on Mike. We only needed one person to say NOT GUILTY. To find him guilty all twelve jurors would have to agree. As we got to day three we got word there was a verdict. I can't tell you the anxiety we were all feeling. Mikey sat next to me and the room was filled with dozens of family members, FBI honchos, US attorneys, and the press. As the jury entered they were very somber as they took their seats. Mike was the first defendant whose verdict was read. Count one, conspiring to violate FARA, NOT GUILTY. With that the entire galley of our friends and family exhaled and relieved. Count two, violating FARA, GUILTY. Oh my God. Count three, conspiracy to commit interstate stalking, GUILTY. Count four, interstate stalking, GUILTY. I put my head in my hands and I felt Mikey start to rub my back. What just happened? I looked at the jury and just shook my head. There was a juror in the front row who stared at me. I just kept shaking my head. I saw Mike shaking his head no and looking at the jury. Zheng, who put the note on the door, was found guilty of conspiracy to commit interstate stalking and interstate stalking. Jason was found guilty of all four counts.

The jury was dismissed and we were left standing in front of the judge. The marshals had been called in prior to the verdict in case the judge decided to remand the defendants to prison right then and there. Thankfully she did not put Mike in cuffs. Larry told the judge immediately we would be filing post-trial motions. Mike was free to go. I walked out into the hallway and let loose. *The New York Times* reporter was recording me. Our friends and family lined the hallway as I went on a tirade. I confronted Karen Zraick, *The New*

York Times writer about the video of Christopher Bruno from the airport making sure "Johnny" didn't miss his flight back to China. The FBI had let Chinese criminals flee, that Mike was a hero, and this was a travesty of justice all around from start to finish. I was in shock. These people had gotten their big win. But did they? Was it really a case that resulted in taking dangerous criminals off the street to protect Americans from foreign adversaries? No. As I finished my tirade the people in the hallway broke into applause. Not because I was saying something worth cheering, quite the opposite. Many had witnessed what I had in that courtroom. A rigged system against an innocent man.

As we walked out to the street Mike and Larry spoke to the press. Larry was very upset and it showed. Genna was in tears. She knew Mike was innocent and she had worked so hard helping us. Larry and Genna took this case personally. We could feel their love and support from the beginning. Larry reminded us Mike was found NOT GUILTY on the biggest charge and we would continue to fight the other GUILTY verdicts with case law which was on our side.

We all gathered outside not able to bring ourselves to leave. When the prosecution team exited they were heckled by our family. I had no problem with that. They were the most hated people on the planet by all of us who loved Mike. There were no winners that day. What Heeren and Bruno had done was a disgrace to the justice system. The war was to be continued.

I don't remember the ride home but I had to call Max and tell him. He took the news well under the circumstances. Thankfully Ann Marie hadn't seen the news on television so I could tell her in person. I told her Mike was not going to prison, we would continue to fight this as long as it took.

I walked into the living room and Mike was crying. He just kept repeating, "I didn't do anything wrong.... I didn't do anything wrong...." He hadn't done anything wrong. He was maliciously prosecuted and beaten daily by a DOJ with too much time and money at their disposal. How could I fix this? Where do I start? Larry and

Genna would be diving into post-trial motions so I didn't expect to hear from them for a while.

I made the mistake of looking online at the media coverage surrounding the case and the verdict. It was extremely painful to see Mike's picture and the "guilty" written next to his handsome face. What have they done to this man? How could they justify what they had put us all through? The media was parroting the prosecutors' talking points but not telling the real story. No one had reported what happened in that courtroom. Why not? There was one headline in *The New York Times* that said the men were guilty of harassing "United States citizens." Really, *New York Times*? After someone called them out on the headline they changed to "people living in the United States." No one seemed to care who these "people" were and the crimes they had been accused of. Who was pulling the strings with the media? My interview with Karen was nowhere to be found. No one cared about the truth. My voice and Mike's innocence, didn't count—that was quite clear.

The next day I was completely drained and shell shocked. I felt extremely tired and decided to take a nap. I managed to fall asleep but forgot to turn off my ringer. My phone rang and the caller ID showed an unknown number. I never answer those and I let it go to voicemail. I listened to the message. It was from *New York Post* reporter Isabel Vincent. The same writer who had written the story about Bo Dietl. I called her right back. She asked if Mike would be willing to speak with her. She felt Mike had been scapegoated and wanted to tell his story. They would come to the house with a photographer and do the interview in person. After we asked Larry if it was OK and he said yes, I scheduled her to come to our home the next day. Our story was about to go in a direction that would make the government doubt whether this entire case was ever worth bringing in the first place.

CHAPTER FIFTEEN

OUR INTERVIEW WITH THE *NEW YORK POST* investigative reporter, Isabel Vincent, went great. She had a deep understanding about Fox Hunt and her overview was that Mike had been scapegoated. The headline read, "Former NYC sergeant says the FBI scapegoated him in China spying scandal." The article was the first one that highlighted the civil lawsuit against Jin Xu. I hoped the jurors who had just wrongly convicted Mike read it and learned they were duped. After the pain of the trial, I was happy for Mike and my children that someone in the media was finally telling the truth. After the verdict, the media regurgitated the one-sided talking points fed to them by the EDNY. Not one outlet wrote about his incredible career while on the NYPD, yet they were more than happy to highlight that he was a decorated cop just to inflict outrage in the story that he was a traitor to the country. This take was not only false, it was dangerous to my family. But that was never considered. It was all about the clicks. Who was dictating the exact same narrative across all media outlets? I always suspected the government was the puppet master from the beginning of this case. Now, having lived through it for a few years, I had a list and pattern of the people behind all of it.

One person I had reached out to was Aruna Viswanatha from *The Wall Street Journal*. As the writer of the original article about the civil lawfare against Jin Xu I believed she would be a great person to connect with to get the truth on the record. We had a great talk on the phone then I sent her all the documents from the civil lawsuit and the EB-5 fraud case. After that initial phone call and my emails, I never heard from Aruna again. Why would she blow me off? I know these publications have editors who dictate stories, so maybe they weren't interested in this topic any longer. Or was it something else?

I went back and researched John Demers, the assistant AG of National Security again. He had led the press conference announcement of Mike's arrest. Just a few weeks after that in November 2020, he spoke at the Aspen Institute, an organization that brings a wide range of leaders together for topical discussions, most often political. When Demers spoke that day the topic was "Assessing the China Initiative" and the moderator happened to be none other than Aruna Viswanatha. Interesting. Was it just a coincidence she was the moderator as well as the writer who wrote Jin Xu and Fang Liu were "victims" of civil lawfare by the CCP earlier that year? The interview wasn't earth-shattering but the information I learned about the Aspen Institute was eye-opening.

In April of 2022 the shocking behind-the-scenes relationship between the DOJ and the media was exposed when Elon Musk bought Twitter and released the Twitter Files. The revelations were minimally covered by a complicit press. On December 21, 2022, the *New York Post* published an explosive article entitled "What is the mysterious Aspen Institute and why did it hold a Hunter Biden exercise?" It detailed how in September of 2022 they conducted scenarios on how the media should handle the laptop. One game was called, "Aspen Digital Hack-and-Dump Working Group." In October 2020, the same month Mike was arrested, the media's cloak-and-dagger plan was executed to keep the American public in the dark about the laptop.

The Twitter Files in 2022 exposed that under Jack Dorsey (the previous owner of Twitter), the *New York Post* had been blocked from tweeting the exclusive article about the contents of the laptop. Not only that, Facebook and Twitter were not allowing users through direct messaging to share the article publicly OR PRIVATELY. Even Kayleigh McEnany, Trump's press secretary, was unable to share the article on a Twitter private direct message. That suggested someone (FBI) had access to an account on President Trump's team.

The fix was in! Secretary of State Antony Blinken managed to get fifty-one former and current intelligence officers to sign a letter saying the Hunter laptop was Russian disinformation. Blinken's move allowed Joe Biden to quote that letter during his debate with Trump. The relationship between the government and the media had become more incestuous than ever over their mutual hatred of Trump. That was it. It was exposed in the Twitter Files that the FBI under Christopher Wray had pressured Twitter and other media platforms to censor info about the laptop and about COVID.

The relationship between the government and the media had become more aligned than ever over their mutual hatred of Trump. An election was coming and it would behoove Director Wray and others working on his backroom misdeeds to get Biden into office to protect his job as director of the FBI. If Trump got a second term it would be problematic for everyone who had participated in the censoring and influencing of the American citizens through the media. If Biden won Wray and many others would remain safe to continue their heavy-handed overreach under Merrick Garland. The FBI was on shaky ground leading into the election. How could Wray convince Trump to keep him in charge? What could Wray do to stop Trump from firing him?

Trump had publicly complained that the United States (FBI/DOJ) hadn't done enough about China. If Wray could prove the FBI was tough on China maybe that would secure his future. Was Mike's arrest part of the Hunter laptop distraction campaign? I may never know. There was never a valid explanation why Mike was arrested just one week before the election. All the main players had already fled to China yet the FBI had many opportunities over the years to arrest them before Mike's arrest on October 28, 2020. Was our case a rush job? It sure felt like it. The FBI managed to round up some low hanging fruit to put a story together. Mike was the only person arrested who would garner any real publicity. The "China Muscle" *New York Post* article with a full-page photo of Mike was a major clue it was all for show and Mike was the star. I also found open letters dated October 28, 2020, from the FBI Agents Association (FBIAA) to both Biden and Trump. The organization was made up of fourteen thousand active and former FBI special agents. The letters were an over-the-top love fest about Wray and how it was vital to the safety of our citizens for him to remain director of the FBI. Secretary of State Mike Pompeo sent out a press release the same day stating the United States was "discontinuing participation in the Memorandum of Understanding between the Government of the United States of America and the Government of the People's Republic of China Concerning the Establishment of the U.S-China Governors Forum to Promote Sub-National Cooperation (MOU), signed on January 19, 2011." It was a slap on the wrist to China for attempting to influence governors and other local leaders in the US. It was all for show and Pompeo knew it! So why was it done on THAT DAY? There was a high-level, coordinated effort on October 28, 2020. How many agencies were involved? I found a clue that seemed way too coincidental not to be connected.

In 2022 *The New York Times* did a FOIA (Freedom of Information Act) request surrounding the use of illegal spyware, Pegasus, by the FBI. The FOIA information revealed that on October 28, 2020, there was a meeting with FBI Intelligence about information obtained though this software. This spyware was housed in a warehouse in New Jersey (after Mike was arrested he was brought to a warehouse in New Jersey). The FOIA documents listed countless emails back and forth between federal agents, all who worked in foreign and domestic intelligence. Months earlier a representative from the FBI and Wray testified in front of Congress about this spyware, which was purchased from Israel for $5 million. They claimed it had only been "tested" internally.

Now there was evidence it had been used in a criminal case, possibly Mike's case. This posed a major problem for the FBI, if true. If they had illegally spied on Mike, the case would have to be thrown out. I had no proof it was used on Mike, but the circumstantial evidence was quite compelling.

Armed with this information, I decided to review the press conference of Mike's arrest from October of 2020. If my theory was true, National Intelligence (Demers) and the FBI (Wray) would benefit the most from an arrest involving a China case with international ties. When I played the video of the press conference, which I hadn't watched since the arrest, I was blown away by what I heard. With the trial over and years having passed since the arrest, the press conference made more sense now that I had years of knowledge under my belt. Demers made a very interesting statement about the targets of Fox Hunt in our case. He said, "...that while some individuals are legitimately sought for criminal activity, although in an illegitimate way, others, in fact, are dissidents, critics, rivals of the Chinese General Secretary." He can only be referring to Jin Xu and Fang Liu. They were the only alleged "victims" Demers discussed in the press conference. By saying they could be involved in "criminal activity," it covers him if any media, not controlled by the government, reports on the case and actually does any research on the "victims."

Then Seth DuCharme, the acting head of the EDNY, said the private investigator (Mike) was "hired to surveil." I didn't hear anything about Mike being part of the Chinese government's organized Fox Hunt team. He made Mike sound like an unwitting participant, which he was. They knew he did nothing illegal but that didn't matter. They had a mission and Mike was sacrificed.

When the floor was opened to questions, the first person called on by Demers was Aruna Viswanatha from *The Wall Street Journal*. Holy smokes! She asked, "Have you seen an escalation in this trend of harassment efforts over the past year or two? Or what kind of change have you seen? Are they being more aggressive about targeting these people? Our understanding is there are at least two dozen sort of publicly identified targets in the US."

There were two things about that question that stood out to me. First, since Aruna was the writer of the article about the CCP using civil lawfare to harass Chinese dissidents in the US and featured the "victims," Jin Xu and Fang Liu in the Fox Hunt case, accompanied by their photographs, why didn't she reference that fact, her own work, in her question? Secondly, who are these "two dozen sort of publicly identified targets in the US"? Where was she getting that information from?

Demers made sure he referred to the "victims" as John and Jane Doe One to protect their identity. By the end of the day when Aruna wrote her piece about Mike's arrest, she included photos of Jin Xu and Fang Liu and a link to her original story from July 29, 2020, about the civil lawsuit. Why would she do that? Was it a preemptive strike to make it appear that the "victims" were not just Fox Hunt targets but also "victims" of civil lawfare? Finding any other media about the civil lawsuit or any of the alleged crimes committed by the couple is virtually impossible. Mike was to be the story all over the world and that was that.

Next Nick Schifrin from PBS asked a great question. He asked if the Chinese agents came to the US under their real names on their visa applications. DuCharme changed the direction in his answer and focused on the people charged who were here in the US legally. We now know why. If he were to be truthful he would have to admit the following. Yes, dozens of Chinese police came to the US starting as early as 2012 under their real names and, by the way, at the invite of the United States. Not a good look.

Associated Press writer, Eric Tucker asked why the CCP wanted the "victims" returned to China. Demers could not answer that one honestly because the "victims" were wanted fugitives accused of embezzlement and bribery. Also the victims were members of the CCP, one highly ranked having held several high-level positions, including in Wuhan, China. This was the first Fox Hunt case ever taken down and the government only took four questions. To this day they have never answered or addressed the real concerns about these Chinese operations.

Aruna Viswanatha clearly had a relationship of some sort with Demers. I decided to email Aruna again and inquire about the nature of their connection. I have yet to hear back. I looked deeper into the writers that I felt were more biased than others when it came to Mike's case. I found an article on NJ.com written by Craig McCarthy, the writer of the original *New York Post* article who called Mike "China Muscle," and to my surprise (not really), the Newark FBI media representative Robert Reilly was quoted in it. Could it be the same Robert Reilly who I learned at trial had been communicating with "victims" Jin Xu, Fang Liu, their daughter Xinxi Xu, and Yan Liu about their immigration and the civil lawsuit? If it is the same Robert Reilly, did he call his old buddy now covering the NYPD at the *New York Post* to write the hit piece about Mike the day he was arrested? I believe he did. Craig McCarthy has never returned any of my emails either. Another disturbing question was why was Robert Reilly, in charge of media relations for the FBI, anywhere near a case involving national security? There was no doubt the media was compromised in our case. I wish the aforementioned examples were isolated incidents, but they are not.

Writer Isabel Vincent is a rarity in the media. She is an excellent investigative reporter who is great at her job. The article she wrote about Mike was the impetus of other outlets having me and Mike on to discuss the case. Greg Kelly from Newsmax interviewed both Mike and I together. Mike was on CNN with Jim Acosta, who did a great and fair interview. I've done more than forty podcasts and appearances on OAN, ABC News, Dinesh D'Souza, and countless others. The narrative was flipping to our side and the DOJ was not happy. Isabel's article was the start of their displeasure. From what I understand they were upset they were not asked to comment on the *New York Post* article. Too bad. Up to that point they controlled how this was covered and now they were pissed. I rode the wave of change and went full tilt on Twitter, calling out the prosecutors and the entire justice system. I tweeted about the New Jersey reporter who wouldn't update his story with the information I had provided due to his relationship with the FBI.

Two days after that tweet our lawyer got a letter from Craig Heeren and National Security representative Matt Olsen about my tweet. They wanted to know who from the press I had spoken to and what documents I had provided to the reporter. They reminded me I was under a protective order and if I shared anything sensitive I had to tell the government what it was. I did not and would not share any sensitive information. That would be against the law. Who knows? Maybe they were so used to leaking to the press themselves they thought everyone did it. I was sick to my stomach that I was now being targeted by these people. Of course I would never jeopardize Mike's freedom and share sensitive information. I had no problem telling the government what I had provided to the reporter because it showed their incompetence. It was my summary of the case, the FBI bulletin that had been released the week after Mike's arrest and the local law enforcement contacts I had spoken to in New Jersey. I would not tell them who the reporter was I had spoken to. It was none of their business. They were trying to bully me into silence and it worked. For two days. Then I was angrier than ever that my First Amendment rights were challenged by these evil, gutless people. They didn't like what I was saying about them so they tried to shut me up. Too bad. I had been in the media business my entire life. I was appalled at how dishonest and compromised it had become. I was grateful for the brave people who pushed back against it but the days of media integrity had been sacrificed to the DC cabal.

I've never had any issue with the press. *The New York Times* and *People* magazine had covered our wedding. I was a frequent guest on national and local news during my career. Every birth of our children was covered with beautiful photo shoots and stories of balancing motherhood and soap life. Every milestone of my life had been covered by the press. I have a closet filled with clippings and archived

VHS tapes, which I treasure. I had been so fortunate to have a positive relationship with the press for decades.

That all changed when Mike was falsely arrested. Before Mike returned from being processed the *New York Post* had "broken" the story online. Photos of the two of us were splattered on the page. The article was written by three people, including the aforementioned Craig McCarthy. There was no mention of his incredible career as an NYPD hero in the article, only he was former NYPD. The details of his career were deliberately left out to paint him in a bad light. Those pesky facts about his heroism and stellar career as a private investigator got in the way of the narrative. The *New York Post* is one of the most read papers in the world. In an instant our lives were dismantled due to lack of journalistic integrity. My family was a victim of "fake news" and blindsided from a literary firing squad.

Over the last four years my education on the press has been riddled with disappointment and optimism. Finding journalists who aren't afraid to tell the truth is not easy. I don't think it's because they don't WANT to tell the truth. They have been put in a position that they cannot. As I said, I don't comment about any subject unless I've lived it. You can't deny someone their lived experiences. The media's spiral into propaganda was painful to witness as an American citizen prior to Mike's arrest but then it hit my home directly.

After Twitter exposed the truth about the media the press has no one to blame but themselves for how they are now viewed. The relationship between the media and the government started out as mutually beneficial. Like the street drug dealer who marks the victim offering, "The first one's on me." This freebie creates a lifelong customer until they die a shell of their former selves. Short-term customers with a revolving door of new ones ready to replace the forgotten corpses. The media fell victim to similar predators: government and politics. Not all members of government or politicians are bedfellows with the press. You only need a few powerful leaders in a myriad of positions. If you're a journalist and get a call from someone who is a "get" you take that call! Of course you do! This could be a big break and a new fancy contact to build your journalism career. It's good business! It's what every journalist strives for: connections. For the journalists these relationships start with good intentions. The addict doesn't have a crystal ball when they take that first hit. They think they can manage and control the demons lurking in the dark ready to cannibalize their souls. When they realize they were prey it's too late. So what's the pattern?

That first call to a journalist disguises itself as purposeful. Get some quotes out there to diffuse a major event such as a pattern of cyberattacks or a shooting in the subway. The journalist is now "in" with the office of a particular official. The honeymoon phase begins and the journalist feels validated. The officials do this to hundreds of outlets so don't think these targets are chosen ones. They're not. The officials will delete their contact info faster than a convicted pervert clears his browser history. They build a go-to slam dunk list of people who will do their bidding. How do they decide who gets the roses on Valentine's Day and who gets ghosted? That's the easy part. They feed the journalist the info and if it's reported without a counterbalanced point of view, these are their people. If they stray from this type of reporting they are cut off. Period. I saw it firsthand during Mike's trial. I was truly shocked how little of the truth made it to print or on the airwaves. It was on full display daily in the courtroom yet no one would print it. The journalists would pop in for an hour then head back to the newsroom next to the snack shop in the lobby. No one ever asked me or any of the witnesses questions unless I initiated it. My quotes never made it to print and my efforts to get the full story out were repeatedly disregarded. How could the media just turn a blind eye to what was happening? Huge revelations occurred in that courtroom which directly affected our national security and no one seemed to care.

The ones truly suffering other than us, were the public who were being fed half-truths. It was terrifying; it still is. The media seemed to be against my family and wouldn't pivot when the facts challenged their dictated position. It's frightening. It's dangerous. The media is in a politically induced coma. If I didn't experience it myself I may have been one of the many fooled by the "fake news."

I knew Trump was the most vilified figure by the media. Mike was also vilified but obviously nowhere on the same scale. When the cases against Trump started to pile up I couldn't help but recognize the similarity to what happened to Mike. Cases created out of thin air for political purposes. Trump was arrested and his mug shot taken. The media ate it up and leaned into the nonsense charges. In New York Letitia James campaigned on "getting Trump" and was creating a case based on nothing. The judges were changing the rules to assure convictions. This was NUTS! I knew exactly what was going on, having lived through it. This was scary for our country's future. If they could do this to the president of the United States and a hero like Mike, no one was safe. The media had it out for Trump and never questioned the actions of the prosecutors. There was only one side of the story dictated by the DC DOJ.

Many people pointed out that Mike had been arrested by Trump's DOJ. That was true but those exact same people had spied on Trump. James Comey, who was the FBI director when Trump took office, bragged about taking advantage of Trump's lack of political experience. These were dangerous and calculating people who liked the status quo and Trump was turning it on its head.

I believe Mike was taken down in a China optics case used as a shiny object to bolster Wray, Pompeo, and William Barr and distract from Hunter's laptop. That laptop was riddled with proof of millions of dollars in Chinese payoffs to Hunter and Joe Biden ("The Big Guy"). Our family held no value to the DOJ; we were disposable but we weren't unique. When Merrick Garland and Wray's FBI raided Mar-a-Lago and went through Barron and Melania Trump's closets, they didn't care about the Trump family either. Why should I think we would be treated better than the former president and his family? I was angry the Trump family had been violated. I know how they felt. I was completely disheartened where our country was but I was willing to fight for it. The Lord was with us. I knew it and held on to my blind trust we would get through it.

When Larry filed our post-trial motions, which brilliantly called out every single example of the prosecution not proving its case, I felt a renewed energy. Our ship had taken on water but I could feel the tides changing in our favor. When Mike was first arrested we were an island and now it felt like the world was starting to learn how corrupt the justice system was due to a man with a red hat who loved this country. When he turned his head to the right the moment a bullet was supposed to kill him, I knew God had plans for this man. As he got up and raised his fist in the air saying, "Fight! Fight! Fight!" I heard it loud and clear. If he was brave enough to take a bullet for this country, we needed to be brave enough to continue our own fight.

Our lives had been merging with warriors who would ultimately fight with us and for us. God had moved the chess pieces into place and was about to reveal exactly what His plan was for us. We had come this far and would not back down. We needed to build our army to finish the job. Who came in to walk beside us absolutely blew Mike and I away. My friend has a saying, "Coincidences are God's way of remaining anonymous." Over the last four years He had been busy and was about to reveal what may be His final chapter to our story.

CHAPTER SIXTEEN

I HAVE NEVER BEEN A POLITICAL PERSON in my life. My understanding of government was minimal until Mike's arrest. I was discouraged early on that trying to get politicians to help us was a waste of time. I was never one to listen to people's opinions. I liked to personally learn what was possible, not be told what is or what is not. As a person of faith I believe that every person who comes into your life is part of God's plan. We all have free will to decide whether to take steps without knowing if it will be worth it or not. From the day this happened to my family I asked God to keep me on track. I wanted to avoid going down rabbit holes that would take time away from getting real answers. I followed every lead but how would I know if a person came into my life was there to help us or to hurt us? I relied on blind faith. I surrendered to God's plan and went all in.

Immediately after Mike's arrest I received an email from actress Kimberlin Brown. Kimberlin played the role of Sheila Carter on the soap opera *The Bold and The Beautiful* for decades. I was not only a fan of her work, but I also thought very highly of her as a person. In 2108 she had run as a Republican for a congressional seat in California and lost. I didn't keep up with her political path but it turned out she was still very much involved with the Republican Party. She sent me an email with just a few lines checking up on me. I responded with my phone number and we had a great conversation. Kimberlin connected me with several members of Congress. I was extremely grateful that I was able to tell our story to people who took time to listen. I felt like I was being proactive but I really wasn't sure what I was looking for from these politicians. I didn't understand the political process at all. I would send emails to members of Congress on the China committees, Republicans and Democrats alike. I never heard back from any of those emails. Since I was not a constituent there was no incentive to respond and work for my vote. Though I was a lifelong Jersey girl, my representatives in Congress Josh Gottheimer (D), Chris Smith (R), and Senator Cory Booker (D) never got back to me either. I was never deterred. I looked at this process like an audition. I went on thousands of auditions and only booked less than 2 percent of them. I didn't quit despite those dismal odds. I had a goal to succeed. That's how I'm wired. I knew there was a political avenue worth pursuing to help us but I had to learn on the job.

In the fall of 2022 the midterm elections were coming up. Mike's brother Vinny wanted to hold a fundraiser at the Pearl River Elks Lodge in Pearl River, New York, to raise money for our defense. Mike was against it but Vinny insisted. Andrea and Eddie Gallagher, the founders of the Pipe Hitter Foundation, said they would fly up from Florida to attend. That was so kind of them. They had been steadfast in their support and we were so humbled. The venue held over four hundred people and our friends and family were happy to attend and support us. The day of the event Vinny came in with a lawn sign that read Mike Lawler for Congress and put it by the entrance. Vinny had gone by Lawler's office earlier in the day, made a donation to his campaign, and invited Lawler to attend. Pearl River was one of Lawler's districts where many members of the NYPD and FDNY live.

The event was attended by friends and family but many members of the Elks Lodge as well. The majority of that particular Elks Lodge are active and former law enforcement. The brotherhood was there in full force. Mike and I were blown away by the support. Cops and firemen filled the room. The former head of the New York Joint Terrorism Task Force was there as well. That was quite a statement. Most federal agents, current or former, would steer clear of Mike due to what he had been charged with. All who showed up knew there had been a great injustice done to us.

Mike Lawler showed up and spoke to Mike, with Mike quickly telling him about what happened. Lawler made a promise that he would help us if elected to Congress. Mike said he felt Lawler meant what he said. We just needed him to get elected. Sure enough, he was elected on November 5, 2022. The day after he was elected he made an appearance on Fox News. I was thrilled. It gave me hope that we may have someone in our corner. I wasn't even sure what that meant but I knew it was a good thing. How could he actually help us? We found out fairly quickly. As promised, he met Mike and I for coffee a few days after the election. He was genuinely outraged by what had happened. Armed with our story and a million other things on his plate, he went off to DC with our blessing. Literally.

Our next political advocate came in a way that can only be called a miracle. My sister-in-law Eileen went on a cruise to the Bahamas in 2022. At the first dinner seating a woman named Shirley came rushing in and took the only seat open, which happened to be next to Eileen. Shirley told Eileen she was delayed coming to dinner because her heel got stuck in the escalator and had broken off. She had to go back to her room to get a new pair of shoes. If she had been on time who knows if the two would have sat next to each other.

As the two spoke, Eileen learned Shirley Maia-Cusick was from New Jersey and running for Bob Menendez's Senate seat, which was coming up for election. Eileen couldn't believe it. She shared Mike's story with her and Shirley promised to help us. Over the next week during the cruise Shirley and Eileen became quite close. She told Eileen about an event being held at Trump National Golf Club Bedminster in New Jersey that Mike and I should attend. The event would be attended by a "who's who" of New Jersey politicians who could be helpful to our case. Eileen bought four tickets for us to attend together. There were several speakers at the event that night including Cynthia Hughes. Cynthia is the founder of the Patriot Freedom Project, an organization that raises money for the January 6 defendants and their families. She is a force of nature and when I heard her speak I was blown away. I could sense she was carrying the weight of the world on her shoulders but rising up to help so many. That night she was the person everyone wanted to speak to. We were briefly introduced and that was it. We connected via phone after that night and after hearing our story she said, "You have to meet Ed." Who was Ed? Ed Martin is the president of the Phyllis Schlafly Eagles, which is a Republican pro-life, pro-family organization. Phyllis Schlafly was a pioneer in Republican politics. She was instrumental in several presidential campaigns including her final endorsement of Donald Trump shortly before her death. Phyllis was a devout Catholic and unapologetically pro-life. The next thing I knew I was on a train to DC with Cynthia Hughes to meet Ed Martin at the Schlafly Eagles headquarters just minutes from the Capitol.

Ed and I hit it off right away. His energy reminded me of that electric feeling I felt in a room full of creative collaborators. People who turn ideas into action speak my language and Ed was fluent in it. He had a million questions about what I did for a living and I for him. On our walk to the Capitol for meetings we were met on a corner by Jeffrey Clark. Jeff had been part of Trump's original administration in the DOJ. First he was the attorney general for Department of Agriculture then Trump appointed him as acting attorney general of the United States. Jeff was one of many arrested in the Fani Willis Georgia election case in 2023. Jeff was falsely arrested for election interference. The former AG was pulled outside his home in his underwear and humiliated in front of neighbors and the world. He was not arrested that day, only served a search warrant. There was no reason to bring him outside in his underwear. True to fashion, the body cam footage of his arrest was released to the public. Jeff committed no crime, he was acting in the capacity of counsel for the president. He was arrested for a draft letter regarding potential election fraud in Georgia, which was never sent. That was his "crime." In Jeff I immediately felt we were both a part of a club no one ever wants to join.

My initial introduction to Jeff on our walk to the Rayburn Building in DC was brief. I got to share how I thought Richard Donoghue was part of our case. I knew Donoghue had testified before the January 6 committee against Trump and was not a fan of Jeffrey Clark. A common thread we shared. Jeff and I parted ways and I followed Cynthia and Ed taking in the sites of downtown DC with the landscape of the White House and Capitol which made me pause in awe. I hadn't seen these landmarks since I was a child. I have to admit I was overwhelmed by the pulse of the city and the power behind every window. It was almost too much to grasp that my husband had been sacrificed by people who had completely forgotten what our Founding Fathers had fought for. How did it all go so wrong? While I was in DC the enormity of what I was up against hit me hard. At the same time I recognized how important the fight had become, not just for our family but the entire country. I felt a tremendous responsibility to never give up on this fight. Then another person entered the picture.

While I was on Twitter I saw that Ed Martin had tweeted a comment from a man named Michael Caputo. When I looked at Michael's profile I saw that he had worked in the first Trump administration. There was a pinned article about him on his Twitter page, which I read with great interest. He was diagnosed with cancer while working in the White House and his outlook wasn't good. While he was suffering with the disease he had his home address in Buffalo, New York, doxxed by Antifa. It was incredibly traumatizing for his children at the time and there were constant threats to him and his family. Antifa would show up at his home and cause havoc. His only "crime" was working for Donald Trump. He explained in the article that on his final day of treatment he had a vision of his family while in the radiation machine. He was always Catholic but that vision started him on a journey even he never expected. I loved the story how his Catholic faith was so interwoven in his life.

I decided to follow him on Twitter. Within a few minutes I checked his Twitter page and there was a HUGE picture of…ME! He tweeted that he was a fan of mine and called me "hot." The picture he posted was an old one but one of my favorites. Michael started following me on Twitter so I could send him a private message. I told him Mike's story and he was horrified. We ended up speaking on the phone for over an hour and I told him how I was visited by the Blessed Mother. How my Catholic faith was getting me through this hell. Caputo had recently joined the 2024 Trump reelection campaign when we spoke and saw the parallels of what happened to Mike and Trump were undeniable. He invited Mike and me to Florida to stay with him, complete strangers. He scheduled a Mass to bless Mike and wanted to host an open house dinner at his home. Mike's uncle Joe who had been recently hospitalized and some cousins lived in Florida and would all hopefully be able to attend the Mass and Caputo was happy to welcome them. We had to get permission from the court to make the trip and give details about who we were seeing and where we would be staying. When Michael Caputo told me where the Mass was to be held I almost cried. Ave Maria Church in Ave Maria, Florida. Ave Maria was a town built to honor the Blessed Mother. People from around the world pilgrimage there to honor her. The residents are devout Catholics and the community is woven with devotion to the faith. I had never heard of Ave Maria before but I recognized the Blessed Mother had put me right where I needed to be with this powerful sign.

We had a beautiful trip to Florida. Caputo had invited the pastor of the Ave Maria church who had said the Mass for Mike. There were other scholars and neighbors who showed up to support us. At the end of the night everyone prayed over us. Mike said he could feel the spirit move through him. That was so powerful. I knew he was struggling after the trial and this overwhelming love from complete strangers was a true blessing. At the time of our visit the judge was reviewing our post-trial motions to possibly overturn the verdict. We needed all the prayers we could get.

The post-trial motion response from the government under the judge's review was shocking. They admitted to misleading the jury (lying) but claimed under the law they can infer something or call it a plain error. That was ridiculous. They had lied to the jury and the judge. How would she take this version of events from the prosecution? Would she be angry they had deceived her or was that just part of the game and she would allow it. As we waited for her answer something horrible happened in DC.

I got a text from a writer that the Committee on China was having a hearing on the Hill to draw attention to Chinese influence in the United States. This committee didn't create policy, only awareness. This session called witnesses to share stories about CCP harassment. The witnesses were political dissidents who had suffered actual harassment. Then Raja Krishnamoorthi (D) put up a GIGANTIC picture of Mike in his NYPD uniform and proceeded to completely destroy him! He accused Mike of harassing Chinese people to line his pockets. It was DISGUSTING! I lost my mind. I went to Mike's office in our house and starting making calls. First was to Raja's office in DC. When someone answered I said who I was and why I was calling. Then I started screaming. I have NEVER yelled like that in my life. "WE ARE WAITING ON A RULING FROM THE JUDGE TO OVERTURN THE VERDICT!! HE WAS FOUND NOT GUILTY ON COUNT ONE!! WHAT THE HELL IS RAJA DOING?!" The woman on the phone transferred me to someone else. I started screaming at THAT person. "MY HUSBAND COMMITTED NO CRIME!! WHO DOES YOUR RESEARCH?!" I said, "I WANT THAT POSTER OF MY HUSBAND! HOW DARE YOU!!" "SAVE THAT POSTER I'M COMING TO GET IT! MY TAX DOLLARS PAID FOR IT!!" That person put me in touch with the head of the Republican side of the China Committee. He told me the Democrat side does their own research separate from the Republicans. I chastised him for the committee not cross-checking their research; this is someone's life. Raja has now reminded the world the US government thinks he is a TRAITOR. "DO YOU HAVE ANY IDEA HOW

DANGEROUS THIS IS?! I HAVE CHILDREN!!" He promised to get back to me. He never did. I was particularly upset with Mike Gallagher, the Republican Head of the China Committee. Republican Congressman Mike Lawler had tried to schedule a meeting for me with Gallagher but he declined. Apparently he believed what the Democrats were spewing about Mike. How can you claim to care about the safety of US citizens and not want to hear our story? A few weeks after he declined to meet me, Mike Gallagher unceremoniously resigned from Congress. The rumblings were that he was involved in a sketchy partnership with Alejandro Mayorkas (head of Homeland Security) surrounding racehorses. Who knows what is true anymore. The optics were that Gallagher was on the fast track to a great political career but then disappeared. That was the truth.

A few weeks later I found myself in DC again and decided to head over to Raja's office. When I walked in I explained to the woman at the front desk who I was. She told me to have a seat and wait for Raja's chief of staff. I was sure I would never meet her but I was wrong. She told me they had destroyed the poster. I remained calm, not wanting to make a scene. I apologized for yelling at the staff but I was very upset. I told her we were waiting on a ruling from the judge to overturn the case and now Raja's actions put that in jeopardy. Mike had not been sentenced yet, so the case was still being adjudicated. She said she understood and apologized. I left her with this. I am a wife and a mother who loves this country. I said, "Mike and I are on YOUR SIDE. We want to HELP and he's been treated like the enemy. We are NOT THE ENEMY." With that I left the office. I'm sure I sounded like a lunatic but I didn't care. They had, again, done the wrong thing. They needed to be reminded there are human beings who are directly affected by every decision they make. Think.

A few weeks later my prediction came true. I believe the judge witnessed, or was privy to from her EDNY prosecutors, what these Congress members did and had no choice but to deny our motions to overturn the verdict. I was right. Not only did she deny the motions, she did not address the prosecutions admission they had "inferred" evidence and committed "plain errors" (aka lies). Why wasn't she angry that the prosecutors LIED to her about the quid pro quo and the communications between the government and the "victims"? I am so disappointed in Judge Chen. Why did she risk her career to back such a horrible and manipulative prosecutor? Her history showed she was an advocate for women. Did she realize she allowed Craig Heeren to use the two freshman female prosecutors for plausible deniability? Heeren was a deputy chief of the EDNY and Attorneys Arfa and Chen's BOSS! They had no choice but to do whatever he said. Was Judge Chen really OK with how he treated these two young women? How can you claim to be a champion of women but let two female prosecutors, in the dawn of their careers, be used in such a manner. Heeren's lies will forever be attached to these two women and their legal careers. Is that why two of the three original prosecutors Matthew Haggans and Ellen Sise, both seasoned prosecutors, bailed just weeks before trial? Shame on them too if they left to save themselves. They left due to claims of having a trial conflict. (Sure.) They had worked on this case, the first international Fox Hunt takedown, covered by the media all over the world, yet BOTH left at the last minute? There had to be more to the story. It didn't matter anymore. Mike would be sentenced and we had to prepare for that.

My intuition told me to look into the civil lawsuit against Jin Xu again. Always trust your instinct. I believed as soon as that guilty verdict was issued in June of 2023 the "victims" would file a motion to dismiss the civil case in New Jersey. At trial Judge Chen stated the case before her had nothing to do with the civil case being reconsidered, as the two were not connected. We had tried unsuccessfully to show the court that was false. I knew Jin Xu had been stalling for YEARS trying to prove to the civil court, unsuccessfully, he was being harassed by the CCP. The guilty verdict in Mike's case now "proved" he and his wife Fang Liu were being "harassed." Common sense told me their first call after they heard the word guilty would be to their attorney in the civil case.

I called Essex County Court in New Jersey, where the civil case was filed, and gave them the case number inquiring about the status of the civil case. The woman on the phone said, "That case was dismissed with prejudice." This meant the case was closed and could not be contested. When I asked when this occurred she answered, "September 4, 2023." I was right again. They wasted no time to file to dismiss and their resolution to close the case seemed to have been expedited. I was so angry. It appeared to me now more than ever they had gotten favor from the government regarding the civil case. I took a trip to Essex County and asked the woman at the front desk about the case number. She returned after looking at her computer and delivered the same news with an additional piece of information. That case was "dismissed with prejudice and impounded." She said she had never seen that before, IMPOUNDED. The definition reads, "to remove all access to the file, record or document except for users authorized by statute or court order." That case was probably in the virtual shredder. I emailed Larry and Genna with the news. Jin Xu, Fang Liu, and Yan Liu won. The details of the case being closed would now have to be addressed through the court to have it unsealed for our appeal.

My next trip to DC was a busy one. I was reeling from all of the psychological beatings. Things were becoming clear that we had started to build quite an army of support to weather these storms moving forward. I sat with Mike Lawler in his office to update him and ask if he would write a letter of support to the judge for sentencing. He confirmed that he would and I thanked him again for his support. Ed Martin got me a meeting with Republican Texas Congressman Pete Sessions. Sessions is a career congressman with a big personality. He has a life-size cardboard cutout of Ronald Reagan in his office. I told him I once sang for Reagan when I was in *Annie* on Broadway (I always try and find the commonality with people). Jeff Clark was also there as well as Ed Martin and Sessions's chief of staff. Ed gave me the floor and I told our story much to the disgust of everyone listening. Sessions said he would help any way he could. Then I got a message from Lawler that the new head of the China Committee Congressman John

Moolenaar would meet with me. Moolenaar only had fifteen minutes but Lawler encouraged me to go. Of course I would go and I took Ed Martin with me.

When I got into Moolenaar's office there were several people who joined us. Then someone on speaker phone said his name but I had no idea what that person said. I knew I had only fifteen minutes so I wanted to make it fruitful. I gave the condensed version of our story but made sure to point out that the "victims" were accused of fraud and wanted in China and they had been sued civilly in New Jersey to the tune of $30 million. I passionately explained that Mike did nothing illegal and he is an NYPD hero. Moolenaar's takeaway was, "It sounds like he was doing his job." Exactly. As we were leaving, Ed explained it this way to Moolenaar. There are members of the CCP living in the US, and CCP members fly in from China to intimidate them. An American gets innocently caught up in the middle and he's the one arrested. Why is America involved in China's problems here in the US?

When we left the meeting Ed showed me the names of the people in attendance, one being the name of the person who was on the speaker phone, counsel for the China Committee, Matt Cronin. Oh boy. That means when I went ballistic about Mike's poster put up at the China Committee hearing a few months prior, there is NO DOUBT Raja called Matt Cronin about my tirade. Upon further review, Cronin was also connected to the EDNY national security representative Scott Claffee. Claffee's name is all over the documents in Mike's case. I'm sure Claffee and Cronin had quite the chat about me after I left Moolenaar's office. Oh well. Maybe it was the first time the China Committee heard the truth when it came to Mike's case.

I felt like I was on fumes trying to get something or someone to pull out a magic wand and end this. I really felt like I couldn't take much more, then I got a tip. I was sent a copy of a letter from Congressman James Comer's (R-KY) Government Oversight Committee which was sent to Attorney General Merrick Garland. The letter alerted him that the Government Oversight Committee was opening an investigation into the ranking of every single federal agency when it came to the CCP. The letter was sent in March of 2024. The letter highlighted Mike's case saying the "hostile efforts of Operation Fox Hunt even overtook a former Sergeant for the New York City Police Department" to "harass U.S. citizens." What the hell was happening? Now the attorney general on the eve of Mike being sentenced thinks the EDNY was the beacon of success? They were continuing to use Mike as their poster boy even after I screamed about it? I realized the date on letter, March 2024, was AFTER Raja put up Mike's poster in 2023 but BEFORE I sat in Moolenaar's office with Ed Martin and Matt Cronin the attorney for the China Committee on speaker phone. Now that Attorney General Merrick Garland had been fed this false narrative of what happened, how could I inform him that he had been misled? I sent information on Mike's case to as many people as I could. I made calls and called out the prosecutors having misled the AG and the Oversight Committee about the truth in this case. If the Oversight Committee was going to do a deep dive into how the DOJ and FBI handled China, our case needed to be investigated for how incompetently it was handled. I sent the information but didn't hold out much hope. We had taken so many hits I struggled and wondered if all the work I had done was worth it?

Prior to seeing this letter something happened that made me question whether the NYPD had been involved directly or indirectly in Mike's case. By God's grace I saw a May 2024 story that was buried in the *New York Post* about an NYPD lieutenant named Steven Li. The article said he had been fired by the NYPD in February of 2024 after an investigation surrounding a Fox Hunt case out of the SDNY filed in 2022. The NYPD investigation revealed he had lied to the FBI when asked about a meeting he had with a Fox Hunt target in December of 2019. This meeting was detailed in the criminal complaint signed by FBI Case Agent Kelsey Palermo in March of 2022, but Li was unnamed at that time. After two years and Mike's trial, information about Li, which would have benefited us tremendously, had finally been unmasked. Steven Li was the law enforcement officer from the

Sun Hoi Fox Hunt SDNY case. I couldn't believe it. Records show the FBI had declined to charge Steven Li in March of 2022 and passed the case to the NYPD to determine whether to discipline him. Why did it take so long for the NYPD to release their decision to fire Li in February of 2024 to the public and the press failed to report it until May of 2024? Why didn't the NYPD do anything to Li in March of 2022? The records were quite revealing.

If we go back to when Kelsey Palermo filed the criminal complaint in March of 2022, "PI FIRM NUMBER ONE" was hired in 2016–2017 and the "law enforcement officer" got involved starting in December of 2019 until October 2020, the exact same week of Mike's arrest. Palermo filed the complaint in March of 2022, then turned over the case to the NYPD. The NYPD did not interview Li until August of 2023, two months after Mike's conviction. Why did they wait so long? Were the NY FBI and NYPD purposely trying to keep Li masked until after Mike's trial? If the FBI had named Li and the private investigative firm in the March of 2022 complaint, it would have COMPLETELY exonerated Mike. Who decided to keep this quiet? Upon further investigation Li was not forthcoming to the FBI when originally spoken to in 2021 and could have been charged with lying to the FBI but was not. Instead, the NYPD decided to use his lying to the FBI to fire Li years later in 2024, which is odd.

I am not saying Li is guilty of anything, but these are the facts. Steven Li met with a Fox Hunt target in December of 2019 while an active member of the NYPD at the behest of Chinese official Sun Hoi. Hoi instructed Li to pressure the Fox Hunt victim regarding alleged stolen money. Why wasn't Li charged? Li claimed he didn't know Hoi was a Chinese official but had visited China and attended several Chinese social events in Queens known for recruiting potential political and law enforcement support. The "I didn't know" excuse was thin on the Li case because the Fox Hunt target was very clear that she knew she was a target and was visibly upset when Li approached her. NY FBI Head William Sweeney had previously praised the NYPD in regard to the EDNY Angwang case, the NYPD officer accused of spying for China, so why was this Fox Hunt case against Lieutenant Steven Li different? It wasn't as if the NY FBI was against charging active members of the NYPD regarding cases involving China. The NYPD clearly had a good standing relationship with the NY FBI, yet the SDNY Fox Hunt case was not pursued. Now we had almost all the information about the SDNY case except for who was the "PI FIRM NUMBER ONE"?

How connected or aware was the NYPD to these Chinese operations? The day of Mike's arrest Brian Neary asked if Mike had worked on any Chinese cases. I remembered a case in Manhattan. Upon further investigation, the job was executed on April 27, 2017, only a few weeks after Mike wrapped his work on the NJ Chinese case. In the Manhattan case, he attempted to serve six Chinese companies at the same address accused of credit card fraud totaling $129,000. Mike's client had been scammed by a law firm who was continually charging his credit card. The next day, a second attempt was made to serve the subjects of the compliant. That day the subjects had hired uniformed NYPD for security. This concerned Mike so he called a lieutenant at the NYPD and alerted him the NYPD was providing uniformed security for a criminal operation. The lieutenant confirmed they sometimes provide security and dismissed Mike's concern. Unlike the New Jersey case, Mike saw multiple red flags in the Manhattan case, felt something suspicious was going on, and he alerted authorities. This chain of events raised me up for two reasons. First, it proved when Mike felt something was of concern he would alert the authorities. Second, that the NYPD was being used by Chinese criminals and didn't seem to care.

Maybe translator "Emily" could shed some light on this for me. There was a connection to a Chinese translation and travel company in the Manhattan case. "Emily" not only operated a translation company but also opened a travel agency at the same address in Queens. Is this a pattern of layering, which is common in Chinese cases, missed or ignored by the NYPD and FBI?

I reached out to "Emily" but I knew if she was represented by counsel I could not continue to speak to her. She answered and I recorded the conversation. I asked if she had counsel, "No." Then I asked for her help. I believed she knew more than what she was saying regarding Mike's case when claiming she was, "just the translator." I said, "I don't believe you." She insisted. I then asked, "Do you know someone named Kelsey Palermo?" She answered, "No." I said, "She was the FBI case agent on the Southern District of New York Fox Hunt case." She got very flustered and hung up on me. Within a few minutes she texted me with her attorney's phone number. Was I right? Was Lina Xu aka "Emily" an informant for Palermo on the SDNY Fox Hunt case? It would explain so much if I was right.

Another unanswered question I always had regarded "Emily's" original email to Mike describing the client. "Emily," said the client, was a "she" and "had been through a lot." We never got an answer why that happened. The female target in the Fox Hunt SDNY case had been harassed many times over the years. Is it possible Mike was sent details from the SDNY Fox Hunt case by mistake? If my theory was right, that ALL Fox Hunt cases lived in the SDNY, a Fox Hunt soup if you will, was "Emily" the catcher of intel? Instead of sending Mike information about Jason Zhu after their initial phone call, did "Emily" mistakenly send the "she's been through a lot" email? If Lina Xu was an informant for Palermo, they couldn't arrest her in Mike's case or any others. Similarly, is that why the California gang member who provided the address in 2018 to put the note on the door in New Jersey wasn't arrested either? Was he a cooperator working with the FBI as well? We knew for sure the PI was a paid cooperator in the California sting operation of this case. It was written in the footnote of the sworn criminal complaint. How many people were on the payroll?! How many criminals were being paid taxpayer dollars to create this case? I assure you I will never stop trying to find out.

By the fall of 2024 Mike's sentencing date had been pushed countless times. We were told that was a good sign. The closer to a new administration the better. Would we be getting a new administration?

Would Trump return to office and help us? The world was a mess and all I could do was pray. Then one day I got an email. The Government Oversight Committee had released its three-hundred-page report on the CCP. As I clicked on the link I saw the report was broken down agency by agency and graded. The FBI report was telling. The committee learned the FBI really didn't have a clue what they were doing in 2016 in regard to the CCP. They were learning as they were going which completely made sense that Mike was used as a guinea pig. Then I got to the DOJ section, which highlighted Mike's case specifically. The committee questioned whether Mike's case should have been prosecuted at all. It was scathing and damning to the EDNY. I could read between the lines. I knew they don't recommend remedies for this overreach but they most certainly strongly suggested they really messed this one up. I couldn't believe it. A bipartisan committee of forty-five members of Congress signed off on this report. The question was would it be enough to end this nightmare? It was a huge win for what I had been saying for years and was now documented forever in the Library of Congress.

At the next meeting at Larry's office, Genna told us some crazy news. Craig Heeren, the man who had destroyed our lives, had left the DOJ. With only weeks to go until sentencing he bailed like the coward he is, leaving Attorneys Afra and Chen to handle the sentencing. This was insane to me. He had spent EIGHT YEARS of his life on this case and he was too afraid to face us again? That was very telling. Had he been interviewed by the Oversight Committee and saw the writing on the wall? Did head of the EDNY Breon Peace finally look into the case and see what a disaster it was? Maybe we'll never know. There were a few things I had discovered that summed up this entire case.

The government claimed Mike was involved in nefarious activity with the CCP in April of 2017. There was only one problem with that. Public documents reveal in 2017 the DOJ was working hand in hand with China to repatriate people. I found a June 2017 video that aired on television in China. This video was taken on a tarmac in China of a hooded man being escorted off a United Airlines plane accompanied by both American and Chinese law enforcement. The news claimed the man had been repatriated with the help of the US. I also found DOJ releases as far back as 2015 where the DOJ THANKED the CCP for their cooperation to repatriate a woman back to China who had committed visa and wire fraud here in the US. As late as September of 2019, there are public documents of meetings between the DOJ and the CCP in China regarding repatriations of wanted fugitives including Jin Xu and Fang Liu. Then COVID hit and our relationship with China was under intense scrutiny. What actions did the DOJ take to disassociate themselves from this long-standing cooperative relationship surrounding legal matters between the China and the US. Did the DOJ retroactively create Mike's case to make it appear as if the US had been on top of Chinese agents involved in repatriations in 2016 (which they clearly were not)? The opposite was true as we saw visual evidence at our trial documenting Chinese police being invited here by the US as shown on the visa records in our exhibits.

One thing I knew for sure: I wasn't going to let my husband go to prison because the United States failed to recognize the danger of Chinese operatives. I wasn't going to let them sacrifice an American hero because they picked the wrong side in this investigation and were clearly played by our greatest enemy. The CCP Oversight report mapped out how our agencies are targeted and used. I had seen so much evidence that the FBI and DOJ had been played. Did they realize at some point they were being played and were too embarrassed to back out? Was spyware tested on my family so the government could "learn" how to capture intelligence?

As we approached the election in November 2024 I had spent every bit of energy I had in my body to fight for my family. I believed that God wouldn't have spared Trump that day in Butler from an assassin's bullet if he wasn't in some way meant to heal our country. I could honestly say I had fought the good fight and left it all on the field. On election night I was exhausted and went to bed not knowing if November 6 would be a dark day for our country and our family. I felt if Biden won, Judge Chen would be emboldened to punish Mike to the extreme. If Trump won, I knew it could be a game changer. This case had the attention of Congress and if Trump won there would be at the very least an investigation into the EDNY's handling of this case.

When I woke up to the news Trump not only won, but he OVERWHELMINGLY won. I was thrilled. I felt my children's future would be paved with opportunity to live the American Dream. I found great comfort in that undeniable fact. No matter what was going to happen with Mike, we would face it.

Right after the election we got word the prosecution had requested Mike's sentencing be moved ahead until March 3, 2025, almost two years after the trial ended. As a glass-half-full person, I hoped this decision was a sign. Moving the sentencing after Trump puts his hand on the Bible to become our forty-seventh president gave me a sense of relief. Like Trump, we had fought the system through the entire Biden administration. Maybe the world was finally turning in our favor. Through it all Trump built an army of support from all walks of life. In him they saw themselves. The net worth of the average man couldn't compare with Trump's. His resilience from the relentless attacks on him and his steadfast belief in the common man are what drew the majority to this man. The lawfare by those who tried to break him had resulted in the opposite intended effect. The actions of the deep state made Trump just like us, the American people. Just like our family. Just Like Mike.

CHAPTER SEVENTEEN

THERE WILL ALWAYS BE THINGS about the trial that will bother me forever. People say hindsight is twenty-twenty, but this is more about trusting my gut. Maybe I should have pushed harder on some issues but because I'm not a lawyer, I didn't want to waste time. It is true that the past is the past and it cannot be changed. This case has proven that's exactly where I need to go to get answers, the past. I looked back at the evidence hundreds of times and it's how I discovered so many important clues. One thing that I couldn't stop thinking about was the Johnny, Tu Lan, and Hongru Jin recording from the hotel room. We never got an answer of how it had been obtained. The circus of the trial didn't help resolve the issue. Hognru Jin's testimony was muddy and confusing, which I believe was intentional. How far did they actually go to deceive the jury? The prosecution had continuously lied, not only leading up to the trial but throughout the trial. I wanted to revisit it. We had the hotel room audio recording played at trial between Johnny and Tu Lan translated by our own translator. When I opened the document of our translated version, my heart sank. Not only was the translation different, it appeared the government had added a line to the text. In our translation (paraphrasing) Tu Lan has no interest in Mike but addresses him as not being Chinese, an American policeman and Johnny cannot speak to him the same way. Tu Lan instructs Johnny that whatever stories Johnny tells Mike just be "thorough." Far from the government's version to "tell Mike everything." This tactic of varying stories supports other evidence of what Johnny told to FBI Agent Christopher Bruno when he was stopped at the airport in April 2017 and lied to Bruno, claiming he was a tour guide. (A tour guide with night vision goggles, but OK.) Even though Bruno had proof Johnny was involved in the activities surrounding Jin Xu's father coming to the US, he was so convincing that Bruno let Johnny get on the same plane as Jin Xu's father back to China that day. Or was it something more disturbing? Maybe criminals don't tell law enforcement, active or retired, they are committing crimes! If Jin Xu's father detailed why he was in the US to the FBI when I presume they interviewed him while he was here and said he felt pressured to come to the states, why on earth would Agent Bruno put the person responsible for this pressure campaign on the same plane?! Was there anything about this case that was honest? Agent Bruno must have panicked after he found out that the "doctor" and "prosecutor" went back to China (fled) sooner than expected once the two lost track of Jin Xu's father in the US. Bruno missed the two women and Johnny was his last hope to save face by stopping him at the airport. Or was he panicking at all? Agent Bruno was not alone when he interviewed Johnny at the airport. There was another FBI Agent who did not work on this case present and the exchange between Bruno and Johnny was all documented on video. Bruno had to walk a thin line. Did the other agent present know Agent Bruno was about to put Johnny on a 15 hour plane ride to China with one of his "victims"? I doubt it. Whatever was SUPPOSED to happen in New Jersey in early April had failed and it had Agent Bruno's prints all over it. Every day I find more concerning evidence on how this case was calculated and mishandled. So many of those involved had gotten away with lying. I have to ask myself, how many people in that courtroom knew Craig Heeren had lied to the jury? Did any of those people have a moral, if not legal, obligation to report it? If they knew what was happening, they were complicit. They allowed an innocent man to be destroyed and face federal prison. The damage was done. It was too late. I couldn't help but wonder if we had a judge who hadn't handed the prosecution every ruling on a silver platter, would the outcome have been different? Even in her last ruling to vacate the conviction Judge Chen ignored the blatant admissions of the prosecutors that they "inferred" evidence. I will never understand how Judge Chen just allowed such obvious lying and favoritism to occur. We had never gotten one favorable ruling since the day of Mike's arrest in 2020.

Another insane turn of events happened in January of 2024 when Secretary of State Antony Blinken rolled out the red carpet here in the US for a man named Liu Jianchao, who was visiting from China. Jianchao initiated Chinese Operation Fox Hunt and was behind the secret Chinese police stations operating across the US, including one in New York City. The *New York Post* wrote an article about his visit in which I was quoted saying Liu should have been "arrested on the tarmac." What a slap in the face to the United States and to our family. His visit made the EDNY case against Mike a complete joke. The DOJ had spent over eight years creating the narrative for this Fox Hunt case, with claims that Chinese agents were involved in dangerous criminal activity on US soil and had gotten multiple convictions. Just a few months after those convictions, Liu Jianchao, the man behind it all, was having a grand ole time hanging out in DC and at the United Nations. This visit was China's way of letting the DOJ know who was in charge. Under Obama and Biden, China was notorious for mocking the DOJ and the United States by taking their "warnings" and throwing them in the proverbial garbage. They were doing it again with Jianchao's visit. I didn't understand how Jianchao, the head of the Chinese Fox Hunt operations, wasn't arrested. It turned out that Liu Jianchao declared himself a diplomat of the US prior to coming here so he could not be arrested. And since he was a diplomat, our government was obligated to provide security and prosecutorial immunity. It's almost too much to comprehend what a complete disaster this entire case had become and how much the DOJ had botched it. The only people who were actually punished were our family.

When I try to find an ending to this story, I realize there may never be one. Over the last four years I have met so many people who have been victims of government overreach themselves. Our stories bonded us. Most are still ongoing, many for more than four years like ours. How did this once-respected government institution get to where it is today? I have met so many former federal agents and prosecutors who are heartbroken to see what the DOJ has become. One former federal prosecutor was adamant that during his time at the EDNY his team would go out of their way to make sure no innocent person was falsely accused. There was no greater failure for him as a prosecutor than if an innocent person became entangled in one of his cases. He said clearing innocent parties from a case strengthened his jury convictions which was his ultimate goal. This is exactly how the justice system is supposed to work but it has gone off course. There is a common thread with those I've met going through something similar to us. We are all fighters but our backgrounds were quite different. I have met CEOs, a Navy Seal, a Wall Street executive, someone fighting Amazon, the Department of Education, a former governor's chief of staff, the list goes on. There seems to be this common unfortunate reality that once the DOJ gets their legal talons in you, they never let go. I have seen that happen to others and it's daunting to think this nightmare will never end for us. The government has the power to bankrupt you both financially and emotionally.

How did my own life experiences thus far get me through this travesty? It would be too simplistic to say that my love for my family, truth, and justice was enough. There's no doubt it was the foundation for this fight, but it was so much more. Who I am as a wife and mother was woven into me even before I met Mike. Early on in my life I knew I wanted to get married and be a mother. I loved being an actor, but career never came first in my life. I was blessed to have found success but my desire to have a family was a priority. With my job on *As the World Turns* I could literally have it all. My life was as normal as you could get. I never felt like a television star and had a very normal life. It was a great job and I loved every minute of it. I came from a family of incredibly hard workers who rarely changed jobs. Work ethic was part of my DNA. My dad was a self-employed tree surgeon. My mother was a teacher and my agent since I was a child. In show business there was basically only one consistent job, soap operas. If your character was a popular one, as mine was, you had job security. I started in 1985 and left *As the World Turns* in 2008. I had a four-year break when I lived in California but the pull to go back to *As the World Turns* was strong. The audience was incredibly enthusiastic about my return in 1993. I will be forever indebted to them for giving me this beautiful life. Without the fans I would not have gotten the opportunity to be creative every single day. The fictional town of Oakdale was a playground of tears and joy I called home for decades. My soap opera life and real life would only intersect when I would get pregnant. My pregnancies were always written into the show. My first two pregnancies with Mikey and Max went smoothly and I returned to work able to balance everything.

On June 12, 2006, I gave birth to our third child, daughter Ann Marie. I went into labor five weeks before her due date. When I delivered our first son Mikey, I experienced twenty-four hours of induced labor, which was brutal and ended in a C-section. He was two weeks overdue and almost ten pounds. Our second son Max was delivered by C-section as well. When I went into early labor with Ann Marie in 2006 I was scared. The doctor performed an emergency C-section and Ann Marie was immediately sent to NICU. Her lungs were underdeveloped and she had to be intubated. I felt a tremendous amount of guilt that she was born into the world too soon. There was no putting her back. She was almost eight pounds, the biggest baby in the NICU and a fighter. I felt helpless. I would pray and ask God to heal her. I'd place my hand inside the incubator and her heart rate would stabilize without me even touching her. I hoped my love would heal her and get her home. Thankfully she continued to defy the odds and two weeks later she left the hospital. The hole in the aortic ventricle had closed without surgery. To this day she has never suffered any repercussions from her early struggles. It had drained me physically but even more so emotionally. I can truthfully say I never fully recovered from that experience.

I was never the same after giving birth to Ann Marie. Prior to my pregnancy the decision had been made to kill off the character of Rose, part of the twin sister dual role I had played for almost four years. I always loved the role of Lily who I had portrayed from the age of fifteen. Following the loss of Rose, the character of Lily had become creatively stagnant and in need of some new ideas to reidentify her. As the time to renew my contract approached, a story idea for Lily, written by a talented production assistant, was submitted to the executive producer and the writing team for consideration. Truthfully, I was struggling with the decision to stay even before my negotiations began. Once started, the communications between my manager and executive producer went back and forth. The show was offering no raises at the time. My request to return to my original show guarantee was a no. My commitment to agree to a three-year contract held no water. While negotiations were still ongoing, the executive producer directed the show's casting director to put out a "breakdown" to agents to replace me in the role of Lily. Negotiations were still ongoing but to me they were now over. As much as I loved my soap family, it would never be the same welcoming place. After some heartfelt discussions with Mike, I made the difficult decision to end negotiations and leave *As the World Turns*. I was recast a few weeks later and, ironically, the story submitted by the production assistant was played out by another actress.

Every event in our lives shapes us. When these things happen you can either see them as an ending or beginning. I made the adjustment and left that wonderful chapter of my life behind. I could now fulfill the most important role as a wife and mother. Since I had worked professionally for decades, we had saved enough money to live comfortably. Not to say there weren't some financial adjustments that had to be made. Mike's business as a private investigator had grown and we had a consistent income to rely on. I went on to explore other work possibilities. I was fortunate to be able to create my own projects that received Emmy nominations, work a short stint on *General Hospital*, and even wrote for a short while for *The Bold and the Beautiful*. I had the perfect balance of work and family. Though I missed my *As the World Turns* friends, I remained close to many after my departure. When the news hit in 2010 that the show was being canceled, I was heartbroken. The show had been a part of my life as a young teenager, a young woman, through a marriage, three children, and the gift of life-long friends. I will always cherish the time I spent on the show but my departure to maintain my integrity is something I will never regret. I would always be able to look back on a wonderful career that started when I was ten years old. I was blessed!

Mike and I were living a beautiful life raising our family when our world was shattered in October of 2020. It turned out my life experiences while playing the fictional character of Lily helped me through what was about to become a reality. Another chapter of our lives was ending and our most difficult one was beginning. I started to apply my skills as an actor and a writer to grasp the legal labyrinth we had to navigate. When I write a script I never take the easy road. I know the audience is not just an observer but a participant in the story. I always wanted to make the reader think. I knew that was a part of the entire creative experience. I dissect every nuance, down to a specific undergarment or perfume choice when I write or play a character. These details give the creative work layers and bring truth to each project. That was my job in life for over four decades. Since I was now seeking the truth in Mike's case I would apply the same thought process. If something didn't make sense, it wasn't true. If it wasn't true, then the question was, what was true? Like a good investigator or writer, you do research. Through my hours, days, weeks, and now years of research, I found answers. As an actor, you read a scene and make choices. You try on these choices and see which one fits right for the character and the scenes. When it comes to getting to the root of the United States government's choices, it's a bit more difficult to get to the answers. I have become a great investigator and I do not say that lightly. I followed the leads and never gave up. I still have so many unanswered questions and I hope one day I will get closure. I will never stop trying until I have hit the final wall. So far we have survived this hell. How will what we've been through shape our future and the future of our family?

When I look at who I am today after what I have been through in the past four years I would have to go back to one of my mantras. My mother always taught me if you are in a position to help others you must do so. That wasn't just a Catholic thing, it was a Mary Byrne thing. She taught me at a young age to donate a portion of my earnings to others in need. As a person who had a large fan base I used that as an opportunity to give back. St. Jude Children's Research Hospital was the charity I focused on. The hospital was started by actor Danny Thomas and became the leading research hospital for childhood cancers and other catastrophic diseases. I ran a fundraiser for years and was more than happy to help raise money for the hospital. The fans and the soap community joined in to support the cause. The power of connectivity I had was rare and I respected the role I was given and tried to use it wisely.

The one thing about soap operas is the generational pattern of fans is unlike any other genre. I would often meet a young woman who would tell me she started watching the show because her grandmother would have it on while she babysat her. Probably every fan I met in the last forty years told me the show had a family connection to them in some way. I have letters from people telling me that watching the show helped them heal after a parent who they had watched *As the World Turns* with passed away. It was ingrained in their DNA and it was a positive in their lives. To have played even a small part in that joy for people has truly been an honor.

When Mike was arrested I immediately went to the internet to see if the soap community was talking about it. They were not. Either they didn't know or were being respectful. In the beginning I was happy it was not being discussed. When I went on Newsmax I knew that would automatically bring a reaction from people. What happened was astonishing. The fans rallied behind Mike. These people had watched me grow up, get married to Mike, have three babies, and had been with us through our entire life journey. They knew us either through soap magazines or meeting us personally at one of my St. Jude or soap opera events. They knew there was no way I would be married to someone who was accused of such horrible things. Unlike a movie star, where the fans see them in one movie a year, I was in their living room almost every single day, a part of their daily routine. They trusted me whether they knew me personally or not. My performances got to their inner selves and left a mark. That experience meant something to the fans and it was precious. The attacks on my family were taken very personally by them. In the last four years I never ONCE have I gotten one negative message. Even when I would compare what was happening to Mike with the lawfare against Donald Trump, the fans would sometimes disagree but were always respectful. Think about that for a minute. I'm not saying I didn't lose some followers, but they went quietly.

Going into the fire of the internet was not easy. The government was literally watching my every move but I had no choice. I was never a political person but what happened to Mike could happen to anyone. I had to speak out. The benefit of speaking out was that the fans would give me suggestions of people to talk to. They would often tag their congressman in a tweet or share an interview of mine on their social media pages. I have no doubt the government had no clue how powerful and dedicated the daytime fanbase was.

When I reached out to members of Congress I would sometimes get a hit on someone who knew who I was. That recognition got me into many rooms and phone calls. Ed Martin would always introduce me to the DC players as being a soap opera star and that I had won Emmys, and so forth. I started calling Ed my "agent." It took him a little while to remember exactly what show I was on but he knew my resume would get attention and I could take it from there. Hollywood and DC are quite similar. I equate the members of Congress to the movie studios and their teams as the producers. You need to get the producers to listen to your pitch then they move it to the studio heads. It's a constant living and breathing mechanism that is insatiable. The pulse of DC had a very familiar energy, one I could easily adapt to once I figured out the rules. Had I lived my whole life for this moment? Had everything I had done in my life prepared me to face this colossal challenge? God had given me a platform to continue on my path. I tried to use it as a positive to give back to others as often as I could. Now my husband was facing a terrible fate and I was using that voice to spread the truth despite so many in our government trying to stop me.

The government media machine was getting outplayed by my base. The soap community had been very respectful. There weren't any salacious stories about what happened and I was grateful for that. The soap press always handled the actor's personal lives with respect. We had a symbiotic relationship with the magazines and I considered the writers friends. If I had been a movie star, Mike's story would have made the tabloids. I was not a big enough star for that to happen but well known enough to have people in my corner. It was a testimony to the loyalty I had from the viewers.

I knew in my heart, if I spoke out, I would have the support of the daytime community. To see it in action was humbling. I knew I had been given this mission of telling our story to help others. I just had to survive it. The world was now closely following along and praying with us and for us. I could feel the shift happen after the jury's verdict. I got a message from Paula Benard, Maurice Benard's wife. Maurice is a soap icon, having played Sonny Corinthos on the legendary show *General Hospital* for years. He had struggled with mental illness and written a *New York Times* bestseller about his journey. I only knew Maurice though mutual friends. I had made a short appearance on *General Hospital* after leaving *As the World Turns* but our paths didn't cross. He had started a podcast called *State of Mind* and invited me on to tell our story. I immediately accepted and booked a flight to California. I don't know if Maurice truly understands how much that meant to me. I had been off daytime since my appearance on *General*

Hospital in 2009 and I wasn't sure his listeners would even know who I was. I knew our story was powerful but would people who didn't know me recognize and care about the injustice? Maurice interviewed me for two hours! He broke up the interview into two parts. The first hour was all about my history in the entertainment business, the second about what happened to Mike. It may be the favorite interview I have ever done. I felt so comfortable, not judged and completely supported. By having me on, Maurice made it OK for other actors to speak up about what happened to us. I didn't expect it but it sure was nice. The government had officially lost the narrative due to the truth overtaking their lies.

Maybe everything I had experienced was fuel for this next chapter of my life. I had used my platform, supported by millions of people, to shed light not only on the injustice against Mike but the corrupt system in general. Due to my small amount of celebrity, DC politicians would listen and many joined our cause. Because of my many years in front of the camera, I could go on television and radio shows and tell a compelling story. Mike is just one of the victims of the DOJ but he is one of the very few with a wife who has no fear of them anymore.

In the beginning, I remained quiet in the hope this would all go away. Despite learning the government hated being called out, I never stopped. Did that backfire in some ways? I will never know. I do know it angered them enough to direct DC intelligence to send a letter to our lawyer in an attempt to silence me. I hit a nerve and they showed their hand.

I was never one to shy away from conflict. I didn't ask for it in my life but when this happened to us I went all in. I committed my life to my husband and family. I wanted to give them the best life possible. That's all I wanted and had achieved it. The day the FBI showed up at our home and violated the sanctity of our family, was the biggest mistake they ever made. I learned that every FBI field office decides how to take down a subject when making an arrest. That meant that Christopher Bruno, Sean McCarthy, and the rest of the Newark, NJ FBI field office chose to arrest Mike knowing full well my children would be home at the time. I will never forgive them for that. I know as a Catholic I am supposed to forgive but even Jesus flipped a table when he saw the greed in others. The trauma suffered by my children on that day will be forever indelible in my mind. I will have to live with that reality as one I cannot change. Evil attempted to dismantle everything we had created as a family and failed. Evil has and will always exist. How we react and handle this evil is in our hands. We can retreat or we can go into battle. I felt with every bone in my body when the Blessed Mother visited me that night in 2020 to give me the strength to get through this. I knew that when, not if, we defeated this beast it would inspire others to do the same. I remembered how it felt when we first got the call from the Pipe Hitter Foundation. We knew then we were not alone. If I can do that for someone else, by writing this book, by offering a listening ear, or going to the front lines with someone by their side, then I accept that purpose. If God leads you to it, He will get you through it.

I know this battle will continue for us but the fact we have never given up has proven successful. To date, the number of people in government still involved in our case are down to very few. Most have left and gone into the private sector. Arresting FBI Agent Sean McCarthy works as an investigator for the New Jersey attorney general, Lead Prosecutor Craig Heeren is a partner at a New York City law firm, US Attorney Matthew Haggans works in a private law firm, Former Assistant AG for National Intelligence John Demers works for Boeing, EDNY Head Breon Peace left government in January of 2024, Former Acting AG and EDNY Head Richard Donoghue is a partner at Pillsbury Law Firm, FBI Director Christopher Wray chose to resign in shame with Trump's election. James Dennehy Head of the New York FBI, was forced to *retire* after defiantly refusing (allegedly) to turn over January 6th documents requested by newly appointed Attorney General Pam Bondi. It is my belief Mr. Dennehy was heavily involved in Mike's case. After the SDNY Fox Hunt case was closed in March of 2022 Dennehy transferred and became the head of Newark FBI. This sheds light on his press interviews about Chinese operations prior to

Mike's trial once he was named Head of Newark. It also explains his inflammatory statement about Mike after his conviction. Dennehy quickly left Newark and returned to head New York FBI. I'm sure many more will exit with the new DOJ taking over.

After four years of being held hostage by a corrupt system and feeling the talons of the DOJ sinking into us deeper each day, we always fell back on the truth. At one time, there seemed to be no chance we could ever win. No one on the other side had any interest in doing the right thing. No one cared about the truth. Then on November 5, 2024, the American people heard us. The forgotten man who had been told for four years that they had no value and were disposable answered back with their vote. When they went after Donald Trump with reckless abandon I felt his fight was our fight.

It brought me hope when I saw the caliber of people Donald Trump appointed to his administration. I would open my phone to check for news and see names like Kash Patel for FBI director, Devin Nunes, chairman of the President's Intelligence Advisory Board, Ed Martin US attorney for D.C., Peter Navarro senior counselor for trade and manufacturing, many who, at one time or another, had been targets of the government themselves. Trump was making it clear he was placing people on his team who were not going to be continuing the status quo. Our journey to the truth was growing and now we had a new beginning. At least I knew no matter what was coming next, we would not be facing it alone.

I hope one day Mike will get the answer as to why the government did this to us. Was the fact that he was an American the reason? If this case was all about taking down a Foreign Agent Registration Act violation, did they arrest Mike because he is the only American connected to this case? The others are all Chinese citizens and will be deported upon serving their sentences or flee back to China over the years with the help of the FBI.

Was the fight worth it? Absolutely. The government thought Mike would cower and take a plea. Ninety-nine percent of the time their arrogance worked successfully with most people. They mistakenly underestimated not only Mike but his wife, who would walk through fire to defend him. Because we were strong enough to speak out, the truth was heard. Not only did the public take notice but DC, including the Government Oversight Committee, made up of forty-five Democrat and Republican members of Congress, did as well. They recognized the outrageous missteps and injustices executed by the FBI and the DOJ against Mike in their three-hundred-page report on the CCP released in October of 2024. I will always be grateful for their willingness to expose the truth. I have met incredible people who can actually implement change in the justice system and will use our story in part to do it. I met military leaders who took notice of our case and saw the terrible laxity in national security dealings with real estate and other fraud perpetuated by Chinese operatives. When we were at our lowest points, I learned who truly had our backs. Sadly, Mike lost some lifelong friends though this. I am angry at those who chose self-protection over friendship. Were they ever really friends to begin with if they couldn't even simply make a call of support? My heart breaks knowing they abandoned Mike when he needed them the most. That may be the biggest betrayal. The government disregarding his tremendous service to this country was brutal. Losing people he thought would have his back was on another level. The loss of some only magnified the tremendous generosity, love, and kindness of our family and friends (both new ones and lifetime ones) who saved us. There aren't enough words in the dictionary to thank them for their financial support, texts, phone calls, food, hugs, laughs, and so much more.

When all is said and done we will ultimately be victorious. We will be bloodied and bruised when we cross the finish line with every scratch representing one battle or another. Joan of Arc was burned at the stake because she refused to recant the truth that God had spoken to her. How could I take the easy road on earth and live with myself if we didn't hold the line of truth? How could Mike? God had given me so much to work with in my life and the Blessed Mother reinforced it with her visit. I hope I have done right by God and shown Him that

I believe He would never leave my side during this fight. I continue to pray for the protection of my children who have been through so much at the hands of dark forces.

We will never get back what was taken from us. If you participated in what was done to us or stood by and did nothing to prevent it, that's between you and God now. You have the rest of your lives to ask for my children's forgiveness but it will be up to them to decide to forgive you, not me. There are four years of life experiences with our children we will never be able to recover. But I can't mourn the loss of something I never knew. It was our path and we had the free will and strength to accept this monumental challenge. We not only survived but I feel we will see God's greatest glory because we trusted in Him. I hope our children recognize our fight for what was right and always stand up for the truth.

People always say they admire my strength. I'm not strong. I love my husband. I have never met anyone as perfect of a human being as he is. I know that's quite a strong review but it's true. We have been married for thirty years and he has been an angel and protector to so many who needed him. He is a great father, husband, friend, cop, brother, coach, and true hero. There was never one second of hesitation, since the day this happened, that I would stop fighting to clear his name. If the good guys aren't given their due respect and honor, what are we doing in this world? Why would the next person put their life on the line for strangers, if only to be thrown to the wolves for someone else's ego. I couldn't let that happen. It is my great responsibility to be an example for my children. I teach them that life is riddled with unspeakable challenges and even the greatest souls like their father aren't immune from being targeted. I teach my children to live their lives like their father has done, as one of service and honor. If you live each day in this manner, when the devil tries to drag you into the fire, you will most certainly win in the end. Mike's pure heart and the people who love him have carried us through this. He will ultimately prevail. We are so blessed.

God bless you all. Thank you for taking time out of your life to read our story. It is far from over. As it says on my dad's headstone, "Life Is One Continual Adjustment." That is the truth. Ride every wave. I promise calmer waters await you on the horizon of your greatest challenges. Every difficulty in your life, at some point, will be in your rearview mirror. You don't know when, but it is guaranteed to happen. Just hold on and never give up. You can do more.... It's going to be OK.

* * *

SENTENCING DAY: APRIL 16th 2025

The day before sentencing our family buried Mike's brother Vincent. Vinny was an Army Ranger, Lieutenant in the FDNY and one of the most unselfish human beings you could ever meet. He attended the trial every day and was my first call when I needed someone. In July of 2024 he was diagnosed with cancer due to toxic exposure from Ground Zero. We could have postponed the sentencing yet another time but Mike wanted to get it over with. I felt the same way. We had fought for over four years, spent hundreds of thousands of dollars, and this was a step we could no longer ignore.

Judge Chen had reviewed our documents including thirty-nine letters from Congressmen, a retired Army Colonel, former intelligence FBI agent, friends, family, all of Mike's medical records and more. We were arguing for probation. The government wanted six and a half years along with a $50 thousand fine. Their sentencing report submitted to the judge continued the narrative that had been disproven pre and post trail with overwhelming evidence.

Here is my letter to the judge.

Dear Judge Chen,

I met Michael McMahon on February 6th, 1993. I had just moved back to NJ from California and met some friends on my first weekend home. When Mike walked in that night, I couldn't take my eyes off of him. He had the most beautiful blue eyes and the "map of Ireland" on his face as they say. I was not one to be shy, so I immediately went up to him and struck up a conversation. I was twenty-three years old, Mike twenty-five. We were young but both had already experienced quite complex lives. Mike as a police officer on the NYPD, me as a professional actress since age ten. We talked for hours the night we met. After more than thirty years and three wonderful children, we haven't stopped talking.

The night we met I learned that Mike had recently lost his sister Ann Marie and father Vincent. Mike and Ann Marie were "Irish twins," with only one year separating their birthdays. I later learned the tragic story of how both family members had succumbed to cancer in the fall of 1992. His father had spent months in the hospital prior to his death from leukemia. Mike was working midnights on the NYPD during their illnesses which spanned over just one year, 1992. He would drive straight to the hospital to bathe and shave his father then head home to his bed-ridden sister Ann Marie who had fatal Neuroendocrine cancer. His siblings shared stories of Mike's empathy at a time when others (he is one of nine children) were paralyzed in disbelief. They were about to lose two members of their family within weeks of each other. Mike stepped up and put his own pain aside to give his father and sister dignity and reassurance, whatever they needed to give them peace.

I met him at a very vulnerable time in his life. The loss of two of his closest family members was written all over his face in 1993. When I met his extended family at their home in New City, NY, they welcomed me with open arms, even during their most difficult time. Many of his relatives, including three siblings, were cops or firemen. It was clearly a multi-generational family of service. You felt it when you walked in their home. There was so much love there and I felt like a part of the family right away. As I got to know Mike I was truly humbled by his goodness. I had never met anyone like him. His perspective and value on the important things in life centered me. During difficult times he would always say, "It will all work out...It's going to be OK." He was always right and my trust in him built the foundation we rely on today. I knew he would be a great father and husband, even after only knowing him for a few months and I wanted us to build a life together. I met a real-life hero and we started planning our future.

Six months after we started dating we were engaged and purchased a home together. I'm sure some people thought we were crazy but thirty years later we're stronger than ever having weathered many storms, none more greater than this current battle.

When we met in 1993, Mike was serving on the Street Crime Unit of the NYPD. He was in constant combat on the job including a shootout in Times Square on New Year's Eve with thieves armed with AK47s holding workers hostage. Mike's partner was shot in the leg that night. Due to Mike's courage and heroism, and that of his fellow cops, no attendees were harmed and the ball dropped right on time. Mike had saved countless lives and no one popping champagne was the wiser. I have a million stories of his dedication to the people of NY. His heroism was a constant occurrence. He viewed it as part of his job and he loved every second of it. Being stationed in the Bronx every day or night was plagued with murder, suicide, assault, gun fire, child abuse cases, human trafficking, stalking, rape and unthinkable horrors only seen in war zones. When the sun went down the gunshots would start until sunrise. The radio was constantly humming with the calls of those in desperate need. He came home with stories of what most people wouldn't believe was going on in their backyard, just a few miles away over the GW Bridge.

He racked up medal after medal building his stellar reputation. He was promoted several times and eventually served as school safety sergeant for approximately 40 public and private schools in the Bronx. With this job came a different kind of responsibility. He was in charge of protecting children from drug dealers, gang recruitment and more. He would often be the only voice for children victimized in the schools and protector for many who otherwise would be forgotten. He hosted a camp for underprivileged kids sponsored by the SDNY and several U.S. Attorneys spent time at the camp with Mike and the children. He was publicly recognized for this work by Mary Joe White Esq., the U.S. Attorney for SDNY.

He helped so many kids during his time on the job. I was always so proud of him. Our lives were quite different but it worked for us. I was a life-long actress on a highly rated soap opera, "As the World Turns' bringing mere scripted drama to life. A cop and an actress made for media interest and Mike's cop stories captivated my soap opera friends. Mike was often brought in to help our soap family over the years when tragedies would strike, which happened far too often. When a co-star of mine committed suicide, the production team called Mike within hours to guide them. He located children of actors who suffered from addiction. One actress sought safe haven in our home for several days after being assaulted by a family member. He was affectionately nick-named "Officer Mike" by many of my friends.

On February 13th, 2001 our lives changed forever. During a high speed chase in the Bronx, a man with nineteen prior arrests was stalking his girlfriend and threatening the victim again. He had broken both of the woman's eye sockets and claimed he was going to kill a cop. Mike got the call and immediately located the perp driving by the victim's home and a high speed chase ensued. The chase was televised on ABC news. I watched in real time the end of my husband's career when the perp ran Mike's police car off the road, hitting a telephone pole at 50 miles an hour. The car looked like an accordion. Mike was removed from the car with the jaws of life and permanently disabled. He suffered a broken hip and a fractured bone in his neck.

On September 9th 2001 after a few months of daily rehabilitation, he returned to modified duty with physical restrictions. Two days later we all know what happened. Mike lost several members of his precinct on September 11th, 2001. Countless funerals became regular events. As the months carried on and the never-ending exposure of toxic dust silently contaminated him, he got the news he was to retire on the disability from the accident. I know this devastated him. I've only seen him cry a few times in our thirty years together. When he got word he was out of the police department was one of them. He never returned to the precinct to retrieve his badge and gun. His brother Brian, also NYPD, worked in the same precinct, took the items home.

He began to recover physically but mentally he was defeated. I knew how much his work meant to him. Truly a loss not just for him but the entire city of NY. With over a thousand arrests and seventy-five medals, including the Combat Cross for a gang-related shooting in the Bronx, the streets were a lot less safe with his retirement. A new unexpected chapter of his life was beginning without a map and he struggled.

The shining light of his retirement was being able to be with our sons every day while I went to work. He not only embraced this time with the boys, he went above and beyond in participating in every aspect of their lives. He volunteered to coach every sport our boys were involved in, baseball, basketball, soccer, lacrosse, track, anything where the boys showed interest, Mike was there. To this day the boys now adult friends, reminisce on how great a coach Mike was to them growing up. When our daughter Ann Marie came along in 2006 he became the best "girl dad". Again Mike volunteered to coach her soccer team, lacrosse and was often the only dad in the mix. I knew how blessed she was to have this time with him and to this day they are inseparable.

The bond he shares with all of his children is precious. As their mother, not a day goes by that I don't recognize the role he plays in their life is immeasurable. Mike has not just been a role model to his own children but to the hundreds of local children whose lives are better for Mike being a part of it. Mike also built our home and a home for my brother after retirement. He found peace and purpose but he missed "the job". I could see it every time he would socialize with his former colleagues. I knew something was missing and had a plan to help. The next chapter of his life began as a private investigator.

Mike started working as a PI for my television "mom" Lisa Brown's husband, defense attorney Brian Neary. His work with Brian led to countless lawyers hiring Mike for big cases, some involving the federal government. Mike worked for the Archdiocese of Brooklyn, on death penalty cases, murder cases and more. There was one type of case he said he would never take, any involving someone harming a child. If he found the accused to be guilty, that was where it ended. I'll never forget him coming home and telling me he returned a check for $1200 to a client after one meeting. The man had been accused of sexual assault on a child. Mike knew he was guilty and pushed the check back to the man across the table and promptly left the meeting. You can change the setting but you cannot change the man. Mike loved his work as a PI and often worked pro-bono when people were in need. It was a part-time job which gave him a tremendous amount of satisfaction. He was using his incredible skills for good and again the community was better for it.

One of the pro-bono cases which has stayed with me involved a young man who had been falsely arrested for murder. Mike met with the young man and his family and knew just by speaking to the family, he was innocent. When the parents struggled to pay, Mike offered to work for free. Something he did more often than not. The case of this young man being falsely accused kept Mike up at night. He did a boots on the ground investigation, placing posters on trees where the shooting took place with his personal cell number. Sure enough it worked. Mike's work led to the young man being fully exonerated when he uncovered the real killers. If not for Mike there is NO DOUBT that young man would be rotting in jail right now. I was with Mike when he got a call from this nineteen-year old, thanking him profusely.

The idea of any innocent person going to jail drove Mike on many cases. His career had nothing to do with financial gain and everything to do with right versus wrong. That's who Mike is. There are countless incidents of Mike doing good for others and expecting nothing in return. He ran into burning buildings, delivered babies, often took on gunfire. He knew what he was called to do in life. Even after his arrest in 2020 that didn't stop him from helping others. In 2022 Mike stopped the robbery of a woman at our local bank. He was driving out of the parking lot and saw a suspicious man lurking by the door to the bank. Despite being unarmed due to this case, he turned his car around and confronted the man who was robbing the 90 year old woman in her car. It turned out there was a pattern of these "lookout" robberies in NJ and Mike had prevented at the very least a robbery; possibly more.

Soon after the event at the bank he intervened on an assault of a woman in Grand Central Station. He could have kept walking and let someone else intervene but he turned around and went back to help. My eighty-six year old mother who has lived with us following my father's death, was recently targeted in a "grandma scam". She got a landline call from a scammer claiming her grandson was in jail and she needed to pay three thousand dollars to get him out. My mother texted Mike on her cell and he instructed her what to do. Sure enough an Uber car showed up to our home just as the local police arrived. Mike and our local police spoke to the driver and quickly determined he was being used as a courier for a criminal organization. Within a few minutes he was cleared of any wrongdoing and on his way. My mother has never received another call from the scammers. The DOJ has recently taken down many of these cases as there was a wave of elderly victims all across the country.

Just saying I'm honored to write this letter in support of Mike, would be minimizing his presence in my life and the lives of our children. We have been given the most incredible life journey because of Mike. I owe him everything. I say that without irony. Growing up in the entertainment industry, my life could have taken a much different turn if not for Mike. I am not naive to think luck had anything to do with it. I had a great support system in my siblings and parents and joining the McMahon family only expanded that support. His mother Pat who we lost in 2007 was the most gentle person and Michael always took care of her. Her dying request was for us to watch over Mike's sister Kathleen who was a single mother with a toddler. Of course we would do that for her without question. She rests in peace. She knew Mike would never abandon his family. Never.

We both grew up in blue collar, hard working families and those values have guided us. Money was never a gauge of success in our homes. A peaceful and joyful home with constant family interactions was our North Star. With hard work came financial stability for us. I worked as an actress since the age of ten and Mike had his first job as a paperboy at age twelve. We were workers and this dedication led to the freedom to spend more time with our children as they were growing up. After I left the soap opera "As the World Turns" in 2008 after a twenty year run and Mike retired from the NYPD, we still worked part-time because we loved our careers, not because there was a financial need. We owned our homes, had saved money for our future and we had no debt. This was also true when Mike was hired in 2016 for the case for which he was arrested in 2020. There was no financial motive in the case for which he was arrested. After decades of hard work on both our parts to be accused of financial greed of a few thousand dollars to betray the country, is not only false, it minimizes our years of dedication to our careers.

Shorty after our daughter's birth in 2006, Mike started to notice he could not smell or taste. He chalked this up to being an allergic person and didn't think much of it. As time went on his symptoms worsened and he saw a specialist. It was discovered polyps had been growing in his sinuses and needed to be removed. He had two surgeries over the next few years to remove the polyps but the symptoms continued and worsened. It was suggested he go to the Mount Sinai doctors treating people for 9/11 illness. After testing we received some very disturbing news. His lack of taste and smell was due to 9/11 illness. His sinuses were growing a specific mold only found in people exposed to the toxic dust from Ground Zero. He would need invasive surgery and a lifelong treatment plan. Since this disease was unique to 9/11 there was no definitive prognosis and what "lifelong" meant. More of a wait and see plan. His most recent surgery a few years ago entailed drilling through his sinus bone to ease draining of sinus fluid. We were warned that this surgery could result in permanent brain fluid leakage through his nose, as the drilling would be extremely close to the membrane protecting the brain. After his surgery we were relieved that did not happen and awaited the results.

Mike was doing better after this surgery and post-surgical daily at-home treatments. He continues to go for constant follow ups where a vacuum scope is inserted inside his sinuses to remove the sinus cavity buildup. The doctor describes the material as a "dense blockage with a peanut butter-like consistency". It is like cement, which if not removed will rapidly grow and cause unknown damage. To date this continues to be the pattern. Up until his arrest his health was manageable and he never complained one day about his pain. The build up in his sinuses would cause tremendous pressure and painful headaches. Mike would only share his physical pain with me and his doctors. We have spared our children the details of his illness. This letter will be the first time we have shared the reality of what he has been dealing with for years. His brother Vincent who is retired FDNY has dealt with some of the same health issues as Mike. Vincent was recently diagnosed with stage four 9/11 cancer and had jaw surgery to remove cancerous tumors. He is currently receiving radiation and chemotherapy treatments as we all pray for a miracle. Every day is a challenge and he suffers excruciating pain . 9/11 did not end on 9/11. Our family continues to feel life long repercussions of that day. The stress of his brother's diagnosis has taken a particular toll on Mike. Vincent has been such an incredible support for him and our entire family since Mike's arrest in October of 2020. Since his brother's cancer diagnosis a few months ago, Mike's nose bleeds from his own illness have increased significantly. The amount of blood is frightening to witness and runs like a faucet until it finally subsides. As always, Mike never complains about his health challenges in an effort to protect us from more concern.

In early 2020, I started a new job and Mike's business was growing. He was getting great cases as a private investigator and his reputation was unmatched. Mike was the go-to PI for top defense attorneys in the tri-state area. He worked for billionaires, cases with the DOJ, FBI and other law enforcement agencies. Our children were thriving despite Covid attempting to dismantle their academic futures. Our oldest son Mikey graduated Montclair State College, Max graduated High School and Ann Marie was finishing up her freshman year in high school. Then on October 28, 2020, the FBI came to our door before dawn and our family's life was destroyed in a moment. Our children were traumatized, especially our then fourteen year old daughter who was terrified in her room as she recounted the sound of "big boots coming towards her bedroom door" and "didn't know what would happen next". After Mike's arrest when he returned after processing, I watched him break down dumbfounded, "How could anyone look at my background and think I would EVER do ANYTHING like this?" The arrest hit our home like an atomic bomb. The same day Mike was arrested the press parked outside our home, took pictures of me and our children, knocked on our neighbors doors, flew drones over our home, pointed bright lights in our windows and the international press called Mike an agent of China. My children had to face their friends and explain what happened. There was never a doubt their father was innocent but every time they exited our home they braced themselves to defend him.

The only light at the end of this horrific tunnel was the trial. We believed the truth would finally be heard, the press would turn, recognize they had gotten it wrong and Mike would finally be free of this. I honestly believed justice would be done and Mike could clear his name. There was mountains of evidence he was unwittingly used, did nothing illegal, so if we had to go to court so be it. Mike would never take a plea deal. It was non-negotiable. If he did he would be perjuring himself and the entire private investigative industry would be finished. He was ready to fight for his life.

At trial I had to listen to the brutal personal and professional attacks on Mike. It was so painful for me and my sons who attended to hear. One day NYPD CCRB complaints against Mike from 2000 were submitted as proof of some character flaw. What the jury didn't hear were the details of those complaints. They involved a known gang member Mike had removed from school grounds who was trying to recruit kids. The other was from the mother of the same gang member who Mike had stopped and vouchered $1400 cash. Mike told the boy if he could prove where the money came from it would be returned. The mother of the boy entered the precinct screaming about Mike and wanted the money back. Mike was not disciplined for these complaints and did not lose any vacation days. This was the prosecutions proof Mike was not one of the good guys.

The prosecutors struggled to find ANYTHING about Mike to paint him was a common criminal. This was also reiterated in the press for everyone, including my children, to read. I feel Mike's tremendous loss of once close friends and the pain he has been dealt as his character was publicly decimated. How could Mike's "good deeds" be suppressed at trial by the court when his entire life IS the unequivocal evidence he would never betray the country. Isn't the content of your character the only thing we leave behind? It enrages me how he was treated and disregarded. Yet, he still holds on to this day and prays for some relief.

I could fill a book with the amount of times Mike has helped those in need but his most important role as father brings tears to my eyes. I don't know how I was so blessed. He is my everything. How he has shown strength though this process of public humiliation and personal attacks is incredible. Our children have looked to him for cues on how to handle all of this and he has managed to stay strong.

We have raised our children to be honest and have integrity in a world which would constantly challenge it. There is no doubt the level of stress put upon them, most children will thankfully never experience. From day one that this happened we continued to fight as a team. I reiterated to Mike and the children that we would fight this until he was fully exonerated. This hasn't been easy for any of us. It was uncharted territory and it got worse as the months, then years, went by. My children have been living with this stigma for over four years and it will now be a part of their forever. I always tried to keep them positive, assuring them that the truth would win in the end.

Heading into trial took our anxiety and stress to another level. Mike wasn't doing well. His panic attacks and night terrors increased. One panic attack occurred while he was driving. Fortunately we were able to pull over and I could drive. Not that I was doing much better. I had never suffered panic attacks in my life until Mike's arrest. I've had several over the last few years. I never wanted our children to witness these attacks as they had already suffered enough and panic attacks are frightening. But my children were scared and trying to keep it together for us. My daughter told me a few months after the arrest, the day the FBI came to our home, she went to school and cried alone in the bathroom, trying to process what happened. I had no idea. I still don't know how she's processing this nightmare. She was only fourteen when it happened. I keep my door open 24/7 for all of my kids. Whatever they need, we are here for them. I continue to remind them of that as often as possible.

Judge Chen, when you were named as our presiding judge, of course I researched your background. I was thrilled to see your history as a civil rights attorney. I believed Mike's rights would be prioritized and protected. His right to defend himself with the full extent of the evidence would be paramount. It gave me some peace of mind in a sea of uncertainty. Coincidently within a few months of you being appointed, I met a former co-worker of yours on a potential film project. During our initial discussion, we realized we had a very odd connection in you. This man had nothing but glowing things to say about you Judge Chen. He reassured me I should not be concerned with you being assigned to our case. That you are a fair judge and an empathic human being. I can't tell you how his words assured me Mike would have a fair trial. Mike was innocent, of course this will end in our favor!

When the prosecutors presented their version of events, I was shocked. Leading up to trial every motion was denied, then negative rulings on admissible and non-admissible evidence felt like a knife to our hearts. As his wife to watch Mike retreat from life, felt like I was watching a slow death. Our life was now filled with emotional landmines I was trying to navigate.

From the first day I entered the court room until the day of conviction was a living hell. I watched the person I love more than anything in the world be called a traitor, a tax cheat, a user of his friends, a stalker, a criminal working for the Chinese government for a few thousand dollars. I heard false statements repeated to a jury. I watched people who are supposed to stand for truth and justice weave a fairytale resulting in the destruction of an innocent man and his family.

People often ask me what it felt like to sit day after day and listen to these attacks on Mike. I can only compare it to one time in 2006. When our third child Ann Marie was born, she was on life support for over a week. Born a month early, her lungs were not developed and she could not breathe on her own. I would have traded places with her in a minute. I would just stare at her and pray she would not take a turn for the worse. Mike was my savior during and after her birth, often sitting with her in the rocking chair for hours with tubes weighing her down as she slowly recovered. As her mother I felt helpless. I felt the same pain listening to the prosecutors paint Mike as a criminal. To smear him and paint him as some horrific person was almost too much for me. Its like when you have a dream and can't reach the person you love who is holding on to the edge of a cliff. Your mouth opens to scream but no sound comes out and your feet won't move. It's debilitating.

I was the person responsible for holding my family together and had to do something. With Mike's support, I started publicly speaking out. I have spent the last three years on a mission to get the truth out and educate anyone who would listen. My children encouraged me. I know they felt helpless and scared. I wanted to teach them not to be afraid and stand up for what's right. We have incredible children who have helped us as much as we've helped them. I have always been honest about the process. I try and protect them from unnecessary pain. When I have panic attacks and mental breakdowns I find a private space to recover. It passes. We are getting through this together.

When my sons wanted to come to court, I warned them their father would be disparaged by the prosecutors but they insisted. The day my daughter was supposed to attend she got physically ill and I made her stay home. I'm glad I did because that day was the closing statement and it was excruciating. My poor children. I have done everything I can to help them but I'm sure I missed signs which will one day manifest. My daughter's entire four years of high school have had this cloud of uncertainty following her every day. She started community college this past the fall to stay close to us. With the sentencing coming, even though I have tried to lessen the reality of what may happen, she has struggled. She's expressed her concern about her dad, as have all of my three children. I'm angry about the time stolen which should have been focused on their future. Believe me, they would be upset at me for even feeling that way because they love their father so much. As their mother, I have greater understanding of what they truly missed. We will never get these years back. I'll never forgive the people who deliberately instilled trauma on innocent children. I can't imagine what they have gone through over the last four years but we have managed because we love each other. There's nothing that can break that love.

I used to joke and ask Mike in all seriousness, "What's it like to be perfect?" He would laugh and respond, "I'm not perfect." But he is. I've known Mike for thirty years and he is a perfect human being. I know that's quite a declaration but I'm a first hand witness to it for decades. I don't think we've spent more than a week apart over that time. He has never raised his voice to me or our children. His way of discipline was through empathy and example. He has been a supporter of mine as a creative person, as a mother and business woman. My children have been given the freedom to grow as individuals, guided by both of us to live lives of paying it forward. We have both given of ourselves through philanthropy and volunteering for countless causes. I served on the professional advisory board for St. Jude Children's Research

Hospital and all of my children have participated in fundraising for the cause. Mike and his retired police officers volunteered for security for my St. Jude events in NJ and NY. We have tried to instill the importance of giving back to all of our children.

My oldest son Michael recently joined the police department in NJ, following in his father's foot steps. Even after what he witnessed, he believes the good guys outweigh the ones who have forgotten their oath. I wept when I heard he wanted to be a cop. I couldn't be more proud of our son. The community in NJ will benefit from the empathy and humanity he learned from his father. A father who is now to be sentenced in your court room.

The thought of Mike being incarcerated is unfathomable to me. If you could only have the opportunity to speak to him one on one. If you met him for five minutes you would love him as so many do. He walks into any room and everyone smiles as he arrives. You would learn instantly he is a man of kindness, unselfishness, with unprecedented integrity and honor who touches everyone he meets. I hope you know people like this in your life. We all should be so blessed.

Since the day he took the NYPD test at the age of sixteen until this very moment he has lived a life of service. He would never put someone in harms way. Never. It is the antithesis of who he is. If he had any idea there was some nefarious purpose when he was hired in this case, Mike would have been the first person to help the victims and help detain the perpetrators. He would never put the former NYPD colleagues turned PIs he hired on this case in a position of criminality. Those men would take a bullet for each other. It kills Mike the long friendships he had with anyone connected to this case have been lost. Many are still afraid to speak to Mike after the way the government treated THEM, with threats of possible charges based on NOTHING. That's very difficult for Mike to reconcile. So many relationships dismantled. Breaks my heart to see it.

I almost lost Mike several times while he was a cop. The multiple shootings, the time he ran into a burning building to save a child, the time he was being choked out and a good samaritan stepped in, the list is endless. When he retired there was a sense of relief knowing the daily risk of death was miraculously over. Then the never ending cloud of 9/11 hit our family as an unpredictable and debilitating illness. His sacrifice for his job never really ended. His body is a constant reminder every day as he suffers nose bleeds and other side affects. I've never heard him complain once. He continues to be an example of humility holding his head high for those of us he loves and determined to protect us through all of it. He's still Mike, no matter how many tried to break him.

Immediately after his arrest in 2020, Mike's main concern was other investigators. He wanted to warn others and help in some way if they had been targeted. We reached out to local law enforcement, national and international private investigation companies and others. I spoke at PI events and met one on one with private investigators to educate and warn them of who was being targeted and for what purpose. One friend who works at an international investigative firm told Mike that due to his case and warnings, the firm turned down a job of potential foreign influence. The job and client showed red flags Mike had warned him about. That's one proven step in the right direction. More needs to be done.

Mike and I continue to warn and educate others, recognizing the purpose of this nightmare may be coming to light. If we could help one private investigator, local member of law enforcement and others by sharing intel, maybe there is a purpose for the greater good of the country. Mike and I have teamed with highly respected former members of law enforcement, federal and local, to structure a national educational program. This program will be presented to local law enforcement, their municipalities and private investigators as a guide to keep communities safe from malign foreign influence. Mike always finds a way to be of service, even in his most dire hour.

He has lost his business, his reputation, his health, his financial stability for the future, friends in law enforcement who are afraid to speak to him, his freedom to live his life as he wishes, our privacy decimated. The only thing that has gotten him through this, how any of us in our family has gotten through this, is each other. We wake up as a family and before our feet touch the ground we know we will get through it somehow. Our daughter Ann Marie has started community college working towards a degree in early childhood education while holding three jobs. She works as a teacher's aide, for the state of NJ assisting a special needs young woman maintain independent living and at a local coffee shop. Our son Max works in the automotive industry and looking to buy his first home and son Mikey graduated the Passaic NJ Police Academy in September to join the Hawthorne NJPD. We were incredibly grateful when Mike was asked to present Mikey with his badge on stage in front of hundreds of people. It was quite a proud moment for us as his parents. The thought of all the future milestones which will be missed without their father there if he is incarcerated is beyond heartbreaking. My children have been through enough.

There is a very important piece of our lives you need to know was you put a picture of who Mike is into your mind. When we married in 1993 I was on the soap opera "As the World Turns" viewed daily by 6.2 million people. My character "Lily" was to ATWT what "Laura" was to the famous General Hospital couple "Luke & Laura". I would receive thousands of fans letters a week at the studio. The day Mike and I got married fans filled the back of the church, despite no public announcement of the location. I have been followed countless times and fans would often park outside our home and take pictures. Being followed at theme parks and supermarkets was common. A few times it became concerning. Unfortunately back in the 80s and 90s, the only way we could be alerted of a potential threat was in the calls to the studio or letters we received. As a young woman, I would get a lot of fan mail from male prisoners. One man serving time in federal prison for arson would write me every week. I still remember his name. Our show aired on CBS but Proctor & Gamble was my employer. When an actor would get a threatening letter, it went straight to the P&G legal team in Ohio. When Anthrax was being sent to news organizations, one letter containing a white powder was sent to my studio. Our security team at CBS studio was always on alert but once I left the security of the building, Mike was my protector. If I got a letter from a prisoner which wasn't threatening but concerning, he researched the person to make sure our family wasn't in any danger. Once inmates were paroled, their footprints through the prison system stopped but their letters did not. Anything that even had a tone of concern was sent to Ohio. Ohio was far away from where we lived in NJ so Mike always had to be hyper aware of our surroundings.

Mike has been with me several times when I was followed. One time at Disney World, a woman followed us for hours. She "hid" behind trees, followed us on rides but never approached us. Thankfully he was by my side in case she had intent to harm. I played a nice character, so I was spared from what other actors/ actresses who played villains dealt with. One of our actresses was slapped in the face outside the studio for something her character did on the show. At the Emmys in 2002 tens of thousands of fans lined the Red Carpet on the streets of NY. The crowd was always enthusiastic and the NYPD had a strong presence to keep us safe. One year I had personal armed security as it was needed, who never left my side. Mike was unable to attend with me that year so I was assigned someone to guard me. Security was always a concern.

When my third child was born in 2006 and the internet was the wild west, I wanted more privacy. Our home was built a thousand feet off the main road, with one way in and one way out. This didn't completely eliminate curious or potentially dangerous fans from finding us, but it was definitely a deterrent. Many people say its part of the job to expect paparazzi and fans to follow you. That is true. It's not a crime but it can sometimes be physically intimidating. As I said I had a great relationship with the fans and enjoy interacting with them here in the U.S. and abroad. They have been so supportive of me for decades and I am grateful. That being said, you still must be cautious.

When we took our boys back to Disney we hired a guide to accompany us so if we had any issue the park employee could address it. This was always a part of our lives as someone in the public eye since I met Mike. He always had eyes in the back of his head as a cop. His intuition and ability to assess danger is truly something to watch. He is wired to protect, not to harm. The idea that Mike would ever put anyone in the same position as what he's seen through his work and as my protector, is just not possible. After his arrest our safety concerns were again raised.

At trial none of the victims could identify Mike and their testimony description of cars they claimed were following them, didn't match Mike's. This was not surprising. I knew Mike and the other two PIs had never been seen but I learned Chinese agents were actually following MIKE and keeping tabs on him during his surveillance. This opened up a frightening reality. I have no idea if Chinese agents ever monitored my home and children since 2016 when Mike worked on this job. As far as Mike knew he was working for a typical client. His home office address was reflected on emails, invoices and paperwork. My family was left vulnerable and I have no idea how close we came to any danger. It wasn't just this revelation which put my family directly in potential harm. There is absolutely no way Mike would share such personal information of his home where his children, wife and mother-in-law resides with people he believes are dangerous. Never. Unfortunately after his arrest that danger immediately escalated.

The afternoon of Mike's arrest in 2020 several photos of us were published in the NY Post online. Within an hour, the press was parked outside our home. Privacy is non-existent these days. With a quick search on the internet, your address is easily accessed. The photographers parked outside for days. When my children, Mike or I would walk to our cars, they would run towards us and take our picture. One day my son Max was photographed as he was leaving. He rolled down his window and told them to please leave, they didn't. My car was followed. The press wasn't breaking any law but it was surreal. Was it the press? Or someone who thinks my husband is a traitor working for the Chinese government? I hoped by ignoring them, they would go away. They didn't. Sometimes the photographers would just stand in the middle of the public street and photograph our home. They finally left after three days.

A week after Mike's arrest, I learned from someone that a man in full tactical gear was stopped in the woods across the street from our home. I still have no idea who that was. Apparently our local police did a threat assessment and let him go. There is no police report on the engagement, which is unfortunate. When the world thinks your husband is a traitor working for the CCP your family instantly has millions of enemies. This label on us will never be removed. It will follow us wherever we go. The case may be nearing an end for many but the threat of retaliation from unknown enemies will be with my family forever.

All of this is to reiterate Mike would never put our family, or any one else at risk. He has seen the reality of what people who are targeted are subjected to. Not just while on the NYPD or with his work as a PI, but as a husband and a father. His level of concern for all of us has been heightened due to this case being so public. The severity of the accusations played a major role in my need to go public. This choice was not an easy one but it had a two-fold purpose. By getting the facts out it could potentially defuse the hate pointed in our direction. Mike received an extremely scary phone call after his arrest. In all my years of public interaction, this call made me shockingly aware all of us could be in imminent danger. I went into offensive mode to protect us any way I could. This unwarranted label of traitor has planted a seed in peoples minds. There is no way to know who or when it could be unleashed.

Judge Chen you have to consider two versions of Michael McMahon. Is he the version of Mike presented over a few weeks at trial? The Michael McMahon who randomly decided one day in fall of 2016 to throw his life away to work for the CCP for a few thousand dollars and betray his country?

Or the Michael McMahon you have been reading about from the ones who know him the best. The man whose selfless actions witnessed for decades by myself and the community he has served while on the NYPD, in the home and as a private investigator, always putting others before himself.

If the prosecution's version is correct, I've spent three decades with a liar, criminal and a fraud. That despite what I have seen with my own eyes, felt with my own heart, the man I have raised three incredible children with, is nothing more than a stranger with deep ill intent for others and disregard for their safety. There couldn't be anything further from the truth. I know this not just as his wife and mother of his children but as someone in the public eye for most of my life. I've seen the best in humanity and the worst. We need more people in the world who share Mike's pure heart. They are rare and often humble as to not draw attention to their kindness. When we are fortunate to cross paths with people like Mike, they should be cherished and celebrated.

Mike has been punished since October 28th, 2020. For four and half years he has suffered tremendous physical and emotional deterioration. My children need their father home to maintain our family unit which has been unbroken and our lifeline for survival. I don't know what I would do without him. I suffer separation anxiety anytime I am away from him for more than a few hours. I worry about his mental and physical health every minute of the day. He has become forgetful and withdrawn at times, which is frightening and completely out of character from the man I know. He will never be the same. I miss the man he was before this happened and I will work the rest of my life to help him heal. I don't sleep and when I do I have nightmares of losing him. The mere thought of what could happen brings an overwhelming sadness and distress, I didn't think I would be facing until our sunset years.

We need to start a new chapter for our family. To try and give back to so many who have shown unwavering belief in Mike's innocence. There is constant concern for the mental health of my children, who could lose their father at a time they need him

> the most. Especially my daughter who relies on her father as protector and confidant. She trusts him on a level I have never seen with other teenagers and a parent. I am so grateful they have each other. Please don't take him away from her, from any of us. We need him.
>
> I am speaking to you as a woman who is trying to keep her family together after unimaginable circumstances. We care for my 86 year old mother, who had two medical procedures during the time of this case, the removal of a cancerous kidney and a heart value replacement. She will need surgery again soon as the value is leaking and needs to be replaced again. She too is a victim of the events of the last few years. Watching her child, grandchildren and Mike who she loves so much suffer, has taken a toll on her as well. I don't know how much time I will have with her. Her heart is breaking for all of us and it shows. I know she prays every day for some resolve to all of it. I would like to give her some peace so we can start anew and put this difficult chapter in the rear view mirror.
>
> Mike and I celebrated our 30th wedding anniversary on November 12, 2024. The vows we made thirty years ago have faced our biggest challenge with this case but we survived. We are blessed with three children who stood beside us and are the reason we never stopped fighting. Our children need to have hope there is an ending to all suffering at some point. I encourage them every day to just hold on, pray and believe. Judge Chen, I humbly request that now be the time to allow that happen.
>
> Respectfully,
>
> Martha McMahon

Mike finally had the opportunity to address the court and have a voice:

> I'm grateful for the opportunity to address the court today. It has been over four years since my arrest. I never thought I would be sitting here today. I got the call for this case in the fall of 2016. It was a routine case to help a client who had money stolen from his

family business in China. He was trying to locate the man and his stolen funds. A simple Google search showed the subject Jin Xu was wanted in China for embezzlement and taking bribes. My job remained the same, find the money and the man to help my client. If I had any indication that I was actually working for China or that Jin Xu and his family were targets of the Chinese government and in any danger whatsoever I never would have taken the case or performed the investigation. I would have done what I have always done, help. I would have been the first person, to rush to his aide and bring him to the police. This whole case has been about the red flags that I should have seen and believe me, I wish that I had. But, there was no indication my clients were anything other than business men who had been taken advantage of and who I was trying to help. Nothing that I was being asked to do was illegal and I never would have done anything to break the law. I wake up every day and go to sleep every night reliving the what ifs and what I would have done if I had only known there were nefarious intentions of my clients. I would never engage in any kind of stalking-that is the kind of thing I have always fought against and tried to bring to justice. I hope now after you have learned about who I am, you see that too. I was just doing what I thought was a routine job.

In that regard I think there needs to be some clarifications on what my job was as a private investigator. After retiring from the NYPD in 2003 I chose the profession of private investigator as a civilian and sole proprietor of my business. I loved it. I found helping those in need of my services as a PI gave me the same role in service I lived for as a cop. This case was a typical case but subject Jin Xu, a wanted Chinese fugitive, was certainly atypical but no more atypical than my work for the Vatican or working security across the country for the Parkland Shooting survivors or working for a presidential candidate or several billionaires. Often I worked for free, especially if I met a client who needed my help and was struggling. I have seen a lot of people in their most painful moments and it felt good to help them if I could. Even though I only served fourteen years due to my injury on the NYPD, I was fortunate to continue using my experiences in law enforcement.

Using public streets for surveillance is part of our job and not illegal. Photographing individuals in a public place is legal. Meeting clients at a restaurant, law office or a coffee shop is normal. I was the sole proprietor with a small part-time business. I have never been sanctioned or ever had any criminal or civil complaints against me in my career as a private investigator. I have earned the trust of attorneys whose work I admire and respect. To have a simple case I worked on or a few days in 2017 end a career I loved is devastating. More devastating than you can imagine. My reputation is forever tarnished and this label as a convicted felon will follow me forever. I certainly cannot work as a private investigator ever again.

After my arrest in 2020, four years after I had worked on this case, I instinctively wanted to help FBI agent McCarthy and John Ross put this puzzle together. When I starting learning that I had been used by Chinese agents I couldn't believe it. Here I was feeling bad for my client for having money stolen from their family business and my clients deceived me. As I processed that reality it was unreal. I looked at all my emails, text messages, invoices, that thankfully I had saved over the years, even transferring the information to a new phone I had purchased in 2018. Who does that if I had committed a crime? I looked through everything a hundred times to see if I could find something I missed. When I heard the evidence in court, I was shocked. There was nothing in my work from 2016 and 17 on this case that aligned with some illegal scheme. A scheme that was unbeknownst to me. If I had known the true intensions of my clients I never would have brought two former NYPD intelligence detectives into the case, never would have discussed this with an active DEA supervisor and an active FBI agent at the gym in 2017, who I had *just met* by the water cooler about it. And most importantly, I never would have participated *at all*. I never thought, not for one minute, that I was working for China stalking anyone. Yet now I have lost everything as a result. This is just a nightmare.

What my family has been through for the last four years is hard to put into words. My oldest son Mikey who chose a career in law enforcement, I am so proud of him, said to me the other day that he can't remember what our lives were like before this. My kids didn't sign on for this and so much has been taken away from them because of it. My youngest Ann Marie who was fourteen at the time of my arrest and is now a freshman at community college. Choosing to stay close to home for financial and emotional reasons. My son Max opted to not go to college as not to put a financial burden on us yet has become extremely successful. They are ok Judge, but forever scarred.

My wife Martha has fought for me every minute of every day since October 28th, 2020. The government criticizes her for that but she believes in my innocence and knows me better than anyone. She continues to fight for me and has taken on multiple attacks by the government, including a disturbing letter from DC national security in 2023 to intimidate her. Ms. Arfa recently had to alert the court she had made an egregious error stating my wife was the cofounder of an organization that raises funds for falsely accused first responders. Our entire family lives with this every day. Unfortunately my son shares my name. I recently received a call from probation that *my* name came up on a hit in the town where he is a police officer. They called my son's police department to inquire and learned of their mistaken identity. I personally received a call from probation minutes after I saved a woman from a robbery at our local bank. This is something my entire family will have to deal with forever. Despite everything my family has faced, my wife and I have used what happened to me to help others. Within days of my arrest the two of us began reaching out to hundreds of private investigators and local law enforcement. A few were large international investigative firms which reached out to us to say thank you as our warnings about red flags stopped them from taking cases which might have been problems. We continue to help and speak out to educate and prevent more innocent people from being unwittingly used.

Judge Chen, I hope after you have read the letters you have a better idea of who I am. I have spent my entire life dedicated to service. I would never harm anyone or put fellow NYPD detectives, who worked every day of surveillance with me, in a position to cause them harm.

I respectfully ask that today you give my family the peace they deserve.

I was so proud of Mike being able to get through that speech. I knew how important it was to go on the record and finally have a voice. Meredith Afra had continued to make false claims to the judge at sentencing and added even more to the lies. Only a few days prior to sentencing Ms. Arfa had to write a letter to Judge Chen admitting she had lied in her most recent sentencing report. She falsely claimed I was the cofounder of The Pipe Hitter Foundation and raising money for our defense. A simple Google search shows that Eddie and Andrea Gallagher were the founders of PHF. I believe Ms. Arfa visited the site due to the fine for Mike she requested, fifty thousand dollars. That number happened to match the amount the PHF had raised for our defense since they started supporting us. Here are a few examples of other lies Ms. Arfa continued in court that day.

1. Ms. Arfa stated McMahon not only saw Jin Xu's elderly father, he was well aware of his ailing health due to McMahon seeing the man with his own eyes. (Mike never saw the father.)
2. Ms. Arfa had to admit the date, April 7th 2017, Jin Xu claimed under oath on the stand he was followed, allegedly by Mike, was wrong. She now claimed Jin Xu misspoke at trial and he meant April 6th. Trial transcripts prove Jin Xu asked for the date April 7th to be read to him twice to confirm the date. (These dates were swapped back and forth as needed for the government's false narrative multiple times.)
3. Ms. Arfa mischaracterizes a sworn statement by Eric Gallowitz where he confirms his salty texts were jokes, yet she used the text exchanges as evidence of malicious intent in this case.
4. It appears Ms. Arfa used sensitive material and manipulated it in her final report regarding a witness statement. This action is completely unethical and its sole intent was to disparage Mike to the judge.

I could fill a book with the amount of lies committed by people who absolutely know better. Their desire to win at all costs is shocking.

When the judge finally began her ruling on the sentence everyone in courtroom was on the edge of their seats. Judge Chen's statements about Mike in her ruling brought the reality of what we had faced for over four years into focus. As with the prosecution team before her, she took all the good deeds of Mike's life, his heroism, health conditions due to his NYPD work, family support, finances, our marriage, children, and turned everything into a negative. She chastised Mike for not showing sympathy for the alleged victims. This opinion was the major factor in her ruling on sentencing, not the facts of the case. She glossed over his 9/11 medical issues, dismissing it as mere sinusitis. Judge Chen made a point of stating my children would be fine if Mike was incarcerated due to their ages and family support. Her position on Mike being a hero and having executed hundreds of good deeds was that there is an expectancy for all people to be good. I believe Judge Chen knows Mike is innocent, which makes her attacks on his incredible character even worse. I won't even ponder what her position truly is on Jin Xu and his family. All I know is the evidence at trial was clear as to who the criminals were and who was not, Mike.

You have now read this book and the letter I wrote to Judge Chen. During her ruling, there wasn't one mention of me, his wife, and how his incarceration would affect me. None. I was dismissed as a factor in her decision to let Mike receive probation and stay home. He absolutely deserved probation for countless reasons.

Finally after over four years, millions of tax dollars spent, countless lives ruined Judge Chen sentenced Mike to eighteen months in federal prison. She fined him 11 thousand dollars, the same amount he had allegedly made on this case.

The alleged victims had not requested any prison time or financial restitution.

There were some serious wins that day for the Byrnes and McMahons. First, the appearance of Craig Hereen at Mike's sentencing. This guy couldn't take a hint. He was the bad penny that kept showing up.

I knew this would be the last time I would see him so I jumped at the opportunity to have one final word. As I walked towards the exit doors during our morning break I looked him dead in the eyes and said, "You have some balls showing up here." There were several FBI agents present when I said it. Mr. Hereen did not return after the break.

Our relatives lined the hallway as the FBI agents and prosecutors left the courtroom. Here are some of the things they heard when confronted by us.

"You should be ashamed of yourselves." "Liars." "You sacrificed the American people for the CCP." "The CCP won today." "You betrayed your oath." "You know he's innocent." "Perjury is a CRIME!" "Repent." "You don't REALLY think he did this for 11 thousand dollars? Come on." Just to name a few gems thrown out by everyone who loves Mike and knows he is innocent. I know if Vinny were alive he would have been ten times more brutal. I hope we made him proud. We had Vinny "The VINMAN" at our backs.

I think Vinny knew what was about to happen in that courtroom that day about a week before he passed. When he was passing away he said he kept seeing swinging doors. He described the doors like saloon doors. This vision happened to him more than once leading up to his death. My interpretation it was relatives on the other side, at the bar, a saloon, preparing for Vinny's arrival. Now I know exactly what his vision meant.

After the sentencing, Mike was in the courtroom where only a few people remained, one being Christopher Bruno. Mike wasn't going to say anything to Bruno but as he was exiting, stopped, turned around and walked back towards the courtroom floor. The only thing between Mike and Christopher Bruno were the three-foot swinging doors, like saloon doors, which separated the galley and the courtroom floor. Mike addressed Bruno as a younger FBI agent stood close by. He said, "Two of my former coworkers work in the same office as you. You never spoke to them. If you had they would have told you that I'm a good person." Hearing this Bruno looked stunned. Was he stunned because Mike confronted him or due to this news that two people Bruno worked with were his coworkers? Then Mike continued, "You're a liar. You lied on the criminal complaint and search warrants. Shame on you. I hope you have a good lawyer." Bruno did not say a word and looked like a toddler getting caught with his hand in the cookie jar. Mike walked out of the courtroom welcomed by hugs from his family with his head held high, having finally been able to confront the man who do this to our family. Mike was the voice for everyone in this country who has ever been accused of something they didn't do. The voice for the countless voiceless who were intimidated and bankrupt, financially and emotionally, due to those who had long forgotten their oath. We will never stop fighting until his name is cleared and every single person involved in this tragic case is held accountable. This should never happen to another an innocent person ever again. Our fight continues. Stay tuned.

UPDATES

On January 15, 2025, Jason Zhu was sentenced to twenty-four months. No fine.

On January 23, 2025, Congying Zheng was sentenced to sixteen months. No fine.

Immediately after her confirmation Attorney General Pam Bondi made changes to FARA laws defining the guidelines. These changes are vital to protecting contractors like Mike by focusing on espionage as it was originally intended. This much needed oversight confirmed FARA is an administrative task to register as a foreign agent.

According to a source, Beau Dietl and Associates was hired to follow Fox Hunt target Miles Guo by a Chinese government official (CCP) back in August of 2017 and was paid high six figures to monitor him for one month. During an interview on Sid Rosenberg's show in March of 2023 Dietl confirms this surveillance and even more shocking details about his work for the CCP. This interview occurred a few weeks before our trial but we were not made aware of it until after Mike's conviction. This is an ongoing investigation by me. I cannot believe Bo looked me straight in the eye in 2021, knowing he had information to clear my husband, and did nothing. Sadly, he is one of many. I don't know how these people live with themselves.

Miles Guo was tried in the SDNY July of 2024 for investor fraud and found guilty. He was sentenced to ten years in federal prison. Surprisingly his defense team did not call Dietl as a witness to prove the CCP was targeting Guo for speaking out against the Chinese government. Dietl's own words during the Rosenberg interview confirmed his directions came from China.

Jedd McFatter released the book *Fool's Gold* March 11th, 2025. The book reveals Jin Xu had contributed to Hillary Clinton's campaign in 2016. This is illegal. A noncitizen wanted Chinese fugitive was engaged in political influence. It also revealed Jin Xu and Fang Liu's immigration attorney Victoria Chan was in communication with John Podesta, (Clinton campaign chairman) regarding fundraising for Hillary Clinton in China. Chan was arrested in April of 2017 and served only one day in prison but was looking at forty years.

Mike and I were invited to the Trump Inauguration on January 20, 2025, and were honored to attend.

In February Donald Trump announced he would be ending the EB-5 program due to "fraud." He will be replacing EB-5 with the Gold Card, which will require a five-million-dollar investment in the United States. Trump has assured the American people the foreign investors will be vetted, unlike the EB-5 program, which was abused by China and riddled with money laundering from foreign adversaries. The majority of the EB-5 applicants are Chinese and the numbers surged starting in 2009 when China was facing economic disaster.

I spoke to Kelly Riddle, the private investigator who had been listed as the expert witness for the government at trial and removed from the list just prior to testifying. He told me after he spoke to the prosecutors and reviewed this case, he could not in good conscience testify against Mike. Thank you Mr. Riddle.

Two FBI Intelligence Agents named in the illegal spyware (Phantom & Pegasus) NY York Times FOIA documents surrounding October 28 2020, unceremoniously retired in February 2025.

When I attended the sentencing for Jason Zhu in January of 2025, I witnessed Jeremy Toner, the person who had prepared Mike's presentencing report, admit to other government employee(s) he had used another colleagues work in Mike's report. He stated he "felt like he had stolen someone's homework" and made other shocking admissions. Mr. Toner did not recognize me sitting only a few feet away, even though he had previously met me, when he made these statements in the public hallway of the EDNY. In April 2025 I filed a complaint with the Office of Professional Responsibility against Mr. Toner.

In April of 2025 I filed a complaint with OPR against FBI agent Christopher Bruno. This complaint was also sent to Attorney General Pam Bondi, FBI Director Kash Patel, FBI Red Bank, FBI Newark, FBI Washington D.C., NJ US Attorney Alina Habba & New Jersey Attorney General.

US National Security Attorney for the EDNY Scott Claffee was relieved of his duties on May 7, 2025 after eleven years with the DOJ.

On May 8, 2025 President Donald Trump posted the following update about Ed Martin on Truth Social.

> *"Ed Martin has done as AMAZING job as interim U.S. Attorney, and will be moving into the Department of Justice as the new Director of the Weaponization Working Group, Associate Deputy Attorney General, and Pardon Attorney. In these highly important roles, Ed will make sure we finally investigate the Weaponization of our Government under the Biden Regime, and provide much needed Justice for its victims. Congratulations Ed!"*

Craig Hereen has blocked me on LinkedIn. How will I ever recover?

ACKNOWLEDGMENTS

THERE ARE SO MANY PEOPLE who helped me make this book possible. I can't thank you all enough. And please forgive me if I left your name off this list.

Starting with family. I'd be nothing without you, all of you, including the McMahon family,

Eileen and Glen, Kevin, Vincent and Haley, Brian, Patricia and Ruben, Kathleen, Stephen and Amanda, Uncle Joe and Aunt Cheryl, Erin and Lynda. Also, the Byrne family, Liz, Fran and Steve, Brendan and Maria, Grandma Mary Adele, McMahon and Byrne nieces and nephews, Patty Leonard, the Callanan family, Johnny and Kim, Michael and Pamela, Brian and Emily, Christine and Bob, the McCullagh family, and the communities of the Pearl River Elks Lodge 2401, the Knights of Columbus 5343 Blauvelt, New York, and the American Legion Post 329 Pearl River, New York.

My friends, who feel like family, thank you: including Elizabeth Hubbard, Lisa Brown, Billy and Melissa Broughton, Dave and Bernie Shirghio, Dave McLachlan, Cliff and Lori Bohling, Dan and Kerry Hurley, Don and Kristy Lucca, Dennis and Amy Fischer, Eric and Jackie Canto, Mitch Greenblatt, Ray and Kathy Curry, John

Hess, Pete and Joyce Streelman, Eileen and Alex Cavegn, Joseph and Madelaine Cavegn, Bieber family, Minogue family, Lonzar family, Steve and Jennifer Laddy, Shannan and Michael Hollingsworth, Lisa Ross, Alexandra Verner Bearslayer, Maureen Walsh, Barry and Shelly Morgenstein, Lauralee and Scott Martin, JD and Chrissy Roth, Eldo Ray Estes, Maura West, Maurice and Paula Benard, Park family, Kim Zimmer, Suzanne Curry, Bill Fitchner, Kin Shriner, Paolo Seganti, Tonja Walker, Christine Taylor, Kimberlin Brown, Gretta and Jimmy Gallagher, Scott Magri, Allison and Randy Grimmett, Eric Gallowitz, Matt Connolly, Amy Nelson, the NJ Fitness crew:

Heather, Michele, Myra, Siobhan, Jamie, Ethel, and Tracey, Suzanne Curry, Mario and Sue Costablie, Kevyn Luff, Genevieve Gorder, Lisa Robertson, Derek Britt, Keith Walker, John Edward, Paul Brickfield, Raphael Rosenblatt, Jason Orlando, Sage Intelligence, Herman Weisberg, Iggy Lacato, Greg Dillon, Timothy Patrick Gill Sr., Nicholas E. Eftimiades, Colonel John Mills (retired), Cynthia Hughes, Ed Martin, Michael Caputo, Jeffrey Clark, James Comer and the GOP Oversight Committee, Peter Schweizer, Jedd McFatter, Phillip Lenczycki, Cindy Groz, Isabel Vincent, Greg Kelly, Newsmax, OAN, Jim Acosta, Cindy Strauss, Sharyl Attkisson, Alpha News, Liz Collin, Post Hill Press, Alex Novak, Caitlin Burdette, Chris Deperno, Frank Moreno, and Matthews Diner in Waldwick, New Jersey. Catturd, Gunther Eagleman.

Thanks especially to The Pipe Hitter Foundation, who helped make so much more possible. Thank you, Eddie and Andrea Gallagher, Sean Gallagher, Rob O'Donnell, Dena Cruden, Bernie Kerik, Mary Vought, Joe Koss, John O'Malley, Dinesh and Debbie D'Souza, Congressman Michael Lawler, Congressman Pete Sessions, radio host Joe Pagliarulo, aka Joe Pags, and my untiring legal team of Gibbons Law Firm, Larry Lustberg, Genna Conti, and the Law Office of Brian Neary.

And, very importantly, all of my fans, and all of the people who have supported us on X, Instagram, and Facebook. You are the army the government could not ignore.

To all of the people who supported us in silence due to the fear of retribution by our government, we see you, thank you.

ABOUT THE AUTHOR

Martha Byrne is a three-time Emmy Award-winning actress, writer, and producer with over forty years in the entertainment business starting at the age of ten on Broadway in *Annie*. She spent almost two decades on the soap opera *As the World Turns*, where she won two Emmy Awards for her portrayal of heiress Lily Walsh, and her twin sister, a Jersey showgirl, Rose D'Angelo. After leaving the soap opera, Martha turned her focus to behind the camera, writing for *The Bold and The Beautiful*, creating and executive producing several digital series including *Gotham* (Emmy nomination), *Weight* (Writers Guild Award), *Anacostia* (Emmy Award), and is currently developing several film and television projects. Martha has been married to retired NYPD detective Michael McMahon for thirty years. They have three children, Michael, Max, and Ann Marie.

www.ingramcontent.com/pod-product-compliance
Ingram Content Group UK Ltd.
Pitfield, Milton Keynes, MK11 3LW, UK
UKHW021651190726
13853UKWH00001B/204

9 798895 651445